The Public Interest In Government Labor Relations

The Public Interest In Government Labor Relations

Richard P. Schick
Jean J. Couturier

Ballinger Publishing Company • Cambridge, Massachusetts
A Subsidiary of J.B. Lippincott Company

Reproduction by the U.S. Government in whole or in part is permitted for any purpose.

International Standard Book Number: 0-88410-245-9

Library of Congress Catalog Card Number: 76-46642

Printed in the United States of America

Library of Congress Cataloging in Publication Data

Schick, Richard P
  The public interest in government labor relations.

  Includes bibliographical references.
  1. Collective bargaining—Government employees—United States—Case studies. 2. Public interest.
I. Couturier, Jean J., joint author. II. Title.
HD8008.S36   331.89'041'35   76-46642
ISBN 0-88410-245-9

Contents

List of Tables   ix

Acknowledgments   xi

Foreword   xiii

Introduction   xv

Chapter 1
Concepts of the Public Interest
and Study Methods   1

Concepts   1
Access   4
Influence   7
Study Methods   8
Literature Search   13
Summary   20

Chapter 2
The Public Interest in Collective
Bargaining in Milwaukee City
and Schools   21

Part I   Milwaukee City   21
Selection of Milwaukee   21

Independent Variables   22
Identification of Interest Groups   25
Definitions of Public Interest   31
Dependent Variables   33
  Part II   Milwaukee Board of School Directors   37
Independent Variables   37
Identification of Interest Groups   38
Definitions of the Public Interest   40
Dependent Variables   40
Summary   42

Chapter 3
The 1972–73 Philadelphia
Teachers' Strike   45

Selection of Philadelphia   45
Independent Variables   50
Identification of Interest Groups   52
Definitions of the Public Interest   58
Dependent Variables   60
Summary   66

Chapter 4
Memphis, Tennessee: Sanitationmen's
Bargaining Climate in 1975 Compared
with 1968 *(coauthored with Thomas W. Collins)*   69

Selection of Memphis   69
Independent Variables   75
Identification of Interest Groups   85
Definitions of the Public Interest   88
Dependent Variables   95
Summary   104

Chapter 5
Public Access to Berkeley's Teacher
Negotiations   105

The Disclosure Law   105
Implementation Policies   107
Selection of Berkeley   109
Independent Variables   112
Identification of Interest Groups   117

Definitions of the Public Interest 123
Dependent Variables 125
Role of the Citizens' Advisory Committee
  in the Fall 1975 Berkeley Teachers' Strike 140
Summary 145

**Chapter 6
Findings** 149

Goals 149
Definitions of the Public Interest 150
Representing the Public Interest 156
Union Political Power 159
Accountability 163
Interest Identification 167
Structural Access 173
Political Access 185
Influence 187
Influence of Structural as Compared
  with Political Access 194

**Chapter 7
Conclusions** 199

Nature of the Public Interest 199
Disclosure 203
Citizens' Advisory Committee 206
Open Negotiations 211
Further Research 213

Appendixes 219

A — Model for the Study of Cases
    of the Representation of the Public Interest
    in Government Labor Relations 221
B — Selected Bibliography 227
C — Public Opinion Poll Data 233

Notes 247

Index 251

About the Authors 265

List of Tables

3–1   Summary of Interest Group Characteristics in Philadelphia Teachers' Strike   54

4–1   Average Memphis Sanitationmen's Salaries Compared with Private Sector Manufacturing, Poverty Threshold, and "Lower" Standard of Living   77

6–1   Summary of Definitions of the Public Interest   152

6–2   Public Attitude Towards Public Employee Labor Relations Decision Making   154

6–3   Person Interviewed Regularly Receives Feedback from (Group Members) or General Public on Public Employee Labor Relations Issues   158

6–4   Community Attitudes Positive Towards Unions, Especially Public Employee (or Teacher) Unions   160

6–5   Labor (Especially Public Employee Unions) Influential in Local Politics   161

6–6   Relationship Between Local Election and Public Employee Labor Relations Situation   162

6–7   Private Sector Unions Locally in Harmony with Public Employee Unions   164

6–8   Elected Officials Should Represent Public Interest in Public Sector Labor Relations Decision Making   165

6–9   Elected Officials Do In Fact Represent the Public Interest in Local Public Sector Labor Relations Decision Making   168

6–10 Availability and Use of Structural Access Points   174

6–11 Availability and Use of Political Access Points   176

6—12   Favor Open Negotiations for Public Employees
       in Some Form   184
6—13   Self-Influence Ratings   187
6—14   Ratings by Others of Influence   188
6—15   Newspapers Influential in Public Employee Labor
       Relations Decision Making   190
6—16   Public Attitudes Towards Public Employee Bargain-
       ing at Federal, State, and Local Levels   194

Acknowledgments

Frank Cassell, Hervey Juris, David Stanley, and Frank Zeidler were generous in their advice and comments on the case study reports. Others who responded to the demands on their time for help in conceptualizing the study were Jack Barbash, R. Theodore Clark, Jr., Ronald Donovan, Paul Gerhart, Raymond Horton, Harry Kranz, Thomas Kochan, Jean McKelvey, Chester Newland, Robert O'Neil, Clyde Summers, Martin Wagner, and Kenneth Warner.

Gilbert Donahue was the Labor Department's technical representative.

Eliose Bodine and Jackie Berman of the League of Women Voters of Berkeley and California, respectively, were particularly helpful with the Berkeley case study.

Principal research assistance was provided by Mark Lehner and Ira Jaffe.

Irene Gordon edited the original draft, and Jeffrey Smith proofread it.

Foreword

It is an unusual impasse, or near impasse, in public sector labor relations in which someone does not make some reference to "the public interest." More often than not, this is done more for emphasis than clarity—as much as the name of the Deity may be invoked in a barroom argument. Parties to the impasse, editorial writers, alarmed citizens all talk about the public interest without saying what it is—or how well it would be served even if there were no labor problems in government. But even if they wanted to argue more rationally, even if they went to the literature for help, they would find little to enlighten them.

This volume is a major effort to fill the gap. Richard Schick and Jean Couturier take the reader through a wealth of theoretical concepts and empirical information concerning how the public interest has been perceived, and how these perceptions resulted in decisions. The discussion concentrates on five case studies in state and local government. In each one they emphasize the extent to which access to and influence upon the political decision making process were enjoyed by the various interested parties. It is clear that what happens between the adversaries at the bargaining table is only part of the picture.

There are in this book no clear-cut answers, no prescriptions for remedies that others may use. However, the examples and the reasoning in this analysis are sure to be helpful to government officials, union officers, and neutrals involved in public sector labor relations. More than that, the authors' research model should be considered by other political scientists who are researching the impact of interest groups on governmental decisions.

It took some nerve for the National Civil Service League to tackle this problem, and for the U.S. Department of Labor to approve its financing, considering the sponginess, immaturity, and emotionalism of the topic. The project has clearly added to our knowledge, and one hopes that other researchers, practitioners, and critics will contribute further evidence.

David T. Stanley
Washington, D.C.
January 1977

Introduction

This study of the public's interest in governmental labor relations is the product of an eighteen-month project which included a literature search, advisory group consultations, and case studies. It was conducted under the auspices of the National Civil Service League for the U.S. Department of Labor, Labor-Management Services Administration, Office of Policy Development. A sense of indifference to the "public interest," together with the desire by many members of "the public" to have an input into governmental labor relations decision making processes, gave rise to the need for a systematic study of both the concept and the facts of representation of the public interest in public sector labor relations. Hence, this beginning exploration.

Fifteen distinguished public sector labor relations researchers and practitioners (listed below) met with the authors in Washington in January 1975. They were asked to advise on the scope of the study, to examine the spectrum of possible study methods and to suggest a feasible research task. There was near unanimity on the difficulty of finding a single broad definition of "public interest." There was also a general consensus that because of this difficulty, the project should focus on the notion of whether a single public interest or several public interests could be inferred from the data developed by the study.

A minority argued that the public interest must be carefully defined, and the analysis based on the definition. Some argued that the study must analyze revenues, resource allocations (expenditures), "economy" of governmental operations, "efficiency and quality" of governmental services to citizens, and other issue definitions that might help describe the effects of collective bargaining upon the costs of government.

A large majority took a more pluralistic view, stressing the potential for access by individuals and interest groups to the labor relations decision making process and their influence upon it. This led to a wide-ranging debate on the concept of representation: who might represent the public interest and in what institutional and related contexts might such representation best be achieved?

The group concluded that the notion of due process—implying the potential access of every citizen to the decision making process—could be used as a criterion or model for analyzing the representation of any public interest, no matter what the policy content of that interest.

The first chapter examines the concept of the "public interest," including the methods by which the public interest may be studied. It also summarizes an extensive survey of the expository literature and other uses of the notion of the "public interest" in public sector labor relations. This is followed by five case studies of jurisdictions where interest groups representing persons who were not parties to the bilateral negotiations between city officials (management) and public employee union representatives (labor) perceived an interest in the outcome of the negotiations and tried to influence it. The final two chapters analyze the findings of the case studies in terms of "interests," access, and influence.

List of Participants and Advisors

Jack Barbash, Professor of Labor Economics, University of Wisconsin, Madison; Frank H. Cassell, Professor of Industrial and Labor Relations, Graduate School of Management, Northwestern University; R. Theodore Clark, Jr., Attorney, Seyfarth, Shaw, Fairweather & Geraldson, Chicago; Paul F. Gerhart, Federal Labor Relations Council; Evelyn Harrison, Board Member, National Civil Service League; Raymond D. Horton, Associate Professor of Business, Columbia University; Roger Jones, Board Member, National Civil Service League; Hervey A. Juris, Professor of Industrial and Labor Relations, Graduate School of Management, Northwestern University; Thomas A. Kochan, Assistant Professor of Industrial and Labor Relations, New York State School of Industrial and Labor Relations, Cornell University; Harry Kranz, Senior Fellow, Brookings Institution; David T. Stanley, Senior Fellow, Brookings Institution; Kathryn H. Stone, Board Member, National Civil Service League; Clyde W. Summers, Professor of Law, Yale University; Martin Wagner, Professor of Industrial and Labor Relations, University of Illinois, Champaign-Urbana; and Frank P. Zeidler, former Mayor of Milwaukee, Wisconsin.

The Public Interest
In Government
Labor Relations

Chapter 1

Concepts of the Public Interest
and Study Methods

CONCEPTS

Citizens are beginning to see a relationship between public employee labor negotiations and the distribution of tax resources for public service delivery. The increasingly fierce competition for scarce public dollar resources is leading to confrontations between citizens, their governments, and the employees of those governments. New York City's fiscal plight, which reached a crisis stage in 1975, and the San Francisco mayoral election of November 1975, which was followed by a public transit workers' strike in the spring of 1976, are among the most dramatic examples of such confrontations. On the one hand, public employees, especially through collective bargaining, are demanding more money, costly fringe benefits, and better working conditions. On the other, citizens are refusing to pay higher taxes, while at the same time they are demanding increased services, or at least are opposing reductions. Governments are responding by moves to cut payrolls, eliminate raises, curtail fringe benefits, and demand higher "productivity" from public employees.

Collective bargaining is the mechanism by which these conflicts are handled in 11,636 state and local governments [1]. The electoral power of public employee unions, many critics argue, gives them disproportionate power over the officials with whom they ostensibly bargain [2]. The unions, on the other hand, often feel caught between conflicting governmental power bases. Citizens are demanding access to the labor relations decision making process, which traditionally has been carried out largely in confidence by the labor and management parties to bilateral negotiations—this access being demanded for a variety of political, economic, and social reasons. Unions counter with arguments over any legal restrictions on employee rights to negotiate with elected officials or their representatives.

Theoretically, citizens have *political* access to the managers who bargain for their governments. It is said that these officials (or those who appoint them) can always be voted out of office by a dissatisfied citizenry. But it is questionable whether voters see the relationship between public employee negotiations policies and elections clearly enough to be motivated to respond in this indirect way of voting for or against officials on the basis of their bargaining decisions. Moreover, sometimes it may be in the interest of the public officials to avoid drawing attention to the real costs of public employee settlements as reflected in taxes and services, especially if they perceive their own employee unions to be an influential constituency. For example, deferred benefits such as pension costs may be particularly hard for the voter to identify. An agreement on a pension plan can take place just before an election but its costs can be deferred for years by underfunding it.

The concept of the public interest has both theoretical and operational or functional dimensions. Theoretically, it refers to an abstract social value that transcends the individual interests of the members of the society (the whole is thus greater than the sum of its parts). At the practical level, the notion of the public interest is value laden—it becomes a standard for judging social actions. For example: "Is what I propose (collective bargaining for public employees) merely good for me (because I am a public employee) or for the whole community (because collective bargaining procedures may provide an equitable way to determine public employee wages and benefits or, at least, may reduce social conflict)?" In analyzing the concept of the public interest, Richard E. Flathman speaks of the "universalizability principle," which:

> ... requires that political actors consider the impact of their actions and demands on the other members of society, reduce idiosyncratic demands, and seek constantly to find common ground with other men. They must perform the difficult task of thinking of themselves as members of a class of people. Through this process they subsume their interests under a larger precept or maxim and thereby begin to transform them into "claims" which can legitimately be pressed in the public forum [3].

According to Glendon Schubert, the identification of the public interest in operation has taken three basic tacs, reflecting major courses of political philosophy: Rationalist, Idealist, and Realist [4]. Rationalists "postulate a common good, which . . . finds expression in a popular will . . . ; the common obligation of all public officials is faithfully to execute the popular will" [5]. Idealists "advise the public official to excogitate the true essence of the public interest by means of a mental act of extrasensory perception. . . . The public interest becomes whatever the still, small voice of conscience reveals to each official" [6]. "The Realists are pro–interest group. . . . 'Public' becomes segmented as 'publics,' in which form it [public], too, merges in the concept of 'interest' group" [7].

The use of the term "public interest" in discussions of governmental labor relations has strong value connotations. With rare exceptions, the concept of the public interest is invoked to give legitimacy to one's own, or to evaluate others' policy prescriptions for public sector labor negotiations. The very assertion of the concept of the public interest in public sector labor relations indicates that there are "interests" other than those of the two parties to bilateral agreements. A search of the literature on public sector labor relations affirms that the term public interest is used to prescribe a standard for evaluating a wide range of governmental labor relations policies and practices. However, the term does not appear to have any universalizable meaning in the context of public sector labor relations.

Nevertheless, there is a shared view among commentators that a considerable segment of the population which is attentive to public sector labor relations matters feels that it has an "interest" in such policies and practices. Moreover, there is a prevailing view among this same group that many "interests" have been excluded from an effective role in the labor relations decision making process. This feeling is expressed as a sense of powerlessness over the input into governmental collective bargaining agreements. It is a feeling of having no opportunity to register opinions or to react to the contents of a proposed settlement. The same feeling exists among many regarding private sector collective bargaining, particularly in areas of potential "national emergencies."

This is a problem of representative government that is not easily resolved. The outcome of governmental labor negotiations has motivated many citizens, both as individuals and in groups, to demand access either to the negotiations process itself or to the parties before they conclude negotiations, in order to try to influence the outcome more directly than going through the electoral process.

Popular notions of the "public interest" tend to be personal, prescriptive views. As such, they cannot be studied empirically. Any party can assert that what they think about the "public interest" is a universal principle. These claims often supply the vehicle for self-interested propaganda. If private interests are couched in such a way as to convince others of a commonly shared interest, an emotionally effective plea has been made for a personal cause. Public policy discussions are rife with such assertions of the public interest, and it is not surprising that public sector labor relations often are discussed in terms of normative, prescriptive claims.

But evidence for these claims is too difficult to produce in order to permit answers that are useful for policy development. It is more useful to consider the "positive" notion of the public interest. This is the question of how the public interest is in fact represented in practice, rather than how it *ought* to be represented. To answer this question fully, however, requires an operational or functional definition of the public interest.

Social science research has not quantified this concept as yet; but "public interest" still may be studied by identifying its components *in action*, without necessarily assigning values or weights to them. These components are the identification of the interests or interest groups that desire to affect the outcome of public sector labor relations decisions, an analysis of the mechanics of that decision making process, and observation of the availability and use of access to the decision making process for such interests, together with an estimate of their influence on these decisions.

ACCESS

Despite the absence of a single comprehensive operational definition of the public interest, the assumptions underlying the concept of democratic decision making are useful as a model for analyzing the representation of the public interest. This concept may be restated as: the potential for each interested citizen to have access either to the decision making process itself or to the persons who are charged with making decisions on behalf of the body politic. According to this concept, the basis for analysis of the public interest in governmental labor relations is *access* to the public sector labor relations decision making process by "publics," "interests," or "third parties" (used synonymously), all of which are defined as the nondirect participants in bilateral negotiations—that is, neither labor nor management. They also may be defined as individuals or groups not directly involved in negotiations but who perceive themselves to be affected by the outcome of negotiations.

In the private sector, labor relations decisions traditionally have been evaluated by their consequences in the marketplace. Only where they have greatly offended a sense of equity have legislators sought to limit them. It has not been the accepted practice to have public access to these decisions. The test is strictly economics as a constraining force on the parties to the bilateral negotiations. For example: a settlement that is "too high" will result in an increase in prices, which will limit the sale of the product, thereby reducing worker income or the demand for labor. Only where the market is not a sufficiently disciplined force (as where there is no substitute for the product) do people go to the government for regulated settlements.

For instance, legislatures such as the U.S. Congress, especially, have attempted to influence collective bargaining through the threat of seizure and, as a matter of fact, actually have prevented railroad strikes through legislative fiat. This action may or may not be related to a sense of equity; more likely, it is the result of concern about the effect of a nationwide strike upon the national economy or the nation's health and welfare. In other words, the test may not be strictly one of economics—it may very well be political. President Truman attempted to seize the steel industry because he felt that a strike would hamper operations in Korea; it was a politically popular move. The assumption that the true test of the "public interestedness" of a private sector labor settlement is strictly economics might hold where the parties to the bargain are not monopolistic—that is, are subject to both labor market and product market competition.*

In the public sector, labor relations are the product of the governmental process where, theoretically, access is a public virtue. Citizen input into public sector decision making processes generally is regarded as a positive social goal, and the democratic political process is supposed to work to provide this access. By contrast with the rhetoric of openness that is applied to most government decision making outside of national security, it is often argued that governmental labor relations decisions, like those in the private sector, must be kept largely secret between the negotiating parties for fear of disrupting the negotiations process by revealing actual bargaining parameters to the other side.

This dilemma posed by the requirements of democratic government for open decision making and government labor relations strategic considerations is illustrated by the fact that the "sunshine" laws in all four of the states represented by the case studies (Wisconsin, Pennsylvania, Tennessee, and California) have not been applied

---

*Frank Cassell, letter to the Authors, July 14, 1975.

to matters under their labor relations statutes. Nevertheless, access is an accepted public sector value, even in the context of governmental labor relations. However, access is conceived of by most interests studied as taking place somewhere else other than at the bargaining table. Here, the public sector interest may begin with a bilateral arrangement between the public employer representing both the citizens and the workers. The labor unions, in the eyes of many citizens, become third party intervenors: it is the union, not the public, that is the third party. This is how some citizens might view the situation, which is similar to the private sector where private employers consider the union to be a third party intervenor into relations between an employer and its employees.**

Access is defined as any opportunity for input which third parties (defined as nonlabor, nonmanagement) may have in the governmental labor relations policy or program decision making process. Access can include formal, institutionalized participation such as serving on a policy advisory board, or informal political participation such as lobbying an elected or appointed official. Institutional participation may be referred to as structural access; political participation as political access. Structural access may be conceived of as having a direct personal role in the decision making process through such means as formal consultations, solicitations of advice, or where agreement or dissent is registered by a third party as part of the decision making process. Political access is seen as having indirect access, through another person who is an actual participant in the decision making process.

Basically, access presupposes a pluralistic political system in which persons or interests who are not in government positions are able to gain a hearing and may influence those who are. However, there is no preconception here that in all instances pluralism extends to the entire body politic or that all interests have equal access and influence, only that the concept of pluralistic decision making can be used as a model for analyzing government decision making.

Those who advocate an elitist conception of government decision making, nevertheless, do so in the context of the pluralistic model. They are simply saying that access to the decision making process does not extend to the entire public and that decisions are, in fact, made among members of a relatively limited group. Only in an absolute dictatorship (which is conceivable but never observed) would decisions be made without reference to any other interest than that of the decision maker and hence be irrelevant to the pluralistic model. Even in such an extreme situation, the pluralistic model

**Cassell, *op. cit.*

would serve as a yardstick for measuring the true extent of the dicta-tor's absolute power. Politics, by definition, implies more than one locus of decision making power, based on the distribution of political resources for influencing decisions.

INFLUENCE

Access to decision making and/or decision makers is a necessary but not a sufficient condition for affecting policy outcomes. Influence on decisions is an indication of the effectiveness of access in terms of an ability to add to or to subtract from them. Influence is a product partly of the kind and degree of access and partly of the methods used to exploit that access. Access, as we have said, is the opportu-nity to participate in decision making; influence is the ability to affect the outcome of the decision. Governmental collective bargain-ing is a form of continuous policy development. Whether the influ-ence of an interest is limited to a single decision or whether it persists (or grows or shrinks) over time is, therefore, an important considera-tion.

Thus the democratic decision making model can serve as the basis for analysis of the public interest. It permits identification of the independent variables (legal and political setting) of the decision making process that affect the dependent variables of access and influence, without having to quantify those variables. Knowledge of the mere presence or absence of an access point or method for exploiting an access point is sufficient to indicate the possibility that a public interest may be represented in governmental labor relations decision making process.

Following the identification of the range of access points available in a given situation, it is necessary to identify those points at which third party access may be most effective. Is such an input most effec-tively undertaken when the collective bargaining laws are formulated, or, as is more usually the case, at the actual crisis or impasse stage? Or could there be an effective third party role during the continuous phase of policy implementation and administration?

This study describes the impact (access and influence) of third party intervention on what is essentially a bilateral bargaining pro-cess. No assumptions are made that such intervention is or is not desirable. Care has been taken not to equate third party access and influence with total public interest nor in any way to imply that union representatives or city officials do not act in the public interest.

It is conceivable that the public interest might well be represented throughout the bargaining process by the principal labor and management bargainers themselves. An immediate step in this direction might be to raise the consciousness of labor and management negotiators with regard to their obligations to interests over and above their own, possibly narrowly conceived interests. A more long range goal would be to ensure that these spokesmen are as representative as possible of all elements of the larger society [8].

STUDY METHODS

Case Studies

Once the concept of the representation of the public interest was defined operationally as the access to and influence upon the governmental labor relations decision making process by third parties (as defined above), the study became one of identifying the characteristics and effects of both access and influence in various jurisdictional settings. The dependent variables are access and influence. These are affected by the independent variables, which are the environmental situations within which access and influence take place, namely: governmental structures, laws, and the economic, social, and political conditions of each jurisdiction studied.

One research design would have quantifiable independent variables that described the characteristics of the decision making process affecting access and influence. This would involve a regression analysis of the independent variables upon the dependent variables. However, not enough is known about these variables to permit quantification.[a] Thorough case studies were needed just to clarify the variables involved in third party access and influence. Hopefully, a major contribution of this study is to identify and classify the factors affecting access and influence and to evaluate these broadly in the context of the governmental and political factors of selected jurisdictions.

Two approaches to the governmental labor relations decision making process were considered. The first was the study of so-called critical incidents. Such a study takes a given law, policy, or bargaining settlement as an output of the decision making process and traces

[a]Knowledge of the dependent variables (methods of access and influence) is necessary before any attempts can be made to quantify them. Quantifiable research may then be done in subsequent studies. A larger sample size also would be necessary to get sufficient degrees of freedom for a regression analysis involving the wide range of variables that may be anticipated. Systematic knowledge of the environmental correlates of public sector labor relations decisions also would have to be developed, for there is no state of the art study of the independent variables of the organization and structure of public sector labor relations decision making and administrative machinery. [Discussion with Hervey Juris.]

its historical antecedents in terms of the opportunities for third party influence. The second method was to consider a jurisdiction as a unit, then to try to identify all the third parties and their methods of trying to influence governmental labor relations decisions generally. The critical incident approach is more easily definable (and therefore controllable) in terms of resources for research. But the unit approach may be more important for what it can reveal about the range of possible third party interests, goals, and methods.

The choice of methods for case studies depends upon whether the critical incident or unit approach is taken. We took a mixture of the two. For a unit study, Milwaukee, which is known to have a long history of governmental labor relations experiences and activities, was chosen. Critical incidents in Philadelphia, Berkeley, and Memphis were selected in order to eliminate as many extraneous variables as possible.

A critical incident, then, is defined as a situation in which third parties manifest concern about the outcome of a governmental labor relations decision. They also may try to influence that decision. The decision can be a law, policy, or settlement of a dispute that led to a strike or other similarly extreme action by either side; in any case, it is a discrete event whose antecedents are identifiable. In Philadelphia it was the 1972–73 teachers strike; in Memphis the 1975 sanitation-men's bargaining compared with what happened in 1968; and in Berkeley the 1975 school board negotiations under the new California disclosure law.

The questions asked were: Who sought access? Whom did they represent? At what point(s) in the decision making process did they try to gain access? How did they try to maximize influence? Were they influential? Were there any indications of persistent interest and influence? In the case study of Milwaukee city and school board bargaining in general, the focus was on the identification of the whole range of possible third party interests, the kinds of government labor relations in which they sought to have input, and a description of their methods and influence.

For both approaches a model representing the range of possible steps in the governmental labor relations decision making process was used to identify the range of potential third party access points and the methods they used to exploit these access points in order to gain representation and influence. Access points may be formal or informal—that is, there may be a specific legal provision for third party input, such as a requirement to hold hearings or a referendum on matters pertaining to a collective bargaining settlement. These are structural access points. On the other hand, third parties may seek to influence decision makers through personal contacts or by attempting to influence the constituents of decision makers through propagandizing them. These are political access points.

A set of five assumed criteria for identifying influence included an identification of direct political contacts, indirect patterns of relationships between decision makers and third parties, whether third party goals are reflected in decisions, descriptions of methods of exploiting access in order to gain influence, and the persistence of influence. Influence may be direct in the sense of contact or pressure by one person on another; or it may be indirect in the sense of affecting the background conditions to a decision, such as economic and political factors, or the mind sets of decision makers, as in conditioning their attitudes.

No objective measures of influence were attempted. Instead, the participants' own evaluations of their own and others' influence was reported. The extent to which an interest's goals were reflected in the output of government labor relations decisions is a necessary but not a sufficient condition of influence, in that reflected interests could be coincidental; absence of an interest's goals in the decision, however, is clearly indicative of a lack of influence. Persistence of influence can be revealed in studies of jurisdictional units over time more easily than in critical incident studies. In both, the indicators of influence are the reputation of the third party among participants in the decision making process and among other third parties, the amount and kinds of activities undertaken to realize goals, and the reflection of policy goals in decision outputs.

The "representativeness" of the interest(s) identified was studied according to such characteristics as the number or kinds of persons reflected in group membership or opinion polls, social and economic characteristics of group members, stated group goals or opinions of individuals as revealed through polls, methods of leadership selection and participation of members in group decision making, profession of the leadership as to what it purports to represent, assessments of other groups and decision makers as to what the individual or group represents, and their perceptions of the interest's goals and their assessments of its effectiveness or influence.

A search of the literature of public sector labor relations, described later, revealed eleven basic definitions of the "public interest." These were categorized as those that supplied prescriptive definitions of the public interest in terms of various community values, such as "efficiency," "maintenance of essential services," or "employee democracy," and those that were concerned with the procedural prerequisites for democratic decision making, such as "due process" and "representative government." By interviewing the decision makers and interested parties in each of the jurisdictions, it was possible to compare the practitioners' and the interest groups' own definitions of the public interest with those cited in the literature.

Besides attempting to define the public interest, the literature contains policy recommendations for achieving the public interest. These may be categorized broadly as those that propose structural changes in the decision making process and those that deal with political changes or changes in approaches toward the existing structures of representative government. The former policies would change the machinery through which governmental labor relations decisions are made in order to facilitate access to this process by various interests. The latter position asserts that the existing system of representative government is sufficient to permit access and influence by those who desire to participate. To change policies requires a changed pattern of political participation by the interests involved.

In the case studies, the attitudes of both the practitioners and the interest groups were considered according to both the structural and political approaches. Generally, the case studies are based on: (1) an analysis of the pertinent newspaper articles, published statements of the interest groups involved, and legal documents; and (2) informal discussions with many key persons active in the governmental labor relations decision making process, persons or group leaders having an interest in influencing these decisions, and uninvolved observers such as newspaper reporters and academics.

Participants, interests, and observers were identified by three methods: (1) a preliminary search of the newspaper files, (2) discussions with local participants and observers, and (3) by asking each person to name other persons thought to be interested or influential in the decisions under study. Discussions—often lengthy—were held with 25 to 40 officials, interest group representatives, and observers in each of the four jurisdictions studied. All of the discussants were accessible; few stipulated that they wished to remain anonymous. Nevertheless, individuals have not been identified by name. None of the mayors of the four jurisdictions was interviewed; however, key negotiators and city council and/or school board members were. The opinions of the unorganized public and other activists were sought through the identification of public opinion surveys, press reports, and expository writing. In the case study analysis, the attitudes and opinions of the 150 persons directly interviewed in Milwaukee, Philadelphia, Memphis, and Berkeley were catalogued by abstracting from the notes of the meetings. One hundred of the more extensive discussions were tabulated and appear below in Chapter 6.

The range of conversational topics included perceptions of community attitudes towards public and private sector unions, questions of shared values between public and private sector union members, the role of labor in local politics, whether any local elections have affected or been affected by public employee negotiations or critical incidents, who is influential in negotiations, how the decision makers take the public interest into account and whom they feel they represent, attitudes towards any tendency to defer bargaining decisions to third parties (in this case mediators or arbitrators), perceptions of public interest or public apathy towards governmental labor relations policies or practices, citizen participation at hearings or other formal access points, feedback received from organized and unorganized publics, opinions regarding who actually represents the public interest (as compared with who ought to do so and whether it is in fact being done at all), definitions of the public interest, attitudes towards such formal policy procedures as open negotiations, disclosure requirements, and other related subjects.

Not all persons had the time or the desire to discuss all these subjects; and some subjects were inappropriate for some discussants. This meant that a complete cataloguing of attitudes and opinions was impossible. The documentation was distilled to include only the basic background information on the jurisdiction's governmental labor relations decision making process and the critical incident studied that is essential for comparative purposes, together with descriptions of the most active interests, the available avenues of access to the governmental labor relations decision making process, and estimates of influence.

The study of interests is limited to those which had made themselves known through their pronouncements or activities on the question of public employee negotiations. Individuals or group leaders who may have had attitudes but did not express them, or who were not perceived by other interests, participants, or observers, fell outside the scope of this study. Probably few such unidentified interests actually exist in the jurisdictions studied. However, many local interests thought to be interested proved not to be; this was often true of local affiliates of national public interest groups.

Interests of unorganized publics can be identified through polls of scientifically selected population samples. These are rare for state and local jurisdictions in the area of government labor relations, as compared with national polls. The national polling organizations have little data on opinions and attitudes on public sector labor relations issues for specific jurisdictions, although they do ask such questions of their national samples. We do have poll data pertaining to three of our four jurisdictions. The Urban Observatory (National

League of Cities, U.S. Conference of Mayors) and metropolitan Milwaukee Association of Commerce polled the city of Milwaukee. The Greater Philadelphia Movement commissioned a poll on educational questions in that community. The California Teachers Association commissioned a poll of the state of California. Pertinent questions from these three surveys appear in Appendix C. None was done for Memphis.

LITERATURE SEARCH

Key elements of the case study design were drawn from a search of the literature on governmental labor relations. Part of the plan was to investigate whether, or to what degree, definitions of the public interest found in selected expository writings and legal documents agreed with the definitions of the practitioners, interests, and observers involved with day-to-day public sector collective bargaining. The expectation was that the definitions found in the literature would be an effective starting point for the field investigations and that policy analyses in the literature would suggest issues that needed further examination. As stated earlier, eleven broad categories of definitions of the public interest in governmental labor relations were found. They ranged from arguments against any public employee collective bargaining to those in support of equal bargaining status between public employers and their employees.

The first step in the literature search was to examine the major bibliographies [9] on public sector labor relations for references to the public interest in titles and for discussions of general public interest policy considerations in legislation, public employee strikes, community participation, and organizational structures for labor relations decision making at the state and local levels. Some 80 articles and books were examined for this initial review. These yielded about 100 definitions of the public interest. In addition, legal documents on file with the Library of the New York State School of Industrial and Labor Relations at Cornell University were randomly examined for definitions of the public interest contained in legal decisions by arbitrators and arguments by plaintiffs. State and municipal public employee labor relations laws and ordinances were examined to see whether there were explicit references to the public interest. Criteria contained in the laws for resolving impasses came closest in most instances to functional or operational definitions of the public interest. Finally, the hearings on proposed federal legislation regulating state and local public employee bargaining were examined.

Two types of definitions of the public interest emerged from these investigations: implicit and explicit. An implied definition of the public interest is one that may be inferred from an author's general attitude towards a specific aspect of governmental labor relations. For example, opposition to strikes on the grounds that they give employees "excessive" powers to determine public policy budget questions is an implied definition of the public interest in the value of maintaining governmental sovereignty in budgetary decision making. Similarly, supporting the right to strike on the grounds that it provides constitutional rights to employees by giving them a voice in setting their own terms and conditions of work is an implied definition of the public interest in the value of "industrial democracy."

An explicit definition is one found in a quotation such as: "It is in the public interest to avoid strikes which would threaten the public health or safety by disrupting essential services, such as sanitationmen's strikes." All three types of literature yielded both implicit and explicit definitions of the "public interest."

From the list of implied and explicit definitions, eleven major headings emerged. These reflect the values of:

1. Continuity of Services
2. (Avoiding) Inconvenience
3. Maintaining Essential Services
4. Public Welfare, Health, and Safety
5. Government Sovereignty
6. Efficiency of Government
7. Constraints on Employers and Employees
8. Constitutional Rights of Employees
9. Equitable Settlements
10. Stable Collective Bargaining
11. Preservation of the Merit System

Within these broad categorical values there are some subdefinitions which will be described. An attempt has been made to shade the meaning from the broadest notion of "Continuity of Public Services" to the more narrow value of "Protecting the Merit System." However, certain ambiguities are inevitable.

1. Continuity of Services means that it is in the public interest to have *no* interruptions of public services whatsoever. This amounts to an absolute strike ban. The continuity of services value usually is stated in order to justify no strikes by public employees. For many holding this view, it implies that *all* governmental services are, by definition, only those which are absolutely necessary. Otherwise, government wouldn't have to perform them in competition with private enterprise. Therefore, no interruption of these absolutely necessary services can be tolerated. An implied definition merely may state that although public sector strikes are, in theory, an anathema to the public, the public in fact generally tolerates strikes. Or, such a definition may imply the desirability of an absolute strike ban.

2. (Avoiding) Inconvenience to the public is an ambiguous subcategory value ranking just below that of continuity of services. A functional definition of inconvenience is highly subjective, although it is conceivable that most people could agree on a least some governmental services without which they would be inconvenienced. Because of the subjectivity of the notion of inconvenience, it may be used more in a propagandistic sense than its successor, "Public Welfare, Health, and Safety." This is because no objective evidence is required to assert an inconvenience in a common sense meaning.

Examples of a cessation of services that might generally be agreed upon as not constituting an inconvenience until after a period of deteriorating conditions might include highway maintenance, tree trimming, or even park services. By contrast, a toll collectors' or bridge shutdown, withdrawing traffic police, or closing some kinds of government offices could inconvenience a large proportion of their users immediately.

As with any of these public interest definitions, whether the public, as a majority of the citizens, would be affected or perceive a problem, or whether only particular publics would be affected, would determine the magnitude of the inconvenience. Some would argue that the inconvenience must be perceived by a large proportion of the community if it is to be classified as interfering with general community values in the maintenance of governmental services in question (traffic circulation valued by more people than welfare payment processing).

Others would assert that inconvenience to any person is against the general public interest in other-regarding social harmony, such that an injustice to one member of the society constitutes an injustice to all; so that even an inconvenience limited to a relatively small number of people is an inconvenience to all. Still others would argue that inconvenience is largely an interest group question of whose ox is being gored and what kind of political action the affected groups are capable of taking in their own defense to remedy the inconvenience.

3. Essential Services are distinguished from those whose cessation would cause merely an inconvenience. Essential services include those whose absence would threaten social stability. For example, to some the interruption of educational services is more than an inconvenience, both because of the possibility of urban disorders in the big cities as well as the unrelenting social and economic needs for functional educational training. Essential services also are ones for which no practical substitutes are available (welfare payments processing), or ones without which the economic infrastructure would be weakened (mass transportation services).

The argument runs that the monopoly role of government in providing certain services such as education, welfare, and mass transportation is largely a function of their expense and the uneconomic nature of trying to provide them through private enterprise. The fact that government does provide them is an index of their "essentiality" in the sense that it is thought that there is sufficient need for them regardless of whether they are profitable in the short run. This economic dependence on government-provided services underlies the potential impact of the cessation of such services in the event of a work stoppage; thus it is argued that their maintenance is in the public interest. Any threat of their cessation by a strike of public employees is taken to be against the public interest. The argument is similar in quality to that of the continuity of services rationale. It differs only in degree—namely that government may provide some services that are not absolutely essential and which, therefore, could be interrupted, in contrast to "essential" services, which must not be.

4. Public Welfare, Health, and Safety is a stronger value than maintaining essential services. "Health and safety" have life-threatening implications more immediate even than essential services. "Welfare" however, shades more evenly into inconvenience or essential services than do those services whose cessation could pose an immediate threat to public health or safety. Hospital, police, and fire strikes are argued to pose such drastic threats. Opponents of this line of argument counter by pointing out that many—perhaps most—of the tasks of even police, fire, and health departments are such that their cessation would not *immediately* pose a threat to life or property.

In the private sector, the Railway Labor and National Labor Relations Acts permit the President and the federal courts to define a threat to the public health or safety in the event of a "national emergency" strike. The functional definition of such a threat is left up to the judgment of specified parties, who must evaluate the specific circumstances and projected (economic) impact of such a strike. The Canadian Public Service Staff Relations Act permits management to define in advance of any work stoppage those employees whose absence would constitute a threat to the national security or safety. The unions may ratify this list. If they object, the controversy is arbitrated by the independent administrative board, which oversees the administration of the legislation [10].

5. Government Sovereignty is a broad category that encompasses two major values. First, collective bargaining is argued to be against the "public interest" in having open and representative government. Decisions made at the bargaining table behind closed doors are said to weaken or destroy the public's control over their elected officials by depriving them of the knowledge of what transpires at the bargaining table. Moreover, it is argued that elected officials cannot constitutionally delegate such decision making power to the appointed officials who do the bargaining. Every time an issue is made bargainable, it is removed from the legislative-executive decision making process. Bargaining rights for labor make employees equal to legally constituted, elected authority. The notion that the electorate's elected representatives would be required to bargain with a group of employees on equal (not to mention disadvantageous) terms is unthinkable to many.

A corollary to this representation argument is the argument that the employees have no right to exact funds from the government— and hence the taxpayer—by bargaining. Only the legislature is empowered to appropriate funds based on its members' deliberative judgments of the requests. Threats to strike over wage or benefit packages that would increase the costs of government are argued to be against the public interest in the legislature's need to weigh all claims made on it for appropriations in the light of their social merits, rather than under the threat of a strike or other concerted job action. According to this view, forcing governments to pay more than they can afford short-circuits the democratic appropriations process.

6. Efficiency of Government is a public interest value that is argued to promote support for the collective bargaining process itself. The efficiency of government argument is used in support of collective bargaining, as are the arguments for equitable settlements, constitutional rights of employees, and stable collective bargaining relationships.

"Efficiency" proponents argue that collective bargaining promotes efficiency by minimizing or eliminating sources of employee dissatisfaction and potential resulting strife, thereby contributing to fewer interruptions of work. Suggestions by employees and employers during the negotiations process are also said to contribute to efficiency by eliminating unnecessary tasks or redistributing them more efficiently. Improved working conditions and benefits won by employees may in many cases be said to contribute to greater efficiency of service delivery through better physical facilities (such as labor saving devices) and "professionalization" of many governmental services (upgrading of teachers, health care personnel, or welfare workers by providing in-service training, for example).

7. Constraints on Employers and Employees are argued to be in the public interest. This is basically the public as third party at the bargaining table argument. It does not accept the implications of the Rationalist view that elected officials, by virtue of the fact that they may have been elected by the largest plurality of votes necessarily represent the public interest. It does take note of the political view of the Realists that other interest groups may get involved in the labor relations decision making process to mitigate the power of labor and management, but rejects this as a value. This is still an Idealist argument for the imposition of restraints on both elected officials and interest groups, as a product of public vigilance and institutional checks and balances. This is an argument for the public regulation and oversight of any public employee collective bargaining.

8. Equitable Settlements imposed by the distribution of power among labor and management is an argument similar to the efficiency argument. In this case, it is collective bargaining that is argued to be the most equitable way to establish employee rights and benefits. Government does not have an absolute right to dictate wages or benefits or conditions of work to its employees, because it does not possess absolute knowledge of the labor marketplace. Either the local private sector (where there is free collective bargaining based on supply and demand) has to be taken as a standard for pay comparability, or public employees must be allowed to bargain with their public employer in order to reach agreements that are based on the supply and demand for public employees in the context of the competition from the private sector labor marketplace. The possibility of overrepresentation of labor (or management) based on their relative political strengths, rather than economic supply and demand factors, is not accounted for by this argument.

9. Constitutional Rights of Employees are closely related to the argument for equitable settlements. It is close to the obverse of the governmental sovereignty argument. These are the familiar private sector positions on freedom of contract, speech, association,[b] and the right to withdraw one's own labor. Sharing in the decision making process that affects one's own livelihood, it is argued, is a basic right of all free people. Recognition of public employee union power is the only basic way to assure equity and justice for employees. Public employers are not necessarily beneficent and their employees should not expect them to be so. In a free society, competing economic groups (management and labor) have a right to struggle in the political arena in order to try to obtain justice for their own side. This is a Realist's argument insofar as it perceives unions as interest groups acting to guarantee employee rights. It is in the public interest not to inhibit this basic democratic method of an interest group (employee union) to organize politically and bargain with governmental office holders (management) for its own ends.

10. Stable Collective Bargaining is the institutionalization of a politically established and guaranteed market system for handling employee-employer conflicts and guaranteeing constitutional rights. This is in the public interest, it is argued, because the institutions of public employee collective bargaining are equipped to deal with problems that otherwise would cause labor unrest and thereby cause an interruption of public services.

11. The Merit System is thought by some to be an impediment to collective bargaining and by others to be a value that must be preserved in the face of collective bargaining. The former argument is used by collective bargaining proponents, who say that the managers of the merit system are not impartial but instead represent management. As such, they cannot be expected to mete out justice to employees. Therefore, employees must organize and bargain directly with their employers for an alternative system of adjudication of employer-employee differences.

Those who would restrict the scope of collective bargaining argue that there is a public interest in preserving the merit system's requirements for nonpolitical hiring and promotions based on fitness for the job, rather than political or other criteria negotiated between politically powerful employee organizations and management.[b] "Merit employment" is an absolute value, which supersedes employee special interests. This is a variant on the Idealist's sovereignty argument

[b]This argument anticipates the "closed shop," which does not yet exist in public employment to any significant degree.

that there is a public interest in keeping public employment decisions solely within institutions of government whose managers are elected or appointed to protect the public interest, rather than permitting political interest groups to influence such decisions simply because they may have political lobbying power greater than the voting power of their members.

SUMMARY

We can illuminate the question of the representation of the public interest in governmental labor relations through case studies of public sector labor relations decision making activities. The object of these studies is to identify: (1) the kinds of third party interests—that is, persons who are not parties to bilateral negotiations between labor and management, who have perceived an interest in the outcome of such negotiations and have tried to influence that outcome; (2) the range of access points, both structural and political, by which such interests sought to influence decisions; and (3) estimates of their actual influence on government decision making.

Case studies can cover a broad range of third party activities, or can be of a single critical incident such as a strike or particular set of negotiations. In either kind of study, labor and management decision makers, third party interests, and observers such as newspaper reporters and academics are interviewed regarding their definitions of the public interest and perceptions as to whether it is a factor in governmental labor relations decisions; the extent to which the existing decision making process, both structural and political, satisfies the interests' needs for access; and the extent to which the parties have experimented with or feel the need for structural and political reforms.

Chapter 2

The Public Interest in Collective Bargaining in Milwaukee City and Schools

PART I MILWAUKEE CITY

SELECTION OF MILWAUKEE

Milwaukee, Wisconsin, was selected because of its long history of relatively stable public sector labor relations. Milwaukee is a major city which reflects many of the strengths and weaknesses that affect public sector labor-management relations. The climate for labor is favorable. Government employee relations are governed by state legislation. The participants are highly experienced negotiators.

Socially, Milwaukee is known as a progressive city, characterized by experimentation and a reputedly high level of public interest in governmental affairs. It was the seat of many of the major governmental reforms of the twentieth century. A major factor in its selection for the first case study was its history of avoiding the excessive public employee labor-management conflicts that have plagued some other cities, and of thus managing comparatively harmonious public sector labor relations over a long period of time. It was felt that a case study of "the representation of the public interest" in such steady, ongoing public sector labor relations would reveal considerations associated with the norm, unaffected by variables found in critical incidents.

Note: The first two of the five case studies document a series of discussions in March 1975 with the principal participants and other parties interested in public sector collective bargaining in Milwaukee, Wisconsin. The first part deals with the city's bargaining with its employee unions. The second part deals with the Milwaukee school board's teacher bargaining.

INDEPENDENT VARIABLES

Government Structure

On paper, Milwaukee's government is characterized as a "weak mayor" form. The common council, besides being a legislative body, confirms mayoral appointees to all operating departments and oversees governmental administration through a 'series of standing and special committees. Council members also form a majority of the eleven-member board of estimates, which in turn supervises the bureau of budget and management analysis. The council's judiciary committee is the liaison to the state legislature and has the sole power to forward legislative proposals affecting city home rule. The civil service commission is notably the only major administrative department over whose five mayoral appointees the common council does not have confirmation powers.

In view of these various constitutional powers, it might be concluded that the common council, not the mayor, would dominate public sector collective bargaining. But, as will be discussed below, there are other countervailing political factors that increase the mayor's powers.

Attitudes Towards Organized Labor

Milwaukee has a record of generally high public and private wages and of high taxes. In 1974 local taxes increased more noticeably than in any year in memory. This could have an impact on the community's attitude toward public sector employees. Over the years, the community has held very favorable attitudes toward organized labor in general, extending to some degree toward public employees in particular. Virtually everyone interviewed volunteered that Milwaukee is a strong union town and this grass roots support was cited as a function of the high degree of union organization in the area.

The AFL—CIO's labor council president claimed that the local work force is one of the most highly organized in the nation, and this claim seems to have valid support. The proportion of private sector workers in both the city and Milwaukee county who belong to unions is about 36 percent, higher than both the national average of 27 percent and the Wisconsin average of 30 percent. Adding the organized public employees in the city and county to this amount brings the total percentage to 39. Eighty-five percent of the 9,450 city employees under the control of the common council are covered by fifteen bargaining units. According to a local public opinion survey conducted in 1970, 18 percent of the citizens of Milwaukee either work for the city or have a relative who does [1].

The fact that both the private and public sector are so highly organized is cited by most observers as a principal reason for the apparent acquiescence of citizens in public sector labor relations developments up to the present. In the 1970 survey a plurality of Milwaukee residents expressed an opinion on behalf of the right to strike for nonpublic safety employees, and a large percentage even supported the right of policemen and firemen to strike. In 1974, however, public opinion polls showed a dissatisfaction with both tax rates and public services. Some of the key participants in Milwaukee's public sector labor relations process think that the community is beginning to harbor negative feelings towards public employees [2]. There is some thought that the local private sector unionized employees, as taxpayers, do not share the same goals and values of public employees, although this was denied by the president of the AFL-CIO's district council.

Political Activities of Unions

It is widely felt that both private and public sector unions play the dominant political role in the Milwaukee community. In fact, the president of a major business interest group revealed that his organization actually worked through local AFL-CIO in endorsing candidates for the common council. This was done in the hope that the business community would have a modicum of influence on the union's selection of candidates, since those whom the unions support were virtually certain to get elected. Other observers were somewhat more cautious in their assessments of the political strength of organized labor. But the consensus is that labor's endorsement is widely sought by candidates. By contrast, some observers remarked that labor's opposition to a candidate could and had backfired; so that labor was not as effective when working against a candidate as it was likely to be on a candidate's behalf.

Labor endorses candidates for both the primary and the general election. These endorsements are widely felt to be crucial to a candidate's success, especially in common council elections in working class districts. Only a minority of the common council comes from districts where union membership is not thought to be a predominant political consideration. Labor's financing of candidates through the AFL-CIO's COPE organization also is regarded as important to common council members. The overwhelming number of council members are Democrats, despite the formality of "nonpartisan" elections. Policemen and firemen appear to be particularly influential in their ability to work on behalf of candidates by "spreading the word" in the neighborhood during the course of their regular contacts with residents.

Since there are no available figures showing the distribution of organized employees by common council district, there is no way of telling which, if any, council elections were—or could have been— affected by the city employee vote. The important point is that such a vote is perceived so widely and strongly to be an influential vote.

Of the 35 key actors in or observers of the public sector labor relations scene, the subject of labor's influence on elections was discussed with twenty. All either volunteered the observation or agreed with the statement that union members, especially public employees, have been influential in city elections. The clear implication is that labor is a force to be reckoned with seriously. In summary, it can be asserted that the political orientation of elected officials in Milwaukee certainly is not antilabor; and is decidedly pro-labor, with some exceptions. Significantly, both the president of the common council and the chairman of the finance and labor committee, while they do not feel that they are antilabor, neither do they think themselves as "pro" city employee union as they perceive most of their colleagues.

Collective Bargaining Structure

The city's negotiating is done under the auspices of the common council by the chief negotiator of the office of labor relations, with oversight from the common council's labor policy committee, expanded to include the mayor and a number of key officials. Negotiating for employees under the city is done the district council of the American Federation of State, County, and Municipal Employees (AFSCME) (3,500) and by representatives of the police (1,890), firefighters (1,000), Laborers' International union (800), and smaller unions (representing 807 other employees). These bargaining efforts have never formally coalesced despite some attempts at informal coordination. This study was limited to AFSCME negotiations. Collective bargaining authority is based primarily on state statute, supplemented by local city charter and common council resolutions.

In practice, the city's bargaining procedure is more complex than is suggested by the formal organizational chart. Certain key officials play more powerful roles than their official status would imply. The personnel director, for example, has unusual status on the labor policy committee because of his previous experience as a chief negotiator for the city. The chief negotiator himself, while technically subordinate to the common council, had had a longer experience with city bargaining than most other participants; this experience, and his personal connections with the council combine to make him semiautonomous in many respects.

The mayor also is reputed to play an important, though offstage role in the collective bargaining process. Since there are no firsthand descriptions of his role, other than a couple of public appearances during the strike situations, it may be inferred to be one of indirect influence upon council members by virtue of political party leadership. He is a Democrat, with strong ties to organized labor. Many observers believe that by abstaining from any direct identification with the formal negotiations process, the mayor is able selectively to use public employee labor relations to his political advantage.

By publicly staying out of most negotiations, the mayor is able to avoid taking the political consequences for bargaining when employees are dissatisfied. At the same time he is perceived by participants and observers as being extremely active politically with members of the common council who have the legal power for negotiations. Also, the mayor is widely perceived as being "influential" in general city policy matters. The 1970 Urban Observatory poll found that 61 percent of the respondents cited the mayor or mayor's office when asked which officials "really run the local government . . . [or] make the most difference in how well the city is run" [3].

In any case, the mayor, the common council, and the chief negotiator all appear sensitive to the constraints imposed by the general political climate including the need for the electoral support of organized labor. Both key labor and management officials also expressed their sense of the limitations on both demands and settlements imposed by the potential for arousing public opinion.

IDENTIFICATION OF INTEREST GROUPS

The political climate in Milwaukee seems to show a preference for individual political contacts with elected officials rather than going through organized groups. The Urban Observatory poll showed that only 14 percent of the respondents thought that organized group activity was the "best way (for people to) make themselves heard by the city government"; while 45 percent would contact officials directly and another 33 percent would use the "regular political processes" [4]. Therefore, it should not be surprising that those third parties working to supplement the electoral and personal lobbying processes through organized special interest or public interest groups had relatively minor impact.

Ten third parties, plus the press, emerged from the procedure of asking each interviewee to identify any person or persons who were not at the bargaining table who had an interest in local public sector labor relations. Few of the persons involved could identify any active groups other than the Citizens' Governmental Research Bureau, the

Chamber of Commerce, the City Club, the Public Expenditure Survey, and the Milwaukee Property Owners' Association. Of these, the City Club, it turns out, is defunct, its membership having died or fallen away. Its former president said the younger generation in Milwaukee does not have the same sense of the public interest or public duty of his generation. Although the list of active groups is small, some of the interest activities are fairly sophisticated, particularly those of the Citizens' Governmental Research Bureau.

Citizens' Governmental Research Bureau

The Citizens' Governmental Research Bureau is a business-sponsored "citizen" nonprofit corporation, founded in 1913. Its several hundred members tend to be upper middle class business and professional men. In 1975 the 51-member board of trustees was entirely male. Nearly all are white and suburban rather than city residents. The bureau's offices are staffed by an executive director and small professional staff.

Despite its composition as a businessmen's organization, the bureau has more of the characteristics of a public interest group than any of the other special interest groups identified in Milwaukee. A public interest group is defined primarily not in terms of the group's composition, but in terms of its goals and methods. Basically, according to Professor Paul Dawson of Oberlin College, the criteria for a public interest group are: (1) the class of beneficiaries of the program or policies sought by a public interest group should extend beyond group members to a broad or narrow class of nonmembers; and (2) the benefits may or may not extend to the group membership itself. One may add that usually these spillover effects to nongroup members are intended or professed, rather than accidental or incidental to the group's other activities.

Although sponsored by businessmen, the Citizens' Governmental Research Bureau both professes goals and works on governmental policies affecting a potentially much broader range of citizens than its own members. The group's interests, largely, are the budgetary functions of the local government body, including the city, county, schools, and surrounding municipalities. It may be characterized in this sense as a "taxpayer" interest. But as will be seen, its interests are not limited to the direct tax impact of government policies upon its own members; that is, it is not merely seeking to lower taxes for local businessmen.

Besides taxes and spending issues of local government, the bureau's interests expand naturally into the areas of government efficiency and productivity. Personnel questions are closely related to this primary interest in budgets. In past years the bureau has done work on civil service reform and related questions. The group has a direct interest in the impact of public sector collective bargaining. It perceives a direct impact upon the budgetary process of personnel costs incurred through collective bargaining. Nevertheless, the group has not been simply "against" all increases in taxes and personnel policies that would cause such increases, as would a special interest group solely interested in the tax rates of its own members.[a] Nor are its personal contacts and services confined to "management," even though it does have a broad "management" orientation.

The Citizens' Governmental Research Bureau has the following general goals for Milwaukee collective bargaining policies (basically, the same goals apply to city, county, and schools bargaining).

1. Revise state budget law and change public hearings so that they are closer to the actual budget adoption date.
2. Revise state budget law so that collective bargaining can be concluded *prior* to budget submission. Sanction delays in bargaining by prohibiting retroactive settlements. Keep the terms of the old contract in force until the new one is bargained.
3. Improve employee productivity.
4. Provide for adequate funding of public employee pensions out of current expenditures. Do not defer costs.
5. Adopt a firm policy of how any increases are to be divided between salaries and benefits, especially in school bargaining where benefits are high in proportion to total costs.
6. Recognize that deferred fringe benefits are "compensation."
7. Provide for direct public access to the labor relations decision making process through increased opportunities for public hearings *before* decisions are made, citizen participation on arbitration and fact finding panels, and disclosure of bargaining positions.

Each of the first five goals would benefit not only bureau members as taxpayers, but the broadest class of taxpayers in general. The seventh transcends even taxpayers and extends to all citizens of the community. It is remarkably close to the premise underlying this study of the representation of the public interest.

[a]Since most members live outside Milwaukee, it might be thought that they have no vested interest in the city whatsoever and that, therefore, their interests were purely beneficient or academic. However, this is not the case for two principal reasons. First, because most members work in the city and are city oriented culturally; second, because they carry out the same kinds of activities in the surrounding jurisdictions in which they do live—although for the purposes of this study, the discussion is confined to bargaining activities of the city and school board.

Besides changing the timing of budget making and public hearings to coincide more closely with collective bargaining, the bureau recommends implementing its goals of due process by requiring written justifications from bargainers on both sides for the proposed terms of settlement as to why they think the terms are in the public interest. These reports of the tentative settlements would be made available to the public at the time of the public hearings.

If "due process" is translated into the need for citizen access to the decision making process, according to one of the fundamental assumptions underlying this entire study, then the Citizens' Governmental Research Bureau's position on due process may be argued to be its most "public interested" goal, inasmuch as access potentially would extend to *all* citizens, not just to bureau members. There is some empirical evidence to show that this same goal of access is part of a local shared community belief structure as well. About 40 percent of the other persons interviewed for this study also specifically cited the value of the need for citizen access to collective bargaining decisions. The same value is revealed in the responses referring to open negotiations, which are predicated on the value of access to information (see Chapter 6).

The bureau's principal activity is to provide studies of the budgetary impact of city and school board employee wage and fringe benefits. This information is regularly supplied to the city and school board officials involved in negotiations and to the press for dissemination to the general public. The executive director ghost writes speeches for some of the parties at interest and candidates, and there is a *mutual exchange of information* between the bureau and a number of participants in the local public sector labor relations decision making process, including both union and city officials. Also there is a direct working relationship between the bureau and the press. The bureau also works directly with service clubs, women's civic, and community groups, activist organizations on social welfare and school policies, advancement associations, and similar community "booster" groups.

Public Expenditure Survey of Wisconsin

The Public Expenditure Survey is a state-level group housed with the state chamber of commerce. It is a businessman's sponsored organization, with goals considerably narrower than those of the Citizens' Governmental Research Bureau in that the survey is strictly concerned with the impact of public employee salaries on budgets and taxes. Wages, salaries, and fringe benefit costs that do not exceed private sector rates are the primary collective bargaining goal of the organization. For the last fifteen years, the survey has published annual surveys of data comparing local public employee remuneration with those of other jurisdictions and private employees having similar job titles. The survey is exclusively research oriented and does not participate directly in any political activities.

Milwaukee County Property Owners' Association

The Milwaukee County Property Owners' Association has about 1,000–1,500 members, many of whom (40 percent) are landlords as well as homeowners. It has been active about fifteen years. The group's president runs its office out of his house and appears to be the organizing force behind its activities.

The association's primary goal is property tax reduction; it wants to accomplish this by shifting the tax burden to a flat 2 percent tax on all earnings (with no exemptions). The president is conscious of any impact of city expenditures on property taxes; therefore, short of eliminating the property tax, he is adamantly in favor of anything that will reduce or slow its growth. So, the group's position on bargaining is translatable into employee productivity—that is, no increases in public employee wages or benefits are justified without a demonstration of increased productivity.

The association is *against* public employee collective bargaining, as such. According to its president, the city government should set wages and benefits according to employee productivity; the voters then should have the opportunity to vote on an increase.[b] The question of other terms and conditions of employment was not discussed.

The aim of shifting the tax burden from property owners is relatively narrow, even though it would benefit other property owners than just the association's 1,500 members. According to Prof. Dawson's concept of a "public" versus "special" interest group, these property owners, especially as landlords, would benefit from such a policy more than a broader class of citizens such as renters and potential income tax payers. In this sense of a relatively narrow class interest, the association's interests in public sector collective bargaining appear more self-interested than those of the Citizens' Governmental Research Bureau or even the Public Expenditure Survey.

By contrast with the Property Owners' Association, the bureau professes a broad public interest goal in promoting the notion of

[b]Of course, prior to collective bargaining, one of the principal functions of civil service systems was to set wages and benefits according to prevailing rates for similar work, subject to legislative ratification. In 1976, salaries for federal employees under the General Schedule were still established in this manner.

citizen access. The survey is not against all tax increases, but professes governmental goals of broader applicability, such as efficiency and economy. But the Property Owners, officially, are strictly concerned with shifting the burden of the property tax. The appeal to new members is single issue oriented, with the theme "Every property owner is a sucker for high government costs."

Metropolitan Milwaukee Association of Commerce

Although the local chamber of commerce has a reputation for being "influential" in local civic affairs, the organization itself does not express an interest or involvement in public sector labor relations. This may seem surprising, as one would expect local businessmen to be more conscious than most citizens of the impact of collective bargaining. As a general goal the association supports the notion of wage parity between public and private sector workers as a standard of the public interest. In 1974, the association did conduct a public opinion survey of Milwaukee residents' attitudes towards public sector collective bargaining questions. The results supported the notion of public–private sector wage parity and exhibited the belief that public employees were more highly paid than private sector workers [5].

The Press

In addition to these special groups, there is the local press, which includes the morning *Milwaukee Journal* and the afternoon *Milwaukee Sentinel*. Although both are owned by the same holding company, they have separate editorial staffs and studiously separate editorial opinions. However, a reading of the newspaper morgue's files indicate that both have similar news coverage of public sector labor relations.

The stance of the *Sentinel* may be overstated by its chief editorial writer as "We are a bastion of conservatism." This translates into policy goals that are "always against the growing control of unions over elected officials." He thinks that management rights have been eroded by collective bargaining, but claims that the *Sentinel* is not antiunion. It is against the right of public employees to strike. The *Sentinel* might accept final offer arbitration as a policy improvement, and is in favor of public access and open negotiations.

This policy on open negotiations is shared by the *Journal*. Its editorial page editor would like to see the antistrike law enforced (which he doesn't think is practical) or abandoned in favor of a limited right of public employees to strike. He thinks that there is too much of a tendency for bargainers to defer settlement to third parties. The *Journal's* management has been very concerned with the fact that the state's Anti-Secrecy Act has not been applied to public employee collective bargaining.

Unorganized Public

Finally, there is the unorganized public itself, whose interests and desires can be judged only by the expression of its will through the election process, or as indicated in public opinion polls. The only poll data available indicates deepening qualms about the rising costs of public services (see Appendix C).

DEFINITIONS OF PUBLIC INTEREST

During the series of interviews participants were asked how they took the public interest into consideration in the course of their public sector labor relations activities. Each individual's definition of the public interest was solicited in the context of what kinds of public sector labor relations policies both *ought to be* and which in fact *are* pursued by the city or school board. Who should represent the public interest and whether that interest is in fact represented were also discussed.

The replies produced fairly consistent support for an operational definition of the public interest in terms of the concept of parity or comparability in wages and benefits between private and public sector employment. Few thought that such comparability was practical, in view of the difficulty of identifying the functional comparability of public and private jobs. Moreover, the unions tended to reject such a notion as irrelevant to their members' interest in using the collective bargaining process to work out a political balance of power between the two parties (management and labor) at whatever level of wages and benefits this produced, regardless of private sector considerations.

Other, broader definitions of the public interest most commonly cited were: efficiency of government, quality of services, level of taxation consistent with the ability of taxpayers to pay, preservation of management rights, and maintenance of essential services. These definitions are similar to the ones revealed in the literature search described in Chapter 1. These definitions from practitioners in the field lend weight to their universality. But, because the definitions are subjective, they elude practical application. Such definitions can be useful to practitioners as well as to expository writers, but the consuming public may not find it easy to use these definitions as standards to hold their representatives accountable for their actions.

There is widespread agreement among all practitioners that the public interest ought to be represented through the elected officials and their appointees. However, there is much less agreement that these officials in fact do represent the public interest. The due process definition of the public interest in access to the decision making process was volunteered by about 40 percent of the interviewees.

Constituency feedback already has been described in terms of the perceived political influence of the local public employees unions and will be considered further in the descriptions of individual interest group activities, below. Apart from these, no one reported any significant feedback from the general public. There was agreement with the notion that "apathy" best described general public attitudes towards public sector labor relations questions. Even work stoppages had not provoked any widespread citizen reaction. One management official described the citizens as continuing to put their nickels in the parking meters five days into the 1971 police "blue flu."

During the 1973, five-day work stoppage by 12,000 combined city and county AFSCME employees, the public hauled its own garbage, volunteers manned the County institutions, the waterworks were operated by supervisors, the Public Library went on a curtailed schedule, and the Public Museum and Zoo closed (animals were fed by supervisors). The *Milwaukee Journal* of January 11, 1973 reported "only minimal citizen outcry." The only "emergency" was cited by the county circuit court judge to whom the city applied for an injunction. He said that the county's suspension of food stamps distribution was the only emergency disruption of service.

Despite the absence of direct citizen feedback in the form of letters, telephone calls, or political support based on public sector labor relations issues, the practitioners have a sense of *potential* constraints. Widespread potential negative reaction to extreme positions is generally regarded as a check on the behavior of the city, school board, and the unions. While none of the work stoppages thusfar has produced such a reaction, the 1975 teachers' strike was perceived as having come perilously close. A citizens' recall petition came in the middle of the school board negotiations and effectively raised the spectre of widespread political dissatisfaction.[c] Most practitioners asserted that the public was interested in public sector labor relations, but not active. Generally, the unorganized public is perceived as acquiescing in the decisions made by its elected leaders and their appointees.

[c] See Part II of this chapter.

DEPENDENT VARIABLES

Access

A general model for access by parties not at the bargaining table includes: (1) direct participation in policy making as appointees to citizen and study committees, or as third party neutrals; (2) consultations with decision makers, as formal consultants or informal advisors; (3) participation in public hearings; (4) obtaining knowledge of negotiating positions during negotiations, prior to agreement, prior to ratification, or after ratification; and (5) direct veto power over regulations as a participant or through referendum [6].

Potential access in Milwaukee is largely political; that is, it consists of attempts to influence the decision makers within the context of their duties and responsibilities, as elected officials. Some structural changes considered possible within the scope of local decision making were considered. These would be largely changes in the dissemination of information to persons not at the bargaining table, including the idea of open negotiations and disclosure of positions. The investigation discovered few structural access points now available and even fewer attempts to use them, especially by the unorganized public. For all practical purposes there is only indirect political access, limited largely to the perceived influence on public opinion by press coverage of reports and positions. Outside parties have extremely limited access to either unions or management. City management does not formally solicit public input into bargaining nor does it hold any public proceedings.

Despite the absence of formal direct access points to the labor relations process, there is a great deal of discussion of the concept of *open negotiations* and the related concept of *disclosure of bargaining positions*. The press and the Citizens' Governmental Research Bureau have actively pursued the concept of public access to negotiations.

Proponents of this concept took heart when in 1969 the state legislature passed an Anti-Secrecy Act, which provided that all meetings involving governmental bodies must be open to the public. The *Journal's* lawyers began to consider litigation to permit reporters to attend collective bargaining sessions, but abandoned the plans after a finding by the attorney general effectively exempted collective bargaining negotiations from the requirements of the Anti-Secrecy Act. No one had litigated the issue, and the attorney general's opinion is widely thought to be definitive. The Wisconsin Employment Relations Commission (WERC) also has ruled that open negotiations are not required by the Municipal Employee Relations Act.

In lieu of open negotiations, mandatory disclosure of the parties' positions has been discussed. There is no present requirement to pub-lish union demands or city counterproposals. No formal distribution system exists for getting copies of the contracts before the public, until after ratification by both sides. Proponents of public disclosure argue that knowledge of proposed terms would be a principal means of access. They assert that without disclosure the public and public interest groups are dependent on—and sometimes purposely misled by—information manipulated by the parties in their own self-interest.

Ironically, the budgetary process provides the only *formally re-quired* public access to input into the public sector collective bar-gaining process, through public hearings on proposed budgets. But because the city charter calls for these hearings to be held by Octo-ber 25, when collective bargaining is usually still in progress, the impact of settlements cannot be studied in conjunction with budgets. Under these circumstances, perhaps it is to be expected that public attendance is reported to be sparse. Only the Citizens' Governmental Research Bureau has a reform of the timing of the budgetary process proposal on its formal agenda.

There is no state law or local ordinance requiring a referendum on proposed tax increases, and the idea of such a referendum is not an active local issue. Public interest groups have no formal access to adjudicatory bodies such as the Wisconsin Employment Relations Commission, which maintains a roster of about twenty fact finder arbitrators. The executive director of the Citizens' Governmental Research Bureau periodically has asked the Employment Relations Commission chairman to use nonprofessional neutrals instead of relying entirely upon professors and professional arbitrators.

Influence

In view of the limited access available to outside parties interested in public sector labor relations in Milwaukee, the interest groups' major recourse has been to use their political influence, both direct and indirect. The study encountered mixed assessments of their influence, which ranged from low to moderate.

Citizens' Governmental Research Bureau. The Citizens' Govern-mental Research Bureau universally enjoys the reputation of a gen-uine public interest group, and the integrity of its executive director is respected. Both management and labor negotiators use the bureau's materials, and the press regularly prints the bureau's "independent" analysis of public sector labor relations issues. Press coverage of bureau positions may be the bureau's greatest influencing asset.

The bureau's direct political influence is limited to an exchange of information with both management and labor, and speech writing by the executive director. The bureau takes no official position on candidates, nor is it permitted to contribute to or work officially on behalf of candidates. Lobbying appears to be limited to personal relationships between the executive director and labor relations decision makers. Since the bureau's sponsors are influential in the community in their own right, indirect influence may be said to flow from them to elected and appointed decision makers. *The Sentinel's* chief editorial writer has asserted that the bureau's executive director and the press are the "only institutions functioning to focus public attention on the inequities of public employment."

Although the bureau has a reputation as a reliable source of information, there is disagreement between its director and most observers over whether the bureau has influenced specific public sector labor relations situations. The director cites instances where he has served on a study committee, appointed by the mayor, to work out a system whereby policemen who take college courses would get points for promotion and more money. Another is a series of studies that the bureau did in the mid 1960s on fringe benefits for public employees, which was widely quoted. The director argues that it is hard to prove or disprove "influence" because there aren't any criteria for measuring this point either way. Key city officials whom he believes do regard him as influential disagreed with this view privately.

Public Expenditure Survey of Wisconsin. The Public Expenditure Survey, being exclusively research oriented, does not participate directly in any political activities. The Survey relies more heavily on its own membership and press coverage than does the Bureau. Survey representatives seldom appear to testify at Milwaukee public hearings, and the organization has undertaken no litigation in public employee bargaining matters. The survey's reports on public employee labor costs generally are perceived as management oriented. But even city management does not take its information without question. For example, the personnel director once issued an eight-page rebuttal of the survey's wage data. His objections were shared by the union.

Despite the controversy over the survey's data, its reports get extensive press coverage. There was also an interpretative article describing the background of the survey and its businessmen's board. But stories on survey data revelations do not question the validity of the data itself. The unions, especially, say that the survey is a highly influential force opposing them in bargaining. This is because the press picks up on charges that generally purport to show that the city pays its employees considerably more in salaries and/or fringe benefits than both local private industry and other governmental units. This kind of information tends to be thrown up by city officials against the unions. In that sense, it is influential with the city, too because it gives them ammunition to use in bargaining. Although AFSCME's executive director may perceive that this data creates an embarrassment and a distortion, there was no evidence that city officials have gotten much direct feedback from their own constituents who have read this information in the papers.

Property Owners' Association. The Milwaukee County Property Owners' Association's activity is aimed toward its own members and state and local legislators. The association's president does not think that the press coverage of his organization is very good. The association has been involved in local elections to the extent of endorsing candidates to its members, and the president estimates that these endorsements may influence 8,000–10,000 votes. The organization's publication is opinion rather than research oriented. It is doubtful whether there is much of an information exchange between the association and decision makers, and there has been no contact between the association and the other interest groups. The president describes his own membership as "apathetic." The group does appear at "all common council" hearings on taxes, but has not been involved in other forms of direct structural access pertaining to public employee labor relations.

The Press. Milwaukee traditionally has been a newspaper town. In 1970 more residents reported that they relied solely on newspapers for their news, rather than on television [7]. Press coverage of local public sector labor tends to be confined to impasse situations. Union demands and official reactions are reported with little independent analysis of long term ramifications. The reactions to union demands by the Citizens' Governmental Research Bureau and the Public Expenditure Survey are reported uncritically. Occasional feature pieces have been done on individuals involved in the public labor decision making process, such as the one about a circuit court judge who played a mediating instead of an adjudicatory or enforcement role in several impasses.

There is a high level of agreement between the management negotiators and the union representatives that the local press is highly influential. Both sides feel that the press is the only channel to inform the general public on public sector labor relations matters. Neither side denies trying to manipulate the press to its own advantage. Attitudes are mixed regarding whether the press coverage is fair.

The press seems to be influential in public sector labor relations for all of the reasons generally cited by students of public opinion. It focuses community attention on those issues its editors and reporters choose to cover, thereby limiting public discussion of the issues to offers, counteroffers, and public demonstrations by third parties. In turn, the editorial staffs say that their readers probably wouldn't pay much attention to more extensive coverage. As for the public itself, its influence is perceived through its tacit restraining effect on bargainers. Both sides seem aware that unusual pressures, particularly tax pressures, could jar the public from its usual apathy by stimulating mass resistance to the causes of those pressures.

PART II MILWAUKEE BOARD OF SCHOOL DIRECTORS

INDEPENDENT VARIABLES

Government Structure
The Milwaukee Board of School Directors (school board) consists of fifteen members, elected at large for six-year staggered terms. The board hires a superintendent and a secretary–business manager. Neither the mayor nor the common council formally get involved in teacher bargaining. However, the common council must approve the board's annual budget.

Attitudes Towards the Teachers Union
Milwaukee teachers are beneficiaries of the same general sympathy towards organized labor that is characteristic of citizen attitude towards other public sector employees. Moreover, there is a tradition in Milwaukee for approval of expenditures for "better schools." The 1970 Urban Observatory poll indicated that support for the public schools, at least in that year, was fairly high. Thirty-five percent thought that the public schools were "very good" and another 31 percent that they were "good enough" [8]. As a result of these factors and the tendency of the public in Milwaukee to rely on the electoral process to protect the public interest, the public's acquiescence to city bargaining processes also prevailed with regard to teachers.

Informal constraints on union bargaining are the union's political sense of what it would take to mobilize public opinion sufficiently to put pressure on the school board one way or another. Given the public climate for public employee bargaining in Milwaukee, the major external constraint on the board in the most recent bargaining was the move by a taxpayers' group to have the school board recalled in retaliation for the increase in school taxes. Although the issue did not arise directly from collective bargaining, the coincidence was widely reported to have inhibited school board bargainers in 1975.

Collective Bargaining Structure

The school board's administrative structure is organized for bargaining through the deputy superintendent's office, which together with the assistant secretary–business manager's office, oversees the chief labor negotiator's office. The school board is under the same legal requirements to bargain as the common council, but compared with the common council, school board bargaining is a simple organizational process. The board has a four-member committee on personnel and negotiations, chaired by the board president. This committee lays down the bargaining parameters to the chief negotiator who, unlike the city's chief negotiator, is not a relatively independent decision maker. The board's chief negotiator appears to have frequent consultations with the board. Board members may—and often do—attend actual negotiations.

The Milwaukee Teachers Education Association dropped its affiliation with the National Education Association. It bargains through its president and full-time professional staff.

IDENTIFICATION OF INTEREST GROUPS

Besides the Citizens' Governmental Research Bureau, whose activities are similar for both the city and school board, there are two other interest groups which have tried to influence school board labor relations. They are the Council of Parent-Teacher Associations and the Citizens' Recall movement. Neither of these may be classified as a *public* interest group in the sense of the bureau,[d] because activities stem from the narrower self-interests of their membership.

Council of Parent-Teacher Associations

The Council of PTAs is a delegate body representing each of the 80 PTA organizations in the city. Council members must have been PTA officers in a local PTA to be eligible for membership. The council has a seven-member committee on negotiations, chaired by the council president. The committee has been active in seeking open negotiations since the 1972 school board negotiations.

The council has tried to take an active role in teacher–school board negotiations by advocating: (1) *Access* to the negotiations by observers, (2) enforcement of the no-strike provisions of state law,

[d] See discussion in Part I of this chapter.

and (3) compulsory arbitration in lieu of strikes. In 1972 and again in April 1975, the board's committee on negotiations held public hearings on the question of open negotiations. Attendance at both meetings was reportedly sparse. No union representatives spoke at the second meeting.[e] Members of the Council of PTAs spoke at both meetings. The Citizens' Governmental Research Bureau's executive director endorsed open negotiations at the 1975 meeting, as did the managing editor of the *Milwaukee Journal.*

The Council of PTAs limited its demands to requesting observer status for its own members, or for a team of representatives. It is not fighting a battle for public access in general, although members anticipate that the press, at least, would have co-access to school board negotiations. The Citizens' Governmental Research Bureau, consistent with its role as a public interest rather than a special interest group, argued for open negotiations and amendment of the budget calendar to coincide with negotiations. In lieu of open negotiations, the Bureau's executive director suggested that the board impose upon itself a responsibility for a "formalized, continuing regular reporting procedure to the public as to the process of negotiations."

Citizens' Recall

The Citizens' Recall movement began with the efforts of one local citizen who, although only peripherally interested in school board bargaining attempted to recall those school board members who voted for the approval of a 26.3 million dollar increase in the school tax. This was done through a recall of each board member. Although the immediate goal was to recall school board members, the long range goal was to lower school taxes. The recall drive failed on a technicality, and the organization then sought to amend the state's initiative referendum law so that the recall drive could resume.

Board Member

One school board member, who is also a member of the Milwaukee Teachers Education Association, sponsored a board resolution in favor of open negotiations. This person has been active in seeking open negotiations since 1972. At the board's meeting of April 7, 1975, it voted to table the resolution pending the seating of newly elected board members.

[e] AFSCME's District Council Executive Director spoke out against open negotiations in 1972, arguing that both sides would "play to the galleries rather than to engage in meaningful collective bargaining," and threatening that the union would pack the hall if the Board held open negotiations. "It is probably a pretty poor union that can't fill a meeting hall when it really wants to" (*Minutes of the Meeting of the Labor Negotiations Committee,* November 27, 1972).

DEFINITIONS OF THE PUBLIC INTEREST

Definitions of the public interest by school interests tend to be single-minded in the sense, almost, of saying "the best for my kids, regardless of cost." This notion, despite its apparent selflessness, boils down to a narrow conception of the public weal as: "my (own) children." It would take a major sociological study to come to any conclusions about this phenomenon, but suffice it that the public interest in schools is perceived as more highly service oriented than for jurisdictions that perform a wider range of services.

The president of the school board sees the problem of the public interest as how to give protection to employees but at the same time assure that services are not interrupted or become too expensive. The consensus of the Council of PTAs committee on negotiations is that parents provide the raw materials for the educational process, namely the children. They pay for this service by paying their taxes and they must live with the product of this service, namely what their children learn. Specifically, they would like to know whether the educational process achieved what it set out to do. Therefore, they would like access to the decision making process regarding such policy matters as class size, teacher efficiency, and general accountability of the educational process. All these matters are affected by collective bargaining.

The chief negotiator of the school board sees the public interest as being represented through elected officials. The elected school board represents many publics (employees, students, parents, and taxpayers) and the role of the board is to balance these. In his view, the public interest is represented by the present system, except that the voice of the special interests are growing, and are being satisfied at the expense of the entire system.

The Milwaukee Teachers Education Association's president believes the public interest is in the quality of education, in getting whatever they need, determining the costs of this level of education, willingness to foot the bill, and fair treatment of employees in the light of the national economy and comparative *professional* wages.

DEPENDENT VARIABLES

Access
The structural avenues of access to the school board's labor relations decision making process are extremely limited. In practice, there are public hearings on the school budget and public board meetings on the contracts. However, like the city, the school board's budgetary hearings are not timed to coincide with negotiations. Con-

sequently, bargaining costs cannot be discussed rationally at budget hearings. Board meetings on formal contract approval are open to the public, but there is no opportunity for members of the public to speak. There are no public deliberations on contract proposals, outside of what occurs at board meetings. Negotiations committee meetings are open for public input, but the level of public interest and participation is said to be low.

The 1970 Urban Observatory poll reflects apparent citizen satisfaction with access to school policy making, but there were indications that a substantial plurality may be expressing a desire for "access" through their preference for more information ("better communication") rather than the channels of direct participation in decision making [9].

Negotiations are closed to the public and the press. Similar problems of disclosure exist as with regard to city bargaining, described in Part I of this chapter. At the behest of the Council of PTAs, the school board did implement a negotiations telephone "hot line" during the teachers' strike. But this is not the same as a legal mandate to disclose positions.

There are no public referenda on school taxes, so that it is impossible even to infer public acceptance or rejection of contract demands or settlements. Until the recall drive, all parties reported little public interest in terms of feedback through letters or other channels, except during the 1975 teachers' strike. The interpretation by local observers of public response to that strike was that parents were anxious to get their children out of the house and back into school.

During the 1975 teachers' strike, one private citizen filed in circuit court to force the school board to ask for an injunction. The procedure succeeded and the board filed suit the next day. The court eventually issued a restraining order against the union, which it obeyed. No one has tested the applicability of the state's Anti-Secrecy Act in school board bargaining.

There is no formal machinery for bringing the general public into labor impasses, and the kinds of activity undertaken by third parties in the event of impasses, thus far, has been sporadic. Only the Council of PTAs actively got involved by marching on the negotiators' headquarters with demands to expedite settlement in order to open the schools.

Influence

Members of the negotiations committee of the Council of PTAs describe their own influence over negotiations as "minimal" but not "nil." (Based on interviews with other participants, their self-evaluation appears to be a realistic assessment.) The members identified themselves as the only organized group attempting to influence school board collective bargaining. They cited three areas in which they felt some changes had been made in bargaining as a result of their efforts. The first was in getting both parties to give them signed statements on their bargaining positions. The second was the board's "hot line" service on the status of negotiations. Third, the board requested the opinions of the PTA council on several bargaining matters. Moreover, this time, both the board and the union showed up at the council meetings to explain their positions.

When asked about other groups which may have had tangential interest in school board bargaining, committee members cited the Citizens' Recall petition. They thought that this effort had had a great influence on the final settlement of the school board negotiations, even though it failed for technical reasons in the courts. Members felt that the recall petition actually had helped to prolong the negotiations because school board members, cognizant of the need to present a public image of economy, were reluctant to give the union the terms it might otherwise have gotten earlier. Nevertheless, committee members doubted that the recall petition would have much influence in the forthcoming school board elections. They cited the low turnout in the recent school board primary, a turnout that was apparently unaffected by either the teachers' strike or the recall petition that immediately preceded the election.

Regarding the Citizens' Governmental Research Bureau, committee members felt that its executive director was treated with deference by school board as well as city officials, and had some influence on matters pertaining to the restructuring of the school board. But on matters of collective bargaining, they said that they did not believe he had any great influence on actual negotiations, although he had asked constantly at budgetary time about school board finances.

SUMMARY

The initial assumption of the study was that the public interest in public sector labor relations would be functionally defined as: the potential for access to the labor relations decision making process for individuals and interest group representatives who are not parties to bilateral negotiations, but who perceive an interest in their outcome.

The Milwaukee studies revealed that many participants and observers agreed with the validity of defining the public interest in terms of this due process right to access. These included interest groups, the press, and some key officials. This community support is not merely theoretical. The emphasis by the press on open negotiations and the push for mandatory disclosure of bargaining positions both are examples of active attempts at access. Such access is one of the goals of the Citizens' Governmental Research Bureau. Its executive director has stressed the "due process" principle in arguing for written justification from bargainers of their proposed terms of settlements, and for bargainers' explanations of why they think their terms are in the "public interest." The executive director's effort to include lay citizens in fact finding and arbitration panels is another example.

Despite community support for the principle of access, there are few actual opportunities for outsiders to participate in the labor relations process. There have been no appointments of outsiders to policy committees or to panels, no public hearings on negotiations other than informal hearings of the negotiations committee, no outside participation in negotiations, and no disclosure requirements until after settlements have been ratified. For all practical purposes, the chief negotiator, primarily, and the mayor, secondarily, are the two parties on whom management depends for final decisions. Access to the mayor is a function of political party give-and-take. Access to the chief negotiator is technical in the sense of providing information useful for bargaining and political in the sense that he perceives the impact of his negotiating positions on the mayor's political coalition building.

The common council, which is legally responsible for negotiations, tends to defer to its chief negotiator, who is in close communication with the mayor. The school board is not formally as inaccessible as the city government, but there does not appear to be any active interest in teacher bargaining outside of the interest groups mentioned. Their access is largely political rather than structural.

Access to the unions is similarly limited and indirect. Under these circumstances, interest group activity has been confined to use of available opportunities to consult informally with union and management officials, traditional lobbying through staff and members, and publicizing their positions and data. They are effectively excluded from the structure of the formal decision making process. Clearly, some degree of public interest is represented by these interest group activities, but it has not manifested itself to any significant degree in Milwaukee. Thus, there has been access with little influence.

The study shows that Milwaukee has traditionally relied on representative government to serve the public interest in public sector collective bargaining, and that there was only limited pressure to open the decision making process to outside parties, in spite of the fact that there is a certain degree of skepticism that elected officials and their appointees are successfully representing the public interest, as well as other signals of political dissatisfaction.

Nevertheless, elected officials received virtually no feedback from unorganized constituents on collective bargaining issues. The perceived political power of the labor movement in general, and public employees in particular, and the predisposition of those already in office to seek harmonious relations with the unions continued to lend great stability to the public sector collective bargaining process. At the same time everyone seemed to be cognizant that there were potential *limits* to the extent to which city officials may agree to public employee demands.

Both labor and management officials realized that if "excessive" demands were translated into significant increases, this could provoke a countermobilization against public officials, as could a prolonged work stoppage that interferred with "essential" or even *convenient* public services. Previous strikes had generated no such massive counterpressures on decision makers, however, and no such test of public tolerance had come about at the time of writing in March 1975. However, the threat posed by the Citizens' Recall Petition during the January 1975 strike was regarded by both sides as influential and as a sign of possible increased public interest in school board negotiations. "Mature" public sector labor relations, basically, were treated simply as another aspect of the political decision making process in which the general public appears to acquiesce.

Whether there may be a new impetus to open the public sector labor relations decision making process and to provide formal access to the public and to public interest groups is a matter of conjecture.

Chapter 3

The 1972-73 Philadelphia
Teachers' Strike

SELECTION OF PHILADELPHIA

The 1972—73 strike by the members of the Philadelphia Federation of Teachers was chosen as a critical incident.

The strike, until that time the second longest on record by public employees,[a] was known to have generated considerable public attention in both Philadelphia and other communities. Numerous interest groups tried to affect the outcome. It was anticipated that a study of these efforts would reveal a broad range of nuances concerning third party access and influence in the governmental labor relations process.

Philadelphia is a major jurisdiction with generally stable, well developed public sector collective bargaining. Union activities go back as far as the early beginnings of the American trade union movement and the city can fairly be called a "union town." In 1972—73, the Pennsylvania Public Employee Relations Act (PERA) was one of only four which permitted public employee strikes. Despite this provision, the context of third party activities during the 1972—73 teachers' strike was similar to that in jurisdictions without such legislation, because the strike was enjoined. The act provides for an injunction of a strike that threatens the public "health, safety, or welfare." In agitating for an injunction, third parties in Philadelphia behaved much as their counterparts do in jurisdictions where strikes

---

[a]The longest was the Newark, New Jersey teachers' strike in 1971. Since then, the Hortonville, Wisconsin (1974) and Timberlane, New Hampshire (1973) teachers' strikes have exceeded this record.

45

are not permitted. Furthermore, when the teachers' strike continued, despite the injunction, the situation was analogous to that in other jurisdictions where an illegal strike occurs.

Financial Constraints Behind the Strike

Philadelphia has a history of high level public wages, moderately high private sector wages, and low property taxes. In teacher bargaining, the strongest constraint on interest activities came from the financial restraints imposed on the board of education. Because the board is unable to raise money independently of the city council, it must rely on the council to implement any collective bargaining agreement that entails an increase in expenditures.

The board's fiscal difficulties were further complicated by the fact that the school budget year is out of synchronization with the school tax year. The school budget, which begins on July 1 of the year preceding the tax collection, does not peak until the following April and May. As a result, the system has been forced to borrow from local banks to make up for the cash flow shortfall. In 1972, unfunded budget increases pushed this gap to approximately $52 million dollars. The banks refused to lend this money because no projected new revenue sources had been provided to pay off the full deficit. This was the situation in late summer of 1972, as the expiration date of the 1970 teachers' contract drew near.

Chronology of the Strike, Phase I
September 1972

Negotiations for a new contract had been going on since October 1971. The board's basic position was that in view of the mounting deficit, no additional expenditures could be made for teacher benefits unless the funds came out of cost savings. The board adhered to the concept of a package proposal on all contract items. The Philadelphia Federation of Teachers' basic position was for maintenance and improvement of existing contractual benefits, coupled with a request for a Bachelor's degree holder's starting salary of $12,000, to a maximum Doctorate holder's rate of $24,000. The need for increases were attributed to inflation, increased productivity, and comparability to other salaries and settlements.

On August 8, 1972, the board unilaterally announced its intention to institute a number of changes in working conditions when school opened on September 7. As a result of the rigidity of the respective positions, the expiration date of the former contract arrived, without a successor agreement and without any realistic negotiations having taken place [1]. The 450 demands put on the table by the Federation remained there through the summer of 1972. On September 1, the board announced that, should a strike occur, its policy would be to keep the schools open and functioning.

On September 5, two days in advance of school opening, the PFT voted to strike. Pickets were in evidence. The superintendent stated that the fault was neither with the school district nor with the union but the apathetic community that was unwilling to respond to the needs of the educational system. These needs amounted to increased funding to carry the system through its annual cash flow crisis. The banks refused to lend this money because no projected new revenue sources had been provided for in order to pay off the projected deficit.

Having run on a platform not to increase taxes, the mayor was adamant in opposing any budget increases that would necessitate new school taxes, or even tax increases that would fund the existing debt. He commented that the strike (over wages, changes in the teaching day, staffing, and class size) was regrettable and called upon the teachers to "sacrifice." On September 6 the union's negotiator warned that the teachers were ready to strike for three months. On September 7 the board announced that it would furlough support personnel. After a three-day lull, a state mediator called a negotiating session, but no progress was reported. Also on September 8, parents confronted the mayor with the responsibility for making a settlement. Educational television was used to supplement classroom work, as the strike became the longest in city history on September 9.

On September 10 there were more protests by parents and students as frustration mounted over the lack of progress. On September 12 the board rejected the Federation's proposals and the next day there were more parents' protests. By September 14, parents demanded that the city council intervene. A committee on education was formed by the council, but the members felt that they could achieve little. Some progress was noted by the union negotiator on September 16. By September 18 there was extensive parent input as protests increased; on September 19 the mayor asked for consideration of the city and claimed that the union demands were outrageous. Also on September 19, the U.S. Secretary of Health, Education, and Welfare said that he would refuse to intervene.

Individual parents petitioned the court of common pleas for an injunction on the grounds that the strike constituted "a clear and present danger or threat to the health, safety or welfare of the public." On September 22 a class action suit was filed on behalf of school children and parents asking for an end to the strike. Other suits were filed subsequently. Named in the first suit were the board, union, city council, and mayor. Plaintiffs were the Union of State Governments, the Educational Equality League, the Welfare Rights Organization, and the Metropolitan Council of the NAACP.

Thus, a public—in this case mostly parents who had a personal stake in the crisis—did gain access. But, they seemed to have little influence on the outcome. Rather, their actions provided a basis for judicial—that is governmental—intervention to mediate and "cool-off" the dispute in a traditional way characteristic of situations in which the parties see advantage in moderation.

On September 25 pupils protested, creating a derogatory song about the mayor. Blaming the union, black members of the Urban Coalition called for an end to the strike. Finally the judge was able to mediate the dispute, in lieu of issuing an injunction. The parties agreed to a "Memorandum of Understanding" on September 28 under which the teachers agreed to continue working without a contract through December 31.

Phase II   January-February 1973

The Philadelphia Federation of Teachers voted a one-week extension of the no-strike agreement through January 7, 1973. On January 3 the membership rejected a factfinder's report by a vote of 8,745 to 1,850. They went on strike on January 8. The board sought an injunction. The mayor again voiced anger with the teachers and parents resumed their protests. The Parents' Union sought a court order to allow them to participate in negotiations. On January 10 the president of the city council put the blame on teachers and on legislators for not granting adequate funds. The Federation rejected the latest board offer and a group of black teachers called for an end to the strike.

On January 11, the judge enjoined the union from striking on the grounds that the deprivation of schooling to the substantial proportion of disadvantaged children and the loss of income to working parents who depended on the schools to care for their children constituted "a clear and present danger to the[ir] welfare." The union leadership stated that the strike would continue and appealed to the commonwealth court of appeals. The board warned that it would seek a contempt ruling. On January 17 the common pleas judge ordered the teachers back to work on penalty of jail. On January 18, 27 PFT members were cited for contempt, including the union president and treasurer (chief negotiator). On January 19 the board, breaking with the mayor, asked the city council for a tax increase. On January 20 the mayor rejected any such procedure. The contempt trial began January 22.

After no progress in negotiations, confrontations between parents and teachers resumed. On January 26 the mayor met with the parties, though there was still no progress. By January 29 the union claimed that it was nearly out of money, and reduced its demands on January 30. However, the Pennsylvania State Education Association vowed to support the PFT. They also called for board of education powers to raise taxes. On February 3, the parties agreed to public "negotiations." These were held on a local television station for four-and-a-half hours and simultaneously broadcast on several local radio stations.

The teachers lowered their demands by 20 percent, but the board rejected this. Also, on February 5 the district attorney was called to see that organizations interested in reopening the schools gain access to the negotiations. On February 6 the school board announced plans to hire new and substitute teachers. On February 8 the mayor said that he would meet with labor leaders. Protestors interrupted a city council meeting. On February 9 the Federation was fined $160,000 and $10,000 for each additional day of the strike. The union's president and chief negotiator were ordered to jail from six months to four years with no release until the strike ended.

On February 10 parents voiced fears of reprisals against their children by teachers. On February 13 it was announced that the teachers' chief negotiator would be freed for negotiations. On February 16 nearly 1,200 people blocked traffic around city hall; some arrests were made. The mayor went on television on February 17 and noted that there was still no progress, calling union leaders "blackmailers." On February 20 pickets continued despite arrests. The board of education's president, who had been the chief spokesman on negotiations, was attacked by local union officials. Characterizing him as a turncoat, they threatened to have him censured or expelled from the AFL–CIO Labor Council to which he belonged as business manager of the local International Ladies Garment Workers' Union. On February 20 he resigned as president of the board. On February 21 the local AFL–CIO Labor Council, together with the Teamsters and United Auto Workers locals, threatened a general strike ("Day of Conscience") in support of the teachers for February 28.

The Assistant U.S. Secretary of Labor entered the negotiations as a mediator on February 22: he urged against a general strike and predicted a settlement. On February 25, Delaware teachers demonstrated to show support. The Assistant Secretary held negotiations around the clock. On February 26, he announced that the 30-hour negotiations had been constructive. Labor leaders met to show solidarity, though the Building Trades voted not to sanction a walkout.

On February 27 the Assistant Secretary announced a settlement in terms of a four-year contract at an additional cost of $107 million. On March 1 the PFT ratified the new contract and the schools reopened on March 2, 1973. On March 14 the fines and jailing of the Federation's leadership were upheld by the commonwealth court of appeals. However, on October 17, 1974, the Pennsylvania Supreme Court negated both the fines and the penalties.

INDEPENDENT VARIABLES

Government Structure

The board of education consists of nine members, appointed by the mayor. Three are appointed every two years from a list of six nominees provided by a thirteen-member nominating panel. The panel itself is appointed every two years, also by the mayor. Panel members are supposed to "represent" various kinds of "city-wide organizations" as spelled out in Section 12–206 of the home rule charter. The president of the board is appointed from the board members by the mayor for a two-year term.

The board has the power to set its own budget, but it must do so within the parameters of available revenues, which include state aid, federal funds, and local taxes. The board has *no* powers to increase its own revenues—it may only recommend increases to the state legislature or city council. There are no referenda on school tax requests. The city council has the sole power, subject to mayoral veto, to increase city funding of the schools.

Attitudes Towards Labor
and the Teachers' Strike

The role of public opinion during the 1972–73 teachers' strike is ambiguous, in spite of the political agitation by organized groups. It seems clear that the mayor and the city council believed their constituents wanted them to hold the line on taxes and consequently resist Federation demands [2]. The board of education's president also believed that he had widespread support for holding out against teacher demands. Countering this perception were the 20,000-strong Philadelphia Federation of Teachers and several thousand parents whose leaders, while they asked that teacher demands be met even if increased taxes were necessary, were determined that the schools be opened.

Political Activities of Unions

Philadelphia is regarded as one of the most "unionized" cities in the nation. The percentage of the private sector work force estimated by the AFL—CIO Council to be organized (47 percent) is notably higher than the national average of 27 percent. The history of organized labor in America has many of its taproots in Philadelphia. The AFL—CIO through its COPE activities is reported to be a considerable force in the mayoral and city council elections. The political position of the Philadelphia Federation of Teachers is growing by comparison with the private sector unions.

The Federation was not a staunch public ally of the mayor, largely because of his 1971 campaign promise not to raise taxes, and the impact of that position on succeeding teacher negotiations and board of education budget deficits. Mutual hostility reportedly ran high during the 1972—73 strike. The teachers openly supported the mayor's chief opponent in the 1975 Democratic primary, together with a slate of city council members also opposed to the mayor. The mayor and Democratic majority of the city council is reputedly "pro" labor. But there are a great many reservations towards the Federation as a result of the 1972—73 strike experience.

Since the strike, the Federation is said to have taken a very sophisticated stance towards private sector unions. They have improved relations by demonstrating solidarity with private sector unionists and a high level of visibility and participation in internal labor affairs. The fact that the teachers have demonstrated a high level of political participation in terms of their ability to get out and work for candidates, as compared with private sector workers, is not lost on local politicians nor on organized labor.

According to a newspaper report, the Federation took credit for the 1973 primary election defeat of the Republicans for control of the board of judges. This was apparently in retaliation for the injunction against the strike and jailing of its members by the board's president, a common pleas judge [3]. A drive to get out the Democratic vote was organized primarily in black areas by black Federation members. The reported voter turnout among blacks was up from 38 to 55.7 percent.

Many observers and participants reported that the strike left an incalculable legacy of bad feelings both among the teachers (many of whom did not support the union or who felt the union's demands were excessive) and among the public at large. There are numerous reports of parents believing that their children were punished by teachers because they came to school during the strike or because their parents were against the strike. Conversely, many teachers are said to believe that parents sabotaged their automobiles and otherwise harrassed striking teachers.

Collective Bargaining Structure

The board of education is the focus of bargaining, which is ordinarily handled by the chief negotiator, who works directly for the board's office of personnel and labor relations. During the 1972–73 strike, however, the board's chief negotiator had resigned, and the *city's* chief negotiator was brought in to bargain for the board. Ironically, the city council, which must fund any budget increases required by negotiated contracts, does not participate in the bargaining process. Key members try to avoid any direct role in bargaining. The mayor is universally regarded as having played a major role in the strike situation, through his political domination of the city council and his influence on board of education members whom he appoints.

Public school teachers in Philadelphia have been organized since 1904, when they formed an association to meet and discuss personnel issues with the board of education. In 1960 they joined the Philadelphia Federation of Teachers, an affiliate of the American Federation of Teachers, AFL–CIO, which won formal representation in February 1965. The treasurer of the Philadelphia Federation of Teachers acts as chief negotiator for the union, under the overall supervision of its president. The union's executive committee sends out notices to individual members and its 26 operating committees requesting suggestions for negotiations. These are sifted by the executive committee, which formally draws up a list of demands. The list is printed and circulated to the membership.

Critics contend that because there is no union shop in Pennsylvania, the union's leadership is in the position of having to take up almost any demand the membership makes, however trivial or counterproductive to negotiations, in order to convince the membership that the leadership is responsive. Each of the 450 or so demands that were laid on the table in 1971 had to be discussed, according to the board president, who complained that it was impossible to separate out the chaff. All demands remained unsettled, in fact, to the very end of the 1973 phase of the strike.

IDENTIFICATION OF INTEREST GROUPS

The study found a high level of third party activity by several sophisticated interest groups. Most interest group activity during the 1972–73 strike came from a coalition of organizations that were basically consumer oriented in their goals, although some could be characterized as public interest rather than special interest groups. Interest activity was almost entirely political in its direction, with groups attempting to influence the parties to the negotiations instead of seeking direct access to or participation in collective bargaining decision making along the lines suggested by the model of the "community at the bargaining table" [4]. During the noncrisis periods, there was considerably less interest activity.

The ten major interest groups studied were the Urban Coalition, Citizens' Committee for Public Education in Philadelphia, Americans for Democratic Action, Parents' Union, Home and School Council, Urban League, Chamber of Commerce, Welfare Rights Organization, League of Women Voters, and Philadelphia Council of the AFL–CIO. Most of these groups, except for the AFL–CIO Council and the press, worked in concert to lobby the city council and board of education to reopen the schools and fund the tax increase. Their individual positions are summarized in Table 3–1, below.

Of these, the Urban Coalition, Urban League, Citizens' Committee, League of Women Voters, and, in this case, the Chamber of Commerce partially met the basic criterion for a public interest group. That criterion is that the benefits of the groups' activities must extend beyond its own membership. The membership of the Citizens' Committee, in particular, extends beyond that of parents to nonparents, such as local and suburban citizens who are generally concerned with the role of the public schools in the community.

The Urban Coalition, Urban League, and the Chamber of Commerce share goals pertaining to the role of public education in the city's economic development. But in this case, the Urban Coalition and Urban League tended to be most concerned with the plight of parents (mostly black) who depend on the school system both to upgrade their children through education and to provide a place for them to stay while parents are working.

Although the League of Women Voters stands for broad policy positions, the impression is that in the case of the strike its membership interests also were parent oriented, as were those of the Welfare Rights Organization. The Parents' Union and Home and School Council are strictly parent organizations. The interests of the AFL–CIO were manifested on the side of the teachers as an interest group.

The rift between the mayor and the parent oriented groups could be explained partly by the notion that the mayor's constituency includes a high proportion of Catholic "ethnics," most of whom send their children to parochial schools.[b] This feeling amongst some is supported by enrollment figures for public and private schools, although ethnic voting data in mayoral elections are not available.

[b] In 1975 the Archdiocese of Philadelphia had a parochial school enrollment of 260,000, almost equal to that of the public schools. Half, or 130,000, were Philadelphia residents.

Table 3–1.   Summary of Interest Group Characteristics in Philadelphia Teachers' Strike

Group	Membership	Strike Goals
Urban Coalition	"Establishment" Business and Professional	Fund deficit and new contract by raising taxes; open schools
Citizens' Committee	Professional, Educators, Parents	Fund deficit and new contract by raising taxes; teacher accountability, management freedom to assign teachers
Americans for Democratic Action	Liberal activists	Fund deficit and new contract by raising taxes; open schools
Parents' Union	Parents	Open schools, fund deficit, and pay teachers more by raising taxes
Home & School Council	Parents	Open schools by funding deficit and new contract
Urban League	Middle level professionals Educators Businessmen	Open schools, fund deficit, and new contract through higher taxes
Welfare Rights Organization	Welfare mothers Unemployed	Open schools, divert federal funding to neighborhood learning centers
League of Women Voters	Civic activists Parents	Open schools, fund deficit and new contract through higher taxes; teacher accountability
AFL–CIO Council	Private sector union members	Support PFT
Press	*Inquirer* *Daily News* *Bulletin*	Open schools fund deficit and new contract through higher taxes; teacher accountability, management assessing of teachers

Table 3–1. continued

Methods	Direct Access	Influence
Contact city council members, organize public demonstrations	City council School board Business establishment Press	Moderate
Contact city council, board of education, testify at budget hearings, research school issues	School board City council Press	Moderate/Low
Join w/Urban Coalition, recall movement against Council Majority Leader	City council Press	(In coalition w/ Urban Coalition)
Contact other parent groups Sue school board & PFT	School board Courts Parents Press	Low
Contact board of education; establish neighborhood learning centers w/Urban League; picket city council	School board City council Parents	Low
Join with Urban Coalition; establish neighborhood learning centers w/Home & School	Community groups City council	Low
Attend school board meetings, work with Urban Coalition, sue school board	Courts	Low
Research school budget issues, work through Urban Coalition	Other citizen groups, board	Low
Threaten general strike	Mayor Council Press Board	High
Editorials, Publicize demonstrations against city council, analyze budget deficit		Moderate

Race was also a factor in the 1972−73 strike, in that 61 percent of the students were black and 66 percent of the teachers were white.[c] The black community's interest in keeping the schools open conflicted with the predominantly white Federation of Teachers' interest in striking. Alternative schools were created under the auspices of the Urban League during the strike, and the predominant number of schools which remained open were reportedly those with a high proportion of black teachers.

Urban Coalition

The Urban Coalition's short range goal was to get the funds for the deficit and necessary contract money. Its longer range goal was "setting public education as a first priority for the city," in order both to upgrade the disadvantaged population and to retain and attract business development. The principal target of the Coalition's activities was the city council. The mass protest demonstration was the primary vehicle for influencing council opinion.

Citizens' Committee on Public Education in Philadelphia

The short range goal of the Citizens' Committee was to reopen the schools by assuring the necessary tax monies. The Committee urged binding arbitration after the strike resumed. It claims to have mobilized about 3,000 persons to demonstrate at the city council for increased taxes and an end to the strike.

Americans for Democratic Action

The leadership of Americans for Democratic Action was part of a coalition led by the Urban Coalition and the Citizens' Committee. In addition, its president started a recall campaign against the majority leader of the city council on the grounds that he had shirked his duties by not supporting a tax increase for the schools. She later led the 1976 recall petition drive against the mayor.

Parents' Union

The Parents' Union formed during the strike as an outgrowth of the Citizens' Committee. Its representatives spoke to parents' groups, and participated in the demonstrations led by the Urban Coalition. The organization sued the board of education over the 1973 contract

---

[c]Of approximately 280,000 children enrolled in Philadelphia's public schools, 60 percent were black. By contrast, the city's population was only 33 percent black.

settlement on the grounds that the board exceeded its authority to bargain away management rights.

Home and School Council

The Home and School Council's primary goals were to reopen the schools "but not at any price," though they did urge raising taxes. The council sought observer status in the negotiations, and were offered a place on the board's bargaining team which they refused on the grounds that they wanted to be neutral third parties. They worked with the Urban League to set up "neighborhood learning centers" as substitute schools during the strike.

Urban League

The Urban League's short range goals were to open the schools, and its long range goals are school integration and functional literacy. The League was part of the loosely knit coalition of parent and community groups that coalesced around the Urban Coalition. The League established 42 alternate schools, attended by 2,500 pupils daily.

Chamber of Commerce

The Chamber of Commerce supported the board of education's position against the strike and supported the board's proposed settlement that would have required additional funds. The Chamber even supported an increase in the general business tax (which constitutes 41 percent of school tax revenues) to fund the schools. Its long range position is that a viable city is dependent upon a viable school system. The organization did not directly attempt to influence the strike situation, but its president addressed the issue of the strike through the press as well as to the membership.

Welfare Rights Organization

The Welfare Rights Organization sought to have federal Title I funds that were being sent to the board of education for special educational programs diverted to the community learning centers established during the strike. Other goals were to end the strike because of the low academic performance of disadvantaged children. They also wanted the city council to be responsive to teacher demands, but in return for teacher accountability. During the first phase of the strike, the Welfare Rights Organization and others sued the board of education for violating their statutory duty to keep the schools open for a minimum of 180 days and depriving school children's state and federal constitutional rights to an education.

League of Women Voters

The League of Women Voters wanted the schools open, with a tax increase if necessary, in return for teacher accountability. During the strike the League joined with the Urban Coalition's movement to persuade council members to support higher school taxes.

AFL—CIO Philadelphia Labor Council

The AFL—CIO Philadelphia Council supported the Philadelphia Federation of Teachers in its strike, espousing the broad goal of "quality of education." AFL—CIO efforts focused on union members, the school board, mayor, and city council. Ultimately, the council involved the President of the United States. According to the council president, it was at his behest that, after the jailing of teacher union leaders and members, George Meany asked the President to send in the Assistant U.S. Secretary of Labor to mediate the dispute. The Philadelphia council also led the movement for a general strike to support the teachers' position.

DEFINITIONS OF THE PUBLIC INTEREST

Key participants and observers were asked to give their definitions of the public interest at stake in the school negotiations. Most respondents expressed the vague criterion of "quality education" as the basic public interest. As translated into the strike controversy, "quality education" meant to management supporters the functional literacy of school children and teacher accountability for such literacy through more flexible management rights. To the Philadelphia Federation of Teachers and most of the pressure groups, "quality education" required increased spending on more and higher paid teachers and smaller classes.

The order enjoining the strike dealt with one aspect of the public interest, the argument that continuation of the strike presented a clear and present danger to the welfare of the substantial number of children of low ability and low achievement. This public welfare definition of the public interest was shared by the predominantly black groups and teachers who tried to keep the schools in the black areas functioning during the strike. This view was shared, less urgently, by most other parent groups who wanted the schools reopened. Of course, everybody professed to be for reopening the schools. It was the level of acceptable costs for doing so that varied.

The desire to open the schools "at any cost" appears to have motivated more pressures than the participants were willing to admit. The prevailing point of view among pressure groups was that the principle of higher costs must be accepted and is preferable to reduced services. Most of the key participants *did* but most observers did *not* believe that the public interest was realized in the settlement of the strike. This is consistent with the view of those who wanted the schools reopened "at any cost." Others who did not share this interest of many parents felt that the $107 million added costs of the settlement outweighed the benefits gained by reopening the schools.

On the major issues,[d] the teachers came out ahead of the fact finder's recommendations, and won most of their original demands. The Federation would not consider questions of class size or teacher work loads to be negotiable as against salaries. In the final settlement, the board of education did not win on the issues of teacher accountability, class size, and teacher preparation time.

Two years later, the interested parties were more prone to side with the board over these issues than they apparently had been at the height of the public furor they generated to force city management to end the strike. These parties did not believe that the board of education or the elected officials "represented" the public interest in school board bargaining either then or in 1975. However, most thought that elected officials ought to have represented the public interest. Most of these persons defined the public interest as increased funding for the schools in order to end the strike. Their position that neither the mayor nor his board appointees and allies represented the public interest should be viewed in this light.

The board's chief negotiator was hospitalized at the time of the case study, so it was not possible to get his definition of the public interest. We can speculate that in this kind of situation, where community peace was perceived by responsible city officials to have been threatened by both the acrimony building between the strikers and the community as well as by the threatened general strike by private sector unions, the public interest in peaceful nonviolent labor relations could outweigh any operational definitions relative to actual service delivery costs. In other words, the high monetary and management costs of the settlement may be argued to have been justified by the restoration of labor peace.

A taxpayer approach to the public interest—a hard line against higher costs and taxes—was embraced by the mayor and more moderately by the board president through most of the strike, even though organized taxpayer activity was minimal. Since there were no public opinion polls during the strike, it is not possible to estimate

---

[d]Wages, length of school day, preparation time, work load, class size, extracurricular activities, and secretarial support.

accurately the depth and breadth of public interest in the strike. If public sympathy can be judged from newspaper reports, it seems that the vocal public blamed city government and felt that the responsibility was the mayor's. The press reported extreme frustration by both parents and students, but not by the taxpayers towards whom the mayor's strategy appeared to have been aimed. Though the teachers' union appears to have acquired a very bad image as a result of the strike, it did not seem to be the target of public protest during the strike.

DEPENDENT VARIABLES

Access

The study revealed that direct structural citizen access to the structure of Philadelphia teacher bargaining decision making is limited to: (1) an indirect role in the selection of board of education members and of the chief negotiator; (2) attendance at board of education meetings at which policies and positions are discussed, but not the specifics of negotiations; (3) disclosure of settlements, but not proposals; (4) board budgetary hearings; and (5) fact finders' reports. In spite of the limited opportunities for structural access, only the League of Women Voters and the Urban League expressed a desire for greater direct access. There has been virtually no demand for direct access by the general public.

This limited structural access to the decision making process supports the hypothesis that the role of interest groups in Philadelphia teacher bargaining was political, rather than that of "the community at the bargaining table." Both private and public opinions appear to have had a high level of political access to the decision making process. This potential access hypothesis was reinforced by the various citizens' lawsuits and direct meetings with the mayor and members of the city council. The chief negotiator had virtually no contact with any third parties. Since regular board of education meetings are televised, it is possible that this unusual degree of access to information alleviates public demands for greater direct input into decision making. During the strike, public board meetings were televised. But none of the decision making was done in public.

All the major interest groups except the Welfare Rights Organization participated either in the nominating panel for board membership or were invited to help consider the new chief negotiator in 1975. A Citizens' Committee analysis of nominating panel dominance by the mayor concludes that this is not an effective vehicle for citizen input. The Citizens' Committee rejected the offer to participate in the selection of a new chief negotiator, because they felt that the board already had decided to choose one of its own staff people. The Citizens' Committee felt strongly that the board should consider nonstaff candidates.

There are no official requirements for disclosing negotiating positions. Interest group spokespersons tended to feel that the publicity given to the initial offers was sufficient to inform them and that the press coverage throughout the bargaining portrayed the broad outlines of the give and take. Nobody outside the negotiating parties themselves seemed to know precisely what happened at the final mediation sessions with the Assistant U.S. Secretary of Labor. Many felt that the mediation was a political strategy to get the mayor to permit his allies on the board to agree to a settlement, rather than a technical breakthrough on the issues.

The president of the board of education was in a sensitive position vis-à-vis both the mayor and the Philadelphia Federation of Teachers. As the business manager of the International Ladies Garment Workers' Union, he was sympathetic to labor. But he played the management role of board president, rather than labor leader, holding out against the teachers' demands to the end of the strike. As the dispute wore on and public pressures mounted, he became critical of the mayor. Strains within the labor movement grew during the strike, putting additional public pressure on him. The private sector union leadership threatened to censure him as antilabor. Ultimately, he broke with the mayor and eventually resigned as president of the board.

Some observers believe that the board president was "the mayor's man" all along and that his opposition to the teachers' demands was evidence of the basic differences between the private sector labor movement and the teachers' union. The press analysis credited him with more independence. The only significant mention of the "public interest" was an editorial tribute that he "placed the public interest first" [5].

The superintendent of schools did not participate directly in negotiations sessions. The board negotiating team does, however, include school principals to represent management directly at the bargaining table.

The city council played an anomalous role in teacher bargaining. Though excluded from bargaining, it held the key to the 1972—73 strike through its exclusive power to raise school taxes. This power helps to explain why the interest groups focused their efforts on the council. The reason these activities were entirely political may have been the absence of any structural access points.

The Citizens' Committee and Parents' Union claimed credit for getting the council to create a committee on education during the strike to consider educational questions in advance of crises. The chairman of this committee, like the council itself, made no inputs into the bargaining. Both the council president and the education committee chairman eschewed any direct council role in school negotiations, although the president would like budget control. The problem of the council's exclusion from teacher bargaining runs deeper than the structural separation of powers, for the council did not participate in city employee negotiations, either.

Although not involved directly in strike negotiations, the council president did get the court of common pleas to delay an injunction hearing in order to keep negotiations going, and he also spoke to union leaders in an attempt to mediate the dispute. He was also credited with the subsequent passage of new tax legislation required by the strike settlement and with the council's overriding of the mayor's veto of the legislation. Interest group pressures directed at the city council during the strike did not focus on collective bargaining structural access or reform. They were directed entirely at the school funding mechanism.

At the time of the strike, the mayor's political leadership of the council may have appeared to be sufficient to guarantee coordination among the mayorally appointed board, his own chief negotiator, and the city council, led by the mayor's political party. The pro-public education interest groups, by concentrating their attention on the city council, built up pressures in conflict with the mayor's constituency, pressures that may have helped to fracture the mayor's relationship with the council.

Most participants and observers opposed open negotiations that would be carried out in public view. The president of the Chamber of Commerce advocated "open covenants, openly arrived at," but other groups' representatives supported some kind of third party presence at negotiations to "represent the public interest." The spokesperson for the Americans for Democratic Action would make the negotiations tripartite, with the public representative required to concur in any settlement. All labor negotiations for public bodies would be conducted by a committee, similar to an arbitration body, without power of reappointment. The Home and School Council wanted to have the opportunity to make written inputs.

The Citizens' Committee took no position that requires tripartite negotiations; on the contrary, they favored negotiations conducted in secret. However, they did recommend that the board have the authority to appoint as members of the school board negotiating team, members of the public who are skilled at labor negotiations but who are not necessarily employees of the school district. Thus the school district would have interests of the public represented on its side, provided there was a unified front between these groups and the board.

There are no referenda on school taxes. Such a mechanism would have allowed the interest groups and the unorganized taxpayer an easier opportunity to register their wishes than through demonstrations before the city council.

By permitting strikes, Pennsylvania law avoids compulsory arbitration. The parties may agree to voluntary arbitration, but the teachers' union would not do so. The president of the board, though a labor man, favored final offer arbitration of school disputes, as did the Home and School Association. The Citizens' Committee called for binding arbitration. The city council president and education committee chairman, on the other hand, complained of the possibility of being bound by outside arbitrators who are not influenced by the local political process.

Influence

The influence of the interest groups that tried to end the strike and reopen the schools may be assessed in two ways: It is true that the strike did end, the council did ultimately approve new taxes to fund the contract, and did override the mayor's veto. On the other hand, the three-week September strike resumed in January and lasted another eight weeks, despite the concerted activities of the interest groups who wanted it to end. In fact, the strike did not end until the Assistant U.S. Secretary of Labor, PFT, and the city's chief negotiator hammered out an agreement, one day before the threatened general strike, using for funding the amount of the cash flow deficit that had been saved by school closings. In sum, there were four factors involved: (1) the political activities of interest groups, (2) the threatened general strike, (3) the intervention of the national AFL–CIO and the federal government, and (4) the alleviation of the cash flow problem through the strike. Various key participants, interests, and observers ascribe different interpretations to these facts.

Interest group activities received mixed evaluations of influence, generally moderate to low. The Citizens' Committee and Parents' Union were the most active independent groups in local school affairs, but even they were not too sure of their own influence in the strike situation. The Urban Coalition leadership was more confident of its influence than most of the other participants. It did play an important role, working in concert with the Coalition was the Citizens'

Committee, Parents' Union, ADA, Jewish Community Relations Council, Welfare Rights Organization, and League of Women Voters. The publicity given to interest group efforts, combined with their demonstrated activism aimed at the city council, was a surprisingly powerful counterforce to the mayor's constituency. However, the council did not vote to fund the deficit or contract prior to the intervention of the Assistant U.S. Secretary of Labor.

The only reported demonstration of antitax forces came after the council finally voted to hold hearings on increasing school funding. The lesson for the council may well have been that once the council was identified as taking positive action to fund the schools, under pressure of the pro funding forces, this would motivate the antifunding forces to become politically active. Most observers agreed that the eventual shift in the political forces probably came from organized labor's strong reaction to the fining and jailing of teacher unionists. Elected officials may have perceived organized union pressures as potentially more influential in their own reelection than an unidentified constituency assumed to be against increased taxes.

The general strike threat was regarded by nearly all participants and observers as influential, and half these thought it was extremely influential in bringing the strike to an end. Others think that the "Day of Conscience" was an empty threat, that labor might not have presented a unified front on behalf of the teachers. In any case, labor's role in bringing in a top level federal mediator was a decisive factor. Both sides agree that the final settlement was the product of the efforts of the Assistant U.S. Secretary of Labor.

The significance of cash flow timing is a matter of dispute. One of the Urban Coalition's leaders said that he forecast the end of the strike "to the day," basing his forecast on the days needed to accumulate the projected savings. The PFT's spokesperson agreed, as did a high ranking member of the board's own administrative services division. The board president denied such a motivation.

One factor in the strike situation that should not be overlooked is the relatively high proportion of teachers who continued to work. On the average for the 35 working days of the strike, 28 percent (3,679) of the teachers were on duty at their schools. Most of these, according to reports, were black teachers.

Both participants and observers remarked on the considerable acrimony within the teachers' ranks which this lack of cohesion produced. The number of strike breakers is a good indication of the differences between the PFT's formal leadership and the nonunion teachers which it represents under exclusive representation. Since to refrain from performing one's duties was a violation of the strike injunction, many union members were torn between union loyalties and their personal desires to obey the law.

A consortium of seven local major banks acted as a significant constraint, in that they held the key to short range financing of the annual deficit. The banks refused to fund the $53 million deficit of the 1974 budget without assurance that a loan of this magnitude would be paid off from subsequent revenues, and demanded a commitment from the mayor and city council. When the mayor refused to support the tax increase necessary to repay the loans, the teachers struck. The strike lasted eleven weeks, during which time the board saved $27.7 million.

As for the press, all three of Philadelphia's daily papers supported an ultimate tax increase to fund a new contract, but tended to support the board's resistance to "excessive" costs. In this sense, they were more of a "constraint" on board bargaining than the organized parents, most of whom wanted the schools reopened at any cost. Observers and participants agreed that the press played the role of keeping the issue of the strike before the general public. The three daily papers generally got high marks for the adequacy and fairness of their coverage. Even the teachers' union representative did not complain about distortions, though both observers and working press thought that the press tended to side with the board of education on the issues of management rights and tradeoffs for higher salaries. Editorially, all three papers opposed the mayor's intransigence while urging a "fiscally responsible" settlement.

The television outlet of the local all-news radio station carried "negotiations" live one Sunday morning in mid February. Both the station manager and other observers expressed the opinion that the TV negotiations were decisive in alienating public opinion from both the PFT and the school board. The station manager thinks this reaction was influential in ending the strike itself. All board of education meetings have been televised on the local educational TV channels for years. Though there is little audience response in the form of letters, this televised coverage during and after the strike could have alleviated public pressure for information by giving a sense of direct participation.

The ultimate settlement of the strike generally is attributed to the mayor, his chief negotiator, the Assistant U.S. Secretary of Labor, and the vote of the mayor's supporters on the board of education. The settlement was generally described as a product of political pressure from the AFL—CIO, reinforced by the political activities of organized interest groups.

SUMMARY

Most interest group activity during the 1972–73 Philadelphia school teachers' strike came from a coalition of organizations that were basically consumer oriented in their goals. This activity was primarily in support of parents who sought an end to the strike, with the implicit goal of opening the schools "at any cost." Because of the limited opportunities for structural access to the public sector collective bargaining process, third party interest activity was almost entirely political in its direction, with groups attempting to influence the negotiating parties.

The peculiar aspect of the Philadelphia situation, which appeared to have the greatest effect on interest activities, was not the law permitting strikes, but the financial constraints on the board of education. Because the board is unable to raise money independently of the city council, it must rely on the council to implement any collective bargaining agreement that entails any increase in expenditures. Since the impasse in the 1972–73 situation arose largely out of the inability of the board to borrow additional money to meet its current cash flow (not to mention additional expenses incurred by a new contract), the city council and the mayor were the focal points for those wanting an end to the strike. These political pressures were resisted by the mayor and the city council, as well as by the president of the board of education, all of whom apparently perceived a preference among their constituents for holding the line on taxes, teacher salaries, and school costs. However, there was no independent "taxpayer" group activity along these lines.

There are conflicting assessments of the crucial influences on the final outcome. In addition to the activities of the third party interest groups, the situation was also affected by the threatened general strike, the intervention of the national AFL–CIO and the federal government, and the alleviation of the cash flow problem through the strike itself. Most observers agreed that the eventual shift in the political forces probably came from private sector organized labor's strong reaction to the fining and jailing of teacher unionists. Through labor's influence, the Assistant U.S. Secretary of Labor was brought into the negotiations, and the ultimate settlement of the strike is attributed to him, the mayor, his chief negotiator, and the mayor's supporters on the board of education. Some observers believe that the public interest was not served by outside mediators, who may have been intent on settling the dispute for its own sake, regardless of the long range impact of the costs of the settlement.

Two years after the strike (in 1975), most of the key interest group participants believed that the public interest was served by the settlement; but most of the observers—such as members of the press and interest group leaders who were not active during the strike—did not think so. Since there were no public opinion polls during the strike, it is not possible to estimate accurately the depth and breadth of the public interest in the strike. Judging from newspaper reports, it seems that the vocal public blamed city government and felt that the responsibility was the mayor's. The press reported extreme frustration by both parents and students, but not by the taxpayers towards whom the mayor's strategy appeared to have been aimed.

It is ironic that the teachers' union, which did not at the time seem to be the target of public protest, later acquired a bad image as a result of the strike.

Chapter 4

Memphis, Tennessee: Sanitationmen's Bargaining Climate in 1975 Compared with 1968

SELECTION OF MEMPHIS

The 1968 strike by sanitationmen in Memphis, Tennessee began as a painful local confrontation; in its final stages it became a national trauma. Martin Luther King, Jr. was murdered in Memphis when he came to support black sanitationmen's demands that they be recognized through their union on matters of wages, hours, and working conditions—a right guaranteed private sector workers one-third of a century earlier. Most participants and observers alike regard the extreme reluctance of city officials to recognize the union as a breach of the public interest in good community relations as well as in harmonious public employee relations. The 1968 crisis gave rise to strong community organization and support for the strikers. This activity may be classified as a critical incident in which third parties manifested concern regarding the outcome of a labor relations situation and attempted to influence it. In this case, the third parties initially were the black community; but as the white business community perceived the deterioration of public order, this group became increasingly involved as well. Ultimately, these groups, together with a shocked nation, forced a settlement.

With this intensive and effective third party involvement as a part of Memphis's public sector labor relations history, the object of the 1975 study was to identify any similarities or differences in third party involvement, together with any changes in the independent

Note: This chapter was co-authored with Thomas W. Collins of Memphis State University.

variables governing the public sector labor relation situation. One of the criteria of influence is the duration of interest activity: would the same persons and groups still be active, or would third party interests and their activities have changed as a result of the possible maturation of the public employee bargaining process?

History of Organized Labor in Memphis

The American Federation of Labor (AFL) has represented the skilled workers in Memphis for most of this century without serious opposition from local business leaders and industry. The Southern Tenant Farmers Union (STFU) was permitted to locate its office in Memphis during the 1930s as a haven from the oppression of the rural areas. In fact, the Crump machine[a] was willing to provide preferential treatment to the AFL—affiliated Memphis Trade and Labor Council in exchange for its political support. Labor unions ran into problems only when they were in conflict with the goals and policies of the local machine.[b] During the 1930s, a prime objective of city officials was economic development through attracting northern industry. A major factor in their pitch to interested companies was low taxes and a surplus pool of low paid labor. There was no quarter given to labor organizers who attempted to organize the few industrial plants and city employees.

City employees who demonstrated any desire for union activity usually were terminated. For example, the city terminated fourteen employees in the fire department in 1936 for attempting to organize a union. The subsequent blacklisting of these men was so thorough that it was impossible for them to gain other employment in Memphis for over a year. Later, the school custodians' attempt to form a union was crushed when they were served with the ultimatum to either give up union activity or face dismissal. An attempt at organization by the police in 1943 met with similar opposition and they were forced to abandon their efforts. Ironically, it was the sanitationmen, the lowest skilled employees in the city, who were finally able to bring a bargaining unit into the government—but, understandably, not until fifteen years after E.H. Crump's death.

The city political machine was equally severe toward organizing efforts in the unskilled private sector. Its attacks on professional organizers were as brutal as any in the South. When intimidation and character assassination did not discourage activity, organizers were

[a]·E.H. Crump controlled Memphis politics from 1919 to his death in 1954; he controlled Tennessee politics to 1948.

[b] Craft unions were part of the machine until they broke with it in the 1930s. In 1948, labor defeated the Crump machine at the state level.

frequently assaulted and often severely beaten by street toughs [1].
As Crump stated publicly in 1940, "I am opposed to the CIO. Their
ruthless methods are destructive and retarding to the group of communities wherein they are active. . . . If the CIO would entrench
itself in Memphis, this city would go back 10 years" [2]. Crump
finally yielded to the organization of a few local plants, but for the
most part they were weak shop unions with black workers having to
contend with lower wage scales for the same job classifications held
by whites.

Over the years, labor power in the private sector has fluctuated
through several elections and contract negotiations. Local industry
tends to be hard pressed to meet competition in national markets.
Therefore, union wage scales in the steelworkers' and meat cutters'
locals generally have been lower than the national level. When unions
have demanded better wages they have been threatened by the prospect of the industry moving to other regions. In short, Memphis has
never had a reputation as a strong labor town, even in the post machine politics era of the 1960s.

Collective Bargaining Background
of Memphis City Government

The first successful union challenge to city power occurred in
1968 with a wildcat strike by the city-employed sanitationmen. Previously the only city employees represented by organized labor were
the few skilled or craft workers such as painters and heavy equipment operators who had been hired out of union halls (about 150
members). For these exceptions, the city simply paid the regional
wage scales. City employees who had attempted collective bargaining
as a unit were ignored and on occasion dismissed. This policy was
clearly evident when the sanitation workers tried to win recognition
for their local in 1963 and 1965. In the former case, fourteen men
were dismissed and several others released to undesirable positions in
the division.

The predominantly white departments of the city such as police
and fire were so intimidated that they did not demonstrate any support for the sanitationmen in any of their strikes. If anything, the
police took the side of the mayor in 1968 when they tended to use
excessive force in dealing with street demonstrations for the sanitationmen. However, once the city recognized Local 1733 as a bargaining unit for sanitationmen in 1968 and again for the hospital workers
in 1969, most of the employees in the other public service departments sought membership in the American Federation of State,
County, and Municipal Employees (AFSCME) or started negotiations

for a separate union. Except for the automobile inspection division, the units of AFSCME have been mostly black. In 1975 over 90 percent of the 5,800-member local was black.

Since 1969, the city has not opposed collective bargaining for any employees. The Memphis Professional Fire Fighters was recognized in July 1972. And the Memphis Police Association became the bargaining agent for the police in April 1973. Organization of the (largely white) police and firemen did not produce a reaction anything like that which confronted the sanitationmen's attempts at recognition. It has been the police unit which has been the most unstable and unpredictable in its negotiations of all the bargaining units. Police bargaining relationships with the city have never been routine. The (mostly white) police have been in conflict with the city over the civil rights of suspects. They have threatened to strike more often since they organized in 1972 over civil rights issues and wage packages than the sanitationmen.

The largely black hospital workers' AFSCME unit also has been very unstable. But it hasn't bargained with the city since the hospitals were placed under a separate hospital authority in 1973. Much of the problem with hospital worker bargaining stems from the lack of a designated chief negotiator for the hospital authority. Consequently, the union is frustrated by having nobody to bargain with. In the absence of collective bargaining legislation, they have no legal recourse on this issue and so must resort to political tactics, including strike threats. Otherwise, labor peace has been the general rule for the city of Memphis since the present mayor took over in 1972. In fact, one of his major campaign boasts in the 1975 mayoral election was the solid relationship that had been established with most city employee unions, including the sanitationmen.

Bargaining in 1968
In retrospect, the 1968 wildcat strike by the sanitationmen was predictable. The leaders of the movement for recognition of their local had labored arduously for nearly a decade. Many men had lost their jobs as a result of these efforts. When the leaders could not gain access to the city commission, they joined forces with other groups to lobby for a new city government in the form of a more responsive mayor-council.[c]

Despite the passing of the Crump machine, groups and individuals

[c]Prior to governmental reorganization in 1966, the city was governed by an elected five-member commission, one of whom was elected as "mayor." The 1966 Charter revision emphasized strong separation of powers between the mayor and the city council.

were still reluctant to put themselves very far out in front on controversial issues. There was never much of an opportunity for political
leadership training or experience under the machine, especially for
Memphis blacks. So, the demise of the machine left a vacuum. Moreover, under the old commission form of government, the buck could
be and was easily passed on issues such as public employee unions.
Even when the reorganization of the city government was accom-
plished in 1966 and a strong mayor elected in 1967, the sanitationmen—as well as blacks in general—reportedly still felt that they were
unrepresented by the new mayor.

During the 1967 election the black and white liberal vote was split
between two candidates. So, a conservative candidate was elected
without receiving many votes from the black community. The new
mayor was all too familiar to the sanitationmen, for in the late 1950s
he had served as public works commissioner, where he had shown
himself to be too conservative for the sanitationmen in employee
policy and budgetary matters. The union leadership considered him
merely paternalistic towards blacks, which was almost worse then
being openly against them. As one worker put it, "Mayor Loeb had
not done anything for us as a commissioner and he sure as hell was
not going to do anything for us now." Others simply considered him
a "southern planter type." Frustration among the sanitationmen was
higher in 1968 than at any time since they had been attempting to
organize a union.

The sanitation union leaders sensed a shifting of attitudes in the
normally conservative black community. Although black leaders had
not supported their previous strike efforts, they appeared ready to
back them in 1968. Thus it was only six weeks after the new mayor-
council government was in operation when sanitationmen hit the
street over a grievance. It took only a few more days to involve most
of the influential black leaders in this labor conflict.

It is unfortunate for the men that they did not plan their action a
little more thoroughly. For example, had they waited six months for
the hot Memphis summer, when garbage turns very ripe within a few
hours, there may have been an immediate demand by the public for
a strike settlement. As it turned out, the public sided with the mayor
"to hold the line." In any case, the sanitationmen were not to be
denied their demands this time. They walked off the job even before
the international headquarters was contacted. Nor was anyone going
to talk (or force) them back on the job without a favorable settlement.

This determination was only matched by the new mayor's resolve
not to yield to what he considered an illegal strike action. Expect-

edly, his first reaction was paternalistic. He prevailed on leaders in the labor council to use their influence to get the men back to work. He wanted the labor leaders to talk them into returning to work. He planned to propose a sanitation fee to the public whereby the city could then afford to increase sanitation salaries. When paternalism did not succeed, the mayor threatened the strikers with outright dismissal. He had resolved not to share any power with a union.

For the first 40 days after the walkout, there were no negotiations. A few men were hired to aid those who had remained at work to collect trash on an irregular basis. Citizens cooperated by carrying their refuse to designated pickup locations and, under police escort, carried it from their trucks to the fill. Had it not been for continual street demonstrations and an effective economic boycott of downtown merchants by the black community, it is possible the strike could have been broken and the men forced back to work. However, the community leaders, mostly black clergy, were determined that "the sanitationmen would achieve dignity in the eyes of city hall."

To strengthen their hand in the conflict, members of the local clergy asked Dr. Martin Luther King, Jr. to come to Memphis to lead a march. By the middle of March, the situation had become so intense that even a leader of Dr. King's magnitude could not keep the crowd's emotions under control. His first march was disrupted by violence when street youths clashed with police. King left the city immediately after the violence, but with a vow he would return for a second march to demonstrate to Memphis and the country that nonviolence was still possible and effective.

By the time Dr. King returned in early April, private negotiations were under way. A sincere attempt was being made by influential community leaders to break the impasse of union recognition. A skilled mediator from one of the local plants was in the final stages of trying to get both parties to negotiate under what was politely called a "memorandum of understanding." Moreover, by April the economic boycott was so effective that the downtown merchants and the local media were privately pressing the mayor's office to take a more conciliatory stand. This is not to say the mayor did not have considerable support in the working class suburbs. He was still receiving cablegrams encouraging him "not to give an inch." In any case, the assassination of Dr. King brought pressure from all levels of government to settle the strike.

The President sent a representative to Memphis to work out a settlement under the details provided in the memorandum of understanding. Major issues were the checkoff system and the full wage package demanded by the union. The task of collecting the dues was arranged by the employee credit union. An anonymous donor contributed $50,000 to make up the difference between the 15 cents the union was demanding and the 10 cents the city was able to pay in the final weeks of the fiscal year. The workers returned to their jobs sixteen days after the slaying of Dr. King, with the first collective bargaining agreement in city history.

INDEPENDENT VARIABLES

Government Structure

The city of Memphis is governed by a mayor and thirteen-member city council. Since 1967, all are elected simultaneously for four-year terms in "nonpartisan" elections. The 1966 Charter revision emphasized strong separation of powers between the mayor and council. This notion persists in the de facto handling of public employee bargaining. The city's taxing powers are still limited by state statute. It cannot pass an income tax.

Workers and Wages

For a city of its size, Memphis is not highly industrialized. Due to its location in the agriculturally rich Mississippi delta, the city developed as a commercial and banking center to serve the entire rural region. The service industry, headed by a large regional medical complex, and an extensive warehousing industry, has employed a large force of unskilled and nonunionized labor in the city. Much of this labor force are former tenant farmers from the northern delta region.

In 1975 the Memphis Standard Metropolitan Statistical Area had 276,700 workers. Of these 37,000 are domestics and self-employed persons and 7,100 are agricultural workers. Of the remaining 332,600 the AFL–CIO estimated that 75,000 were unionized. This includes 6,000–7,000 local public employees, Teamsters, independent unions, and AFL–CIO private sector affiliates, or 23 percent of the labor force (including local government). This is lower than the national average of 27 percent of the work force which belongs to unions. The Steelworkers are the largest AFL–CIO affiliate, followed by the AFSCME and the Meat Cutters.

Following their first contract in 1969, sanitationmen, on the average, made less than 2 percent over the federal poverty threshold for a family of four. Prior to the 1968 strike settlement, they made even less (6.7 percent below in 1967). In 1975, the percentage was 33 percent *over* the poverty threshold—that is, sanitationmen made almost one-third more than the poverty threshold. In that same year, however, sanitationmen made only about three-quarters as much (75.3

percent) as the average annual wage of production nonsupervisory manufacturing employees in Memphis. Also, they made only 89.3 percent of the *minimum* income for a family of four to maintain what the U.S. Bureau of Labor Statistics defines as a "lower" standard of living. By comparison, manufacturing employees in Memphis made 117.6 percent of the "lower" standard. (These figures are shown in Table 4–1.)

The economic situation in Memphis can be described as one of low level public and slightly higher private sector wages, and low level property taxes.

Community Attitudes Towards Labor

The attitude in Memphis following the industrialization which has taken place over the last 30 years or so has been one of general disinterest or even apathy. Union representatives have stated that the city is not particularly hostile to their private sector organizing activities now, but that paternalism still persists. This point is illustrated by union activity involving small, family owned plants. Generally, these plants pay only minimal wages, but the owners also tend to be very personable and protective of their employees, a relationship reminiscent of that between the old tenant farmer and the landlord. The most frequent response to organizing activities is one of disbelief. A common question is, "Why do you want to give your hard earned wages to outsiders?"

The larger plants that locate in Memphis usually bring established unions with them. Thus they have little problem maintaining a stable relationship between labor and management. In some cases, plants have only to threaten to move out of the city to get what they want from both labor and the city government. Politically, the private sector unions are not seen as particularly threatening to the existing power bases. Community leaders state that an endorsement from labor groups is not beneficial to a political candidate. Hence, power brokers generally have been uninterested in what the private sector labor unions do in Memphis.

There were no available public opinion polls reflecting community attitudes towards public sector unions. Reportedly, people are split along racial lines. The white community is said to be apprehensive about AFSCME, based on the union's reputation for mobilizing the black community in support of its goals. In 1968, this was perceived not only to have been effective against downtown merchants, but to have led to the King assassination and the further damage to Memphis's image as a desirable place for new businesses.

In 1969 and 1971, attempts to organize city hospital workers

Table 4–1. **Average Memphis Sanitationmen's Salaries Compared with Private Sector Manufacturing, Poverty Threshold, and "Lower" Standard of Living**

	Sanit.¹	Manuf.²	Poverty³	Lower⁴	Sanit. % Manuf.	Sanit. % Poverty	Sanit. % Lower	Manuf. % "Lower"
1967	3,182	5,373	3,410	5,032	59.2	93.3	63.2	106.8
1968	3,494	5,806	3,553	n.a.	60.2	98.3	n.a.	n.a.
1969	3,806	6,091	3,743	5,491	62.5	101.7	69.3	110.9
1970	4,181	6,360	3,968	5,776	65.7	105.4	72.4	110.1
1971	4,805	6,908	4,137	6,011	69.5	116.1	79.9	114.9
1972	5,429	7,806	4,275	6,212	69.5	127.0	87.4	125.7
1973	6,053	8,414	4,450	7,170	71.9	136.0	84.4	117.4
1974	6,843	9,018	5,040	7,671	75.9	135.8	89.2	117.0
1975	7,322	9,723	5,500 (Est)	8,194	75.3	133.1	89.3	118.7

Sources: 1. City of Memphis, Sanitation Division.
2. U.S. Dept. of Labor, Bureau of Labor Statistics.
3. U.S. Bureau of the Census.
4. U.S. Department of Labor, Bureau of Labor Statistics. Standard of Living Figures are available for Nashville only. They were corrected informally by taking the 1970 median income comparison of Memphis to Nashville of 91.3 percent and multiplying the Nashville "lower standard of living" figures by that percent. The choice of 1970 was dictated by the availability of that figure.

(subsequently transferred to the hospital authority) necessitated another massive black community campaign in support of the public employees. This time a "spread the misery" tactic was more threatened than executed. Black community leaders and AFSCME representatives organized a boycott and general disruption of suburban[d] shopping centers. They also threatened to ship ghetto rats to the largely affluent white, quasi-suburban community of East Memphis. The dramatic overkill of the rat threat appears to have stuck in the minds of white people, who are said to be fearful and resentful of AFSCME.

Heretofore, the black community has looked upon AFSCME as an organization fighting for community causes. Hence the black public interest role and image of the union. Its economic successes for its own members have been perceived not only in terms of the economic justice won for its own members but as a harbinger of economic justice for blacks in general, though spillover effects. The leadership of AFSCME still participates in community affairs; but it is now an open question whether they will risk damaging their political relationship with the elected officials with whom they bargain by allowing union affairs to spill over into such community activities as financial support of black community charities and registration of black voters.

Editorially, the local press is "pro" city management in its opposition to union demands. It also deplores any strike threat, raising the spectre of 1968. This helps to keep the fear of a repeat of 1968 alive and to constrain the bargainers on both sides from risking an impasse. The press has had nothing to say about sanitationmen's bargaining since 1968. Its attention has been focused on hospital bargaining, which has been far less harmonious than was the sanitationmen bargaining. However, the implication is that if the sanitationmen threatened a walkout, the public would be incited to put pressure on elected officials and the union to avoid anything that could provoke a replay of 1968.

The sanitationmen's union is constrained in making demands by its "garbageman image." In both the black and white communities, there is a feeling that as long as the sanitationmen are making a living wage and are being treated fairly in their grievances, there are limits on the demands which they can make on the public. As AFSCME has not yet demonstrated to elected officials its power of election (in that it does not have its "own" people in key elective offices), com-

---

[d] In Memphis, many of the affluent "suburbs" legally are incorporated in the city.

munity attitudes towards unions in general and public employee unions in particular retain overtones of paternalism.

Even the black community leadership sees AFSCME constrained by "reasonable" wage requests limited by the city's ability to pay. As representatives of the poorest elements of the community, the black ministerial leadership is keenly aware that poor people, especially poor blacks, will have to help to pay more than their share of any additional city expenses entailed by wage and benefits settlements with AFSCME. The regressive nature of city taxation is felt to put a disproportionate burden upon the poor and black taxpayer. Furthermore, inflation and unemployment have hit Memphis blacks hard since 1972. These economic facts of life were very clearly expressed in the statements made to the local membership by the union leadership in the final voting for contract ratification in 1975. For example, one leader is reported to have told the workers, "it would look very bad for sanitationmen to be out on strike when people could not find jobs." Black leaders have indicated that it would be impossible to generate the type of support the sanitation workers enjoyed in 1968. In the event of a strike today, it is not inconceivable that most blacks would simply ignore the economic issues and press the employees to return to work.

Political Activities of Unions

The political activities of organized labor in Memphis fall into two categories: those of the private sector unions and those of AFSCME. The controversy over whether AFSCME behaves like a civil rights movement or a labor union is central to this distinction.

By 1968, sanitationmen had been trying to unionize for almost a decade. That year, events coalesced to convert this struggle for recognition as a labor union into a civil rights movement. This change began when the mayor's intransigence and police tactics in handling demonstrations on behalf of sanitationmen's recognition ultimately involved a large segment of influential ministers. Civil rights organizations like the NAACP had been interested in sanitationmen's recognition all along, but their activities were not decisive.

When the local black ministers got involved, they helped to rally political support for the sanitationmen by mobilizing the black community. Some segments of the local AFL–CIO Council, especially the meat cutters and retail clerks, also were trying to assist the sanitationmen by providing facilities for meetings and logistical support. According to a knowledgeable and deeply involved AFL–CIO commentator, the national AFSCME was not interested in the Memphis sanitationmen prior to the burgeoning of the civil rights movement.

The AFSCME reportedly embraced the struggle only when it became a national *cause célèbre*.

The tactic of the economic boycott in support of the sanitationmen generally is regarded as the most influential instrument at their disposal. It was supported by the black ministers, who mobilized the black community and some of the white community. The downtown shopping area, then the main shopping area in the city, was severely hit by an economic slowdown. The peak of the boycott hit just before Easter, ruining sales. Fathers' Day sales were threatened next. Although the presence of Dr. Martin Luther King, Jr. and his subsequent assassination dramatized the situation and served as a catalyst to the recognition the sanitationmen had been seeking, several participants claimed that the strike eventually would have been settled as a result of the negotiations which had been going on for months.

Thus the emergence of the AFSCME Local 1733 was the result of a major *political* struggle. With its roots deep in the civil rights movement, the Local became a symbol of the black community's growing political awareness and political power. In 1975, local ministers and civil rights organizations involved in the 1968 struggle still laid great claim on the AFSCME unit for its continued activities as a black political force. All participants and observers agreed that in 1975 the AFSCME Local 1733 was the largest and by far the most powerful black political organization in town. Most believed in its potential political influence in terms of electing candidates to the city council and the mayor's office.

Feelings were more mixed regarding AFSCME's demonstrated political muscle. The local private sector labor movement was not perceived as very supportive of AFSCME. Only the AFSCME leaders themselves claimed unqualified support. A highly placed local AFL–CIO Council member thought that private sector union members were becoming increasingly resentful of the gains of AFSCME members at public expense, for which they paid as taxpayers. This attitude could weaken the support for any future tests of strength between public employees and the city. However, except for the AFSCME and AFL–CIO Council members, few observers thought that the AFL–CIO had given much real support to the sanitationmen's organizing efforts in the first place. One participant characterized it as "more lip service than manpower."

Besides the potential economic conflict of interest between private sector union members and their perception of having to pay increased taxes to support public sector union members, there has been a difference in racial composition which is crucial to a mid South political situation. The AFL–CIO has been dominated by the craft unions and other unions which historically in Memphis have been white. Not only is there the potential for a manifestation of white indifference or hostility towards black dominated public sector unions, but the historical racial exclusivity of the labor unions in Memphis engendered black hostility towards organized labor in general.

Except for AFSCME, which is perceived as a black civil rights and political movement by the leadership of the black community, unions do not get much sympathy from the blacks, nor from the majority of white citizens used to an antiunion business and machine "boss" (Crump) political culture. The ability to elect candidates to public office is a fundamental test of political power. A secondary test is the ability to influence the behavior of elected officials by convincing them of the *potential* for affecting the outcome of their next bid for reelection. The power of AFSCME in the former sense has not been conclusively demonstrated. The NAACP's executive director attributed her election to the school board to AFSCME's support. The AFL–CIO Labor Council executive said that labor in general had spent $500,000 on the 1971 mayoral election to try to defeat the man who was elected as the hand-picked successor of the man who was mayor in 1968.[e] The AFSCME executive asserted the "tremendous" political power of his organization, not only in electing officials but also in voter registration drives and campaign financing.

The Landrum-Griffin law's restrictions on political activities by organized labor do not apply to public employee unions. Moreover, the absence of a Tennessee statute governing public employee collective bargaining means that there are no restrictions on AFSCME political activities. There is a general consensus that labor endorsements are now sought after by candidates; but whether labor can defeat a candidate it opposes is still an open question. It was not able to do so in the previous mayoral election, although its candidate lost by less than one percent of the vote.

Except for AFSCME's animosity during the incumbent mayor's election campaign, no local election was identified as having been influenced by a public sector labor situation. Few persons outside of the unions even mentioned the 1971 mayoral race. The mayor's reelection in 1975, however, was a potential test both of the strength of AFSCME as a political force and of its self-image as a labor, rather than a civil rights movement. The outcome of the 1975 election could have had as profound an effect on the Memphis political power configuration, as did the 1968 crisis, which mobilized the black community politically for the first time. Ironically, the test was whether

[e]A local newspaperman thinks that this amount is "preposterous—one hundred thousand dollars will buy a handsome mayoral campaign today."

AFSCME would endorse or tacitly support the reelection of the incumbent mayor over a black candidate who was supported by the civil rights movement and the ministers who were active in 1968. Most perceived themselves as having been decisive in the fight for sanitationmen's recognition.

In spite of AFSCME's opposition in the 1971 race, labor relations under the incumbent mayor were regarded as harmonious to the extent that the leadership clearly perceived its economic self-interest in his reelection. As in 1971, his opponent was a white juvenile court judge again in 1975. In 1971, the opposition candidate had the strong support of AFSCME and the black community. However, in 1975, a third candidate, a highly respected black criminal court judge, was catapulted into the race literally at the last moment before the filing deadline. His stature in the black community made him a much stronger contender for the black civil rights–led vote than either their former candidate or the incumbent mayor. The mayor's image in the black community was not bad; but there appeared to be no enthusiasm for him as someone who would work vigorously to support black community economic and social causes.

The city charter provides for a runoff election where no candidate receives an absolute majority of the votes cast. With a black population of only 38 percent and a white community that is described almost universally as highly polarized, no one expected the black candidate either to gain an absolute majority on the first ballot, or to beat the incumbent mayor in a runoff. This posed a dilemma for AFSCME. If it acceded to the demands of the black community to support the black candidate, it risked alienating the candidate with whom it most likely would have to bargain for the next four years. At the same time, some AFSCME leaders argued that to oppose him would negate the political power they had already gained by what are perceived as his attempts to win their support by his handling of AFSCME thus far. Moreover, they argued that to support a candidate simply because he is black, while punishing an incumbent whom they could live with, would prove to the white majority political community that there is no point in attempting to win black dominated AFSCME political support through policy concessions, since they wouldn't support a white candidate anyway, when a black man is running.

On the other hand, by supporting the incumbent mayor, AFSCME would clearly signal that its primary goal in the economic self-interest of its members, as opposed to the broader civil rights and black community economic development issues pushed by the black ministerial and civil rights leadership. Such behavior would be consistent with that of a labor union, but it would doubtless alienate a substantial portion of the black community's political leadership. They would almost certainly think twice about lending support to AFSCME in any future power struggle with the city. The gap between black *public* employee demands and benefits and other private sector black employment could become a source of resentment if the members of the black community did not feel that by supporting AFSCME they were supporting the long range betterment of the black worker in general, through AFSCME's considerable political power. The question is how much of that political power could be risked for long range community benefits at the expense of short range union member benefits.

In a sense, AFSCME is perceived by much of the black community—and certainly is expected by the black ministerial leadership— to behave like a black public interest group, not strictly a self-interest group. In the end, the membership of Local 1733 voted to endorse the black opposition candidate for mayor in 1975. However, the union leadership was not active during the campaign. The incumbent mayor won reelection. Clearly, there were differences between the black membership's perceptions of its interests in a civil rights oriented candidate and the leadership's interest in strengthening its bargaining relationship with the mayor.

Collective Bargaining Structure

Benjamin Aaron points out that American labor relations law is primarily statutory, as opposed to being founded on common law or judicial precedent as it is in the United Kingdom [3]. There is no Tennessee law authorizing collective bargaining for state or municipal employees. Several Tennessee State Supreme Court cases asserted the illegality of public employee bargaining prior to 1968. The absence of such an enabling law, together with the case law precedent against bargaining, were grounds for the mayor's initial refusal to recognize the sanitationmen's union or provide for dues checkoff in 1968. However, political circumstances forced him into a de facto recognition. No legal challenges have been made subsequent to the 1968 recognition. The form of the "memorandum of understanding" between the city of Memphis and its employees was used to circumvent the legal technicalities impeding formal recognition and bargaining.

In the absence of state enabling legislation, the Memphis city council passed a resolution in 1969 stating:

1. That all departments and divisions of the city, including all separate boards, commissions, divisions and authorities *will meet and confer*

with employees, or employees' designated representatives, to discuss wages, hours, and working conditions, provided, that such designated representatives shall have been appropriately selected by a majority of employees.

2. That employee rights will be protected and their grievances corrected by a meaningful grievance procedure, as uniform as practicable.

The mayor has de facto authority for bargaining. The 1967 city charter provides for strict separation of powers. The mayor is responsible for management through a chief administrative officer (CAO). Personnel functions are handled by a personnel officer appointed by the mayor at his pleasure and responsible to him. The civil service commission operates only to hear employee grievances not covered by collective bargaining agreements.

Prior to 1975, the personnel director was the mayor's chief negotiator. However, this official carried the chief negotiator's role with him when he became the chief administrative officer. In 1975, the personnel director played a secondary role in bargaining. It was the CAO's intent to divest himself of bargaining responsibilities by hiring a full time chief negotiator. The CAO wants bargaining to remain closely coordinated with personnel.

There are no formal management collective bargaining policy making bodies which include members of the city council, and the council members generally have seemed to prefer a "hands-off" position. In 1974, the mayor settled wage increases with the unions without even consulting the council. As a result, the council in 1975 demanded and got informal consultations with the mayor regarding pay increases. The council also created a labor committee to consider collective bargaining policies and budgetary implications.

Sanitationmen bargaining was headed in 1975 by the chief of the sanitation division. Representatives of the other four city divisions with employees in Local 1733 were on the bargaining team. Local 1733 is affiliated with the AFL–CIO Memphis Labor Council, but not with the state AFL–CIO. Bargaining is done by the local's acting administrative officer. A master contract was bargained for members throughout city government in parks and recreation, general services, automobile inspections, and public works, as well as the sanitation division.

Local 1733 has 55 of the 350 delegated to the AFL–CIO Memphis Labor Council and two members of the Executive Board of 21. Local 1733 is the AFL–CIO's largest local in Memphis. But the steelworkers, with several locals, outnumber the public employees. The AFL–CIO Memphis Labor Council has 35,000 members of which 6,000 are AFSCME.

Local 1733 has close ties to the national AFSCME. The area director for AFSCME operates out of the Memphis Local 1733's offices. Most observers and participants perceived the area director to be the spokesperson for Local 1733. In fact, he was out of the office on organizing trips throughout the South about four days each week. Technically, he is not part of Local 1733.

Local 1733's executive board consists of the chairmen and secretaries of each of its bargaining units, elected at large by the local's 6,000 members. Negotiations policies are suggested by the board, subject to ratification by all members. In 1975, the acting administrator was the negotiator. No national AFSCME representatives are said to be at the bargaining table; nor does AFSCME use any lawyers in bargaining.

IDENTIFICATION OF INTEREST GROUPS

In 1968, the three major black community interests, which were not parties to any bilateral negotiations but who perceived an interest in the outcome of the situation, were (1) the National Association for the Advancement of Colored People, (2) the Memphis Urban League, and (3) the ad hoc Ministerial Alliance and Committee On the Move for Equality (COME) [4]. The national organization of AFSCME and members of the AFL—CIO Memphis Labor Council also became involved. The Memphis business community was not formally organized to influence the strike, but as the principal target of the union's business boycott strategy, individuals in the business community definitely had an interest. Other businessmen, particularly family owned, locally controlled companies dependent upon low cost labor, had an interest in keeping down local wages, particularly unskilled wages.

In addition to the above, one local business personnel director acted as a mediator and the Under Secretary of Labor eventually was dispatched by the President to mediate the final settlement. Subsequent to 1968, two new groups, reputedly interested in sanitationmen's bargaining, emerged: The Concerned Women of East Memphis and Shelby County, and People Unified to Save Humanity (PUSH).[f] Local staff of the Federal Mediation and Conciliation Service (FMCS) were active in mediating disputes between hospital workers and the Memphis—Shelby County Hospital Authority. The Chamber of Commerce professed an interest in public employee bargaining. Another businessman's group called Future Memphis became active politically.

---

[f]PUSH is a spin-off of the Southern Christian Leadership Conference's "Operation Breadbasket," a black economic development, political, and social movement.

Since 1968, all of the third party "interests" have receded to the background in matters concerning sanitationmen's bargaining. The NAACP, Urban League, and PUSH were most frequently identified as the organizations which tacitly "monitor" sanitationmen's bargaining on behalf of the black community. However, PUSH proved to be only generally interested in public employee bargaining, as a function of black economic development. The feeling in the black community is that AFSCME members now have achieved economic justice for themselves and that they owe a duty to the rest of the black community to help to achieve the same goals for everybody.

National Association for the Advancement of Colored People

The NAACP's executive director was kept informed of the details of the 1975 bargaining. She was one of three people mentioned as being active in city–AFSCME bargaining affairs. In fact, she was not active in the sense of initiating any activities on behalf of AFSCME, but she was "on call" in the sense that her daily political relationships kept her in touch with AFSCME and its activities.

Urban League

The Memphis Urban League did not aid the sanitationmen publicly in 1968. The League's low profile during this conflict was in part due to the narrow base of its funding and the makeup of the membership. The League is probably the most integrated public service organization in the city. Its leadership was reluctant to take a firm stand on issues that could drive off membership. In 1975, the leadership was in a more independent position, but the organization continues to be conservative in most of its policies. There was little interest demonstrated in the 1975 AFSCME negotiations with the city.

Ministerial Alliance

In 1969, the black community organizations became active again on behalf of AFSCME, supporting the economic boycott aimed at the new shopping centers in the outlying affluent sections of town where many had moved after the 1968 boycott downtown. As sanitationmen's bargaining has become routinized, the goals of the black ministers have broadened to include economic development and social (employment) justice for the entire black community.

The individual ministers previously involved in AFSCME bargaining indicated that they were not "on call," nor in any way directly involved in sanitationmen bargaining in 1975. In short, no third parties could be identified who currently play an active role in AFSCME bargaining with the city of Memphis, since the Concerned Women of Memphis and Shelby County were involved in the 1969 sanitationmen's strike and AFSCME's hospital organizing drive. Some are still active on behalf of hospital workers in the Memphis-Shelby County Hospital Authority and the Memphis board of education.

This is not to say that these individuals and groups were no longer "interested" in sanitationmen bargaining. However, the absence of conflict and AFSCME's growing political strength have meant that these groups have not had to engage in the kind of political mobilization efforts on behalf of AFSCME which they made in 1968 and 1969. Their activities have been aimed, instead, at the board of education, the county, and the hospital authority, with the goal of getting these units to treat their AFSCME workers in the same way the sanitationmen are treated by the city government. For various reasons, these units are less vulnerable to political pressure. In the case of the hospital authority, its relative autonomy gives it considerable immunity. The county and the board of education, in the other hand, are difficult political targets because power in these units is diffused and factionalized.

Concerned Women of East Memphis and Shelby County

The Concerned Women of East Memphis and Shelby County grew out of a group of about 50 East Memphis women who formed a local chapter of the Panel of American Women. The Panel was founded out of concern for the aftermath of the 1968 strike. Its aim was to educate the upper middle and upper classes in the community on race relations and problems of low income people. The following year, during the 1969 sanitationmen's strike and the threatened strike by city hospital workers, the Panel's leader organized the Concerned Women. Their goal was to support the efforts of AFSCME to gain higher wages ($2.00 an hour) for sanitationmen and to gain recognition for hospital workers. They were also concerned about the avoidance of violence.

Business Community

The business community again was the target of union effort to get pressure put on the mayor to settle with the strikers. Their goals were to end the boycott and avoid any repeat of violence. The union strategy forced them to subordinate any taxpayer goals or general desire for depressed wages to the expediency of ending organized harrassment of their shops and avoiding violence. The Chamber of

Commerce recently has expressed an interest in public employee bargaining in terms of possible impact on city taxes. But its foremost goal in terms of public employee bargaining is still a concern for harmonious labor-management relations and the avoidance of violence, rather than a concern for the substance of bargaining. The head of Future Memphis lamented that he still "can't convince people that there's any connection between collective bargaining and city policy making."

AFL—CIO Labor Council

The AFL—CIO Memphis Labor Council has no official position, but its leadership is keenly interested in the issue of "comparability" between public and private sector wages and benefits. The feeling is growing that public workers are "getting a better deal at the expense of the working taxpayer."

DEFINITIONS OF THE PUBLIC INTEREST

The notion of the public interest is fundamental to the analysis of Memphis public employee relations. It was implicit in the social struggle that emerged from the sanitationmen's attempts at recognition and was still at the crux of the black community demands upon AFSCME Local 1733 in 1975. Historically, there are at least five major public interest definitions in the Memphis situation with many ramifications. The black and white communities do not share the definitions completely, although there is some overlapping.

The most important definition of the public interest is the white community's desire for civil peace. Ultimately this transcended the original fundamental principle of governmental sovereignty held by the mayor and his supporters. The other major, white, public interest is in economic development of business relocation in Memphis. It is perceived as largely a function of civil peace. Black community interests are in the self-respect of black workers and economic justice for black city employees. A sixth public interest, originally articulated by the fiscal managers of city government, but increasingly shared by the black community as its interests in black worker self-respect and economic justice are met, is the classic notion of the "ability to pay."

Implicit in the reactions by the city council, business community, and black community to the resistance of the mayor to recognize the sanitationmen's demands for bargaining in 1968 was the concept of the public interest in harmonious public labor-management relations. This view transcended the strictly legalistic interpretation of governmental sovereignty by the mayor who asserted that he had no authority to recognize the union. Technically, he was right: strikes by public employees were tacitly illegal. Recognition of public employees for bargaining purposes had been ruled unconstitutional, in the absence of specific enabling legislation. Practically, as fears of increasing black violence grew, the white political and business communities asserted strong pressures on the mayor to subordinate the value of governmental sovereignty to the value of civil peace.

Because the public interest value of civil peace is so widely and deeply held in Memphis, incidents which could jeopardize that peace are strongly feared. Public employee labor conflict, or disharmonious public employee labor-management relations are at the top of the list because of the conditioning from 1968 and subsequent disputes over black employee organizational demands. Ironically, there were no such fears expressed when the mainly white police and firemen organized. In other settings, however, fear of police and fire work stoppages, which might leave the citizenry at the mercy of unorganized social violence, have proved a strong asset to employees in winning their economic demands.

In the case of Memphis public sector bargaining, the fear of violence has been focused on the workers and their supporters themselves. So, attitudes of the white and business community have not been quite the same as they might be towards a police or fireman's strike. Nevertheless, the prime motivating factor in resolving both such disputes is fear of a breakdown of civil order.

The fear of the possibility of new violence arising from the boycott by the black community against the white business community in support of the sanitationmen and, subsequently, hospital workers forced the white community influentials to put pressure on city government to accede to black worker demands. Thus, the tactics of the sanitationmen's supporters forced the white community to reorder its public interest values. The supporters of the sanitationmen did not so much convince the opposition to adopt their values as to coerce them into settling in order to preserve a higher public interest in civil order.

The boycott and the possibility of its escalating into violence raised a new hierarchy of public interest values. Violence proved to be inherent in the situation as it developed, not a planned strategy of the sanitationmen supporters. Nevertheless, its existence was the catalyst in reordering the community's priorities. The interest in preserving governmental sovereignty which was the crux of the mayor's position, was superseded by the value of civil peace. When the strike at last threatened a breakdown of civil order following the assassination of Dr. Martin Luther King, Jr., many of the members of the city council and influential members of the business community, as well as the sanitationmen's supporters, counseled recognition in order to defuse the situation. This value, ultimately, was expressed by the President of the United States when he dispatched a top level Labor Department mediator and personally telephoned the governor and the mayor and told them to settle.

The economic boycott by the black community started many pressures in motion on behalf of recognition. Many believe that it ultimately would have succeeded in bringing sufficient white business community pressure on the mayor, without the aftereffects of the King assassination. The reaction to the boycott was more a self-interested reaction of the business community to loss of business income than a notion of the public interest. But the threat of violence was and is perceived as deterring new business from locating in Memphis. This has public interest connotations in economic development and jobs for the entire community. Concern for Memphis's image is a public interest value which grew out of the 1968 situation and, in fact, was a function of the blow to the city's reputation which was perceived by the business community and the community leaders in general. In 1975 the city's image was a major public interest value not limited to the white community. This may help to explain the fear of both black and white community leaders of any repeat of 1968.

In 1969, the fear of incipient violence was the key to the success of the city hospital workers' organizing attempts. Again, the tactics included a boycott by the black community against the business community, in order to force the community influentials to pressure city government to accede to black worker demands. The white business community's self-interest in economic survival was expanded to include the entire community's interest in civil peace when the leaders of the black boycott threatened to "spread the misery" (including the rats) from the black ghetto into the affluent white quasi-suburban areas of the city.

While civil order is the overriding public interest of the white community, self-respect is at the heart of the black community's definition of the public interest. In 1968 the black community rallied to the sanitationmen's cause in demanding self-respect. "I am a Man" was their slogan. These demands were operationalized in terms of better working conditions, including equipment and uniforms, new grievance procedures, and equal treatment with white sanitationmen in terms of paid hours and leave. Foremost was the demand for a mechanism through which to gain this self-respect. That mechanism was union recognition and dues checkoff. As is usually the case with unions seeking recognition, the demands for wage increases actually were less important in the short run than was the cause of recognition and union security through dues checkoff. Paternalism might have provided the substance of the demands in the long run, but recognition was deemed vital to the fundamental demands for worker self-respect and employee equity.

Unfortunately, it was the black public interest goal of recognition that was antithetical to the white community value of governmental sovereignty. Connotations of racial economic conflict underlay these positions. Black labor was cheap in Memphis. Sanitationmen were not making an average wage high enough even to put them over the poverty threshold. Many were on welfare. Their demands for recognition, besides being technically illegal, threatened to revolutionize the image and costs of "black" labor. The business community, reinforced by the local press, doubtless used the legal situation to bolster its own opposition to any higher taxes that might result from a new wage settlement.

"Ability to pay" is a classic management value, shared by a large segment of the taxpaying public. Even many members of the black community leadership are reluctant to support additional demands by organized employees that would raise the regressive tax burden on black taxpayers. This underlines the contemporary differences in interests between the leadership of AFSCME Local 1733 and the black community. Demands for increases in union members' wages and benefits beyond what the community regards as a fair wage for sanitationmen would not be supported by the black community because such demands are perceived as against the interests of black taxpayers. At the same time, black community social and economic public interest goals that require AFSCME members to sacrifice their own bargaining power with the city are not likely to be supported by the union's leadership.

Representing the Public Interest

City officials believe that they should and do represent the public interest in Memphis public employee labor relations. There was less support for this notion among the black community leadership. Community organizations and the union were suggested as the representatives of the public interest. Especially in 1968, the union could be said to have represented the public interest in equity for employees. Whether it is perceived to represent other public interests, beyond the self-interests of its own members today is a controversial question.

Until he received a telephone call from the President, following the King assassination, the mayor had remained steadfast in his opposition to recognition and dues checkoff. A large segment of the political and business community already had elevated the value of civil order above that of governmental sovereignty. But the mayor reportedly did not feel that he could condone policies that he believed to be illegal.

The parties to contemporary bargaining were asked how they took the public interest into account. Management's participant replied that employee negotiations were an administrative process that was handled "just as we would negotiate any item of city business." This reflects the position that the elected officials and their appointees represent the public interest by virtue of their positions. No direct access is needed, according to this view. Officials are accountable at the polls.

Having lost the support of the business community, as a result of the effect on Memphis's image by the King assassination, the previous mayor could be said to have heeded the notion of the public interest being represented through the electoral process when he did not run for reelection in 1971. Many segments of the community were said to have been upset by his handling of the sanitationmen's situation, perhaps to the extent that he perceived that they would not reelect him because of it. A spokesman for AFSCME responded: "What 'public interest'? We look out for the public employees' interest." This casts the union's position in the classic mold of labor-management relations. It underscores the potential differences with the black community leadership's notions of the public interest.

Three key elected officials, the chairmen of the city council's finance and newly created labor committee, and the council's representative during the 1968 negotiations, shared the conception of the "public interest" that salaries and benefits for sanitationmen and other city employees in 1975 were very good, by comparison to the private sector and that the city ought to hold the line against future increases. Although the two committee chairmen have potentially important roles, they both eschewed any direct role in bargaining; hence they didn't consider "taking the public interest into account" directly regarding collective bargaining. The role of collective bargaining in achieving the sanitationmen's goals may be judged through union "gains" since 1968.

As shown in Table 4–1, above, sanitationmen's wages edged over the poverty threshold in 1969. In 1975, they made an estimated 14 percent below the average of other City employees and almost 25 percent less than private sector workers in nonsupervisory positions.[g]

[g]The city's personnel director estimated that the average city employee's wages were $8,500 in 1975, compared with $7,322 for sanitationmen and $9,723 for nonsupervisory manufacturing.

But pay gains were not the only—or even the primary—issue of the 1968 drive. The primary issues were worker dignity, including grievance handling and a myriad of working conditions, which the union leadership argued could only be achieved through recognition.

In analyzing the three agreements since 1968, it is important to realize that before 1968 no bargaining relationship existed between the parties. As a result, the 1968 agreement met only two major purposes: First, the city agreed to recognize Local 1733 of AFSCME as the bargaining agent for the sanitationmen. Second, the city agreed to set up a grievance system with advisory arbitration as its last step; therefore, *any* gains made by the union since 1968 must be viewed as important ones.

The most important of these gains have been: (1) exclusive (rather than designated or acknowleged) recognition, (2) payroll dues checkoff, (3) no subcontracting, (4) time and one-half for overtime, and (5) a formalized agreement by the city to promote sanitationmen out of the bargaining unit into higher level and supervisory classifications. Under this agreement the city joined with the union to establish training programs leading to promotion.

The director of the sanitation division takes credit for implementing the concept of on-the-job training for promotion. He says that it is more efficient than trying to train new supervisors who do not have experience on the jobs they are supposed to supervise. Moreover, he reports that turnover in his department is down to three percent from 14 percent as a result of the practice of upgrading sanitation over the past three and one-half years. During this period, only three new people were hired from outside the bargaining unit.

All employees are eligible for promotions. When a vacancy occurs, preference is given to those in the division where the job is located. The person with the most seniority wanting the job is temporarily promoted on six months' probation. At the end of that time, if not rated satisfactorily by his new supervisor, the person returns to the former classification. No one risks a job by taking a promotion. There are no written civil service examinations, and employees are evaluated by their on-the-job performance.

Except for crisis or potential crisis situations in which a work stoppage is supported by an economic boycott or there is the threat of violence, none of the participants or observers reported any feedback whatsoever regarding the ongoing bargaining between the sanitationmen, in particular, and the city. Only the AFL—CIO Labor Council member said that he got "lots of feedback" from his members regarding public sector wages and fringe benefits. He described pensions as "astronomical." In view of apparent apathy, the opposition of private sector labor to increased public sector employee benefits is highly significant. Apart from the public employees themselves, private sector labor is potentially a powerful political force.

None of the third party interest group people said that their membership had expressed any interest in sanitationmen's bargaining since the 1968 settlement. The organization of the hospital workers in 1969 produced some of the same kind of interest as the sanitationmen strike of 1968, and continuing flareups in hospital negotiations have mobilized the black community on occasion.

Reportedly the mayor received a great number of supportive letters and telegrams during the 1968 strike. They urged him to hold the line. Initially the business community strongly supported his opposition to recognizing the union, but this waned as the situation grew more tense. Councilmen reported the only interest came from AFSCME members and city employees themselves and that they were never contacted by constituents or others who were not parties to the bilateral negotiations.

Press Coverage

According to previous accounts of the 1968 strike, the two daily newspapers were adamantly against the strikers and with the mayor. One of the key participants said that when a settlement finally had been agreed to, he called the editors of the two papers to enlist their editorial support for it. Near the end of the strike, even the editors were trying to "soften" the mayor. Since then the press has paid virtually no attention to the sanitationmen's bargaining, as such.

In 1969, the sanitationmen's agreement was renegotiated. The union mobilized community support again and organized a boycott of white-owned stores, this time in the more affluent quasi-suburban areas of East Memphis. This was treated negatively by the press but, apparently, not with the degree of hostility that the 1968 strike originally had been treated. At the same time, hospital workers were bargaining. They represented a similar group of underpaid, unskilled blacks. The press placed heavy emphasis on the "share the misery" campaign and the rat-export ploy of the union leaders. This incident and its effects was the most intensively covered story since the 1968 strike.

The Concerned Women of East Memphis and Shelby County (who organized to put pressure on the city council to accede to hospital workers' demands for recognition and a raise) were at first treated cavalierly by the press. But when the members of the city council expressed this kind of attitude and the women became outraged at the council, the press took on a more sympathetic tone towards the group.

In 1972, the city raised the possibility of contracting out sanitation services, particularly in some newly incorporated areas. The sanitationmen threatened to strike over this issue. The press was sympathetic with the city; but the entire incident received little coverage. The papers consistently expressed "dismay" at any strike talk. Hospital bargaining has been most widely covered, probably because labor relations with the hospital authority are not as harmonious as those between the sanitationmen and the mayor and city government. The press is quick to remind its readers of the threat to the public health and safety and the possibilities for a breakdown in civil order should AFSCME members go on strike, thereby keeping alive the public fear of civil disorder. Ironically, this kind of treatment may reinforce the union's bargaining power. No one wants a repeat of 1968. Leaders in the black community are as anxious to avoid being caught up again in a potentially violent strike as the white business leaders are fearful of the results.

DEPENDENT VARIABLES

Access

Access to the public employee collective bargaining process in the city of Memphis was entirely limited to the political process. The question of direct access by persons who are not parties to bilateral negotiations between the city and its employees was not even an issue. With negotiations as a de facto, rather than a de jure process, in the hands of the mayor, the city council—through which indirect public access might be sought—until most recently has been effectively excluded from the decision making process.

Besides the self-interested reasons of management and the union to operate with as little outside interference as possible, the formerly activist community (black) appears to support the lack of opportunities for direct structural access. This may be in part because of its perceived political weakness in the (white) community as a whole. With black community interests still identified with AFSCME interests, it is generally felt that AFSCME represents the black community at the bargaining table. There is also the fear that any attempts at more direct public access might provoke conservative, white attempts to interfere with AFSCME. Any action that would tend to take away or reduce gains by black employees would, in turn, be perceived as hurting the blacks in general.

Since 1968, sanitationmen's negotiations have been in the hands of a person rather than an official, in that the personnel director continued to serve as the mayor's chief negotiator when he became chief administrative officer. As a mayoral appointee, he was able to represent the mayor in bargaining. So, there have been no problems with "end runs" by the union around the negotiators; nor do they try to get around the mayor by going to the city council. Both mayors or their staffs have personally dominated negotiations policy making for the city. The negotiators had no direct contact with any interest groups or persons not at the bargaining table. Management holds no public hearings on negotiations. Third parties have no opportunity for direct participation or observation. No public disclosure of demands or positions is made, except through informal press contacts at the discretion of either side.

In practice, negotiations have been carried out *after* the formal adoption of the annual budget by the city council. But there is no disclosure in the budget of labor costs. Public attendance at budget hearings reportedly is minimal. No taxpayer interests ever have shown up to discuss city personnel costs. The public is permitted to speak at budgetary hearings only at the "third reading" stage; however, only union representatives are said to attend.

The 1975 "negotiations" were so deeply imbedded in the budgetary process, that the chairman of the labor committee described the process as having precluded negotiations for all practical purposes. In December 1974, the International Brotherhood of Electrical Workers demanded a 12–13 percent increase from the quasi-independent Memphis Gas, Light, and Water Board (MGL&W). The board had offered only 4.75 percent. The city council, which has to provide the funding, began to take the position that *no* increase could be given. The mayor and council finally agreed that the city could not go above 6 percent and forced the Memphis Gas, Light, and Water to hold to the same ceiling. The 6 percent limitation was based on the maximum amount available in the 1975–76 budget without increasing any taxes. It was extended to *all* city employees, regardless of whether or not they were in a bargaining unit. New equipment purchases scheduled for 1975 were deferred to compensate for the $2 million additional salary costs.

Informal negotiations apparently took place with AFSCME prior to the implementation of the 6 percent increase. The city council's demands for no increases extended to consideration of possible salary reductions. The mayor, personnel director, and city administrative officer met with all city labor organizations and told them that the council was opposed to any increases. However, based on the Memphis Gas, Light, and Water precedent, the mayor included a 6 percent increase in his 1975–76 city budget. Apparently, the unions were convinced that there were no hidden funds or other possibilities for exceeding this budgetary ceiling and they acquiesced in it. The budget committee chairman stated that he had not consulted with the union before agreeing to the increase. The "memorandum of agreement" negotiated under these constraints was for three years and provided for the reopening of wage negotiations in one year. Union officers claimed that, with fringe benefits, they actually got 7 percent for the sanitationmen.

The city council's budget committee considers the annual budget, submitted by the mayor. Although council approval is required, the attitude of the council has been strongly supportive of the separation of powers in labor negotiations. Whether this is based on a desire to let the mayor take the political responsibility for potentially unpopular labor negotiations is not clear. In 1973, the council defeated (seven to six) an ordinance which would have required it to "advise and consent" by a resolution of concurrence by an absolute majority of seven (of thirteen) members. However, the council leadership's attitudes towards organized labor appears to be more conservative than that of the current mayor.

In 1974, when the mayor made the 6 percent settlement with the Memphis Gas, Light, and Water Board (later extended to all city employees), the negotiations were concluded without the council's being informed. The council was in the position of having to fund an agreement in which the members had no input. Following this episode, the council formed a committee on labor. Members were advised of the mayor's desire to give a 6 percent increase to all city employees based on the budget limitations. Still, the council never held public hearings on labor relations matters. The labor committee chairman said that no one had ever asked for them. However, he would hold hearings "if it got to be a radical situation."

The "open meetings" law was circumvented during the negotiating process between the mayor and the city council over the 6 percent increase. Council members discussed the proposed increase individually by telephone instead of meeting together on the subject. The council member who had participated in the 1968 negotiations thought that this was "a terrible way to conduct city business."

There is no requirement for formal ratification by the city council of the memoranda of agreement, which are technically strictly between the mayor and the unions. They represent a position by the executive on personnel administration which is taken as strictly an executive branch function. Ironically, the council "ratified" the Memphis Gas, Light, and Water agreement by appropriating the funds for it three weeks before they realized what they had done.

Council members, including the chairman of the labor committee, do not have access to the union's demands or to information on the bargaining. Both AFSCME and the city take the position that bargaining is strictly confidential between them until after the union has ratified the agreement. It is then signed by the mayor, without formal referral to the city council. Through 1975, funds either have been in the budget to cover the increase, or the agreement was concluded prior to budget submission date so that the mayor merely includes the additional labor costs in the next budget, as in 1969 and 1972. The memoranda are printed by the city and the union, but there is no public distribution.

Council members reported virtually no feedback from constituents on sanitationmen's bargaining since 1968 and 1969. City labor relations generally produce no constituent interest except when there is a strike threat.

Since 1968, the Federal Mediation and Conciliation Service (FMCS) has been directly involved with AFSCME negotiations with *other* local jurisdictions (county and hospital authority), but not city bargaining. It was the 1968 sanitationmen's strike which finally prompted the President to order the FMCS to lend itself to state and local public employee disputes. Since then, the city has not had occasion to use them.

During the 1968 strike, a local citizen, who was personnel director for a major local corporation, played a key role as mediator. He was called in on a personal basis by virtue of his employment with one of the mayor's closest friends. The black minister who was one of the key black community leaders also sat in on the negotiations as an observer-mediator. He was reportedly eased out by the union during a conflict over whether the union should get explicit formal recognition, or whether a memorandum of agreement would give an operational definition of recognition instead.

No one involved in Memphis governmental labor relations favored open negotiations. The black community seems to feel that the less attention paid to negotiations, the less likely incipient racial hostilities will be provoked. Since the black community shares the basic goals of AFSCME, the tacit oversight by the black community leadership of the city's willingness to bargain apparently obviates any demands for access to bargaining information. Public disclosure of the parties' initial or subsequent bargaining positions, therefore, is not a salient issue.

Persons sympathetic to the union were adamantly opposed to the notion of a public referendum on public employee contracts. (Even the city council doesn't exercise this power.) They thought that a referendum would give the majority white population the opportunity to vent their anger at union members, who are perceived as mostly blacks. Management's argument was that a referendum would undermine representative government. Persons interested in governmental cost cutting supported a referendum on the grounds that any public employee salary or other cost increases would be defeated. It is conceivable that, as the racial composition of union membership becomes increasingly white, public attitudes towards public employee bargaining gains could soften. Since there are no polls that reflect public attitudes, it is probably more accurate to say that the perceptions of participants and observers regarding public attitudes may change.

The failure of a July 1975 referendum on increasing the local sales tax was not interpreted as a reflection of community attitudes towards public employees, even though the money would have gone far for teachers, police, and fire salaries. Rather, it was perceived as a rejection by the white community of an increased aid to a black-dominated school system.[h] Voter turnout was extremely low: only 17 percent of the registered voters turned out. Ten percent of the black voters and 20 percent of the white voters participated. Of those who voted, 58 percent of the blacks but only 40 percent of the white supported the referendum. While the AFL–CIO, AFSCME, and NAACP supported the referendum, only the NAACP actually got out and worked for it. Other black organizations opposed it on the grounds that the sales tax is regressive and would put the heaviest burden on the poor and blacks. Some of the black opponents also held the view that the schools should not be further subsidized until they provided more effective services to the black community.

Compulsory arbitration of "interests" disputes is not a salient issue for most in Memphis. The collective bargaining authorization bill passed by the Tennessee House provides for compulsory arbitration of any interest impases [5]. The chief administrative officer opposed this bill because of his opposition to compulsory arbitration. AFSCME would rather have no legislation than that which would limit it regarding such matters as campaign financing, scope of bargaining, or the right to strike (which, in the absence of specific prohibitions they feel is at best ambiguous.) The National Labor Relations Act model would be acceptable. If applied to public employees, it would permit the right to strike as an ultimate recourse.

The ministerial black community leadership was extremely reserved regarding the "right" of public employees to strike. This rein-

---

[h] The population of Memphis is 62 percent white, but the public school system is 71 percent black.

forces the differences in values between AFSCME and its third party support during the 1968 strike. In the context of public employee strikes, the black community leadership sounds more like a concerned taxpayer group than an advocate of AFSCME's economic goals. Ironically, while not endorsing the right to strike, the executive director of the Chamber of Commerce recognized its inevitability under certain circumstances, as did the chief administrative officer.

Influence

No third parties who are not labor and not elected city officials or their appointees have any direct influence on Memphis city labor relations policies. The mayor retains a very tight rein on labor relations decision making. Even the city council has been effectively excluded, for all practical purposes. The possibility of increased AFSCME electoral influence on the mayor, who is generally regarded as more "pro labor" than the council, is an important consideration. But the membership's 1975 endorsement of his opponent seems to dampen this prospect.

City council members are growing increasingly conscious of labor relations and are trying to exert influence through their power to approve or disapprove the mayor's annual budget (which includes the costs of labor settlements). They are doing so in the context of their own perceptions of the relationship between personnel costs and taxes, rather than out of any overt constituent pressures regarding labor relations policy.

The business and black communities, including both secular and minister led groups, remain key potential third party influences, despite the fact that in 1975 they appeared to exercise virtually no direct influence on bargaining. Their indirect influence, respectively, is limited to a tacit concern for Memphis's image as a community conducive to business and for the dignity and economic security of black city employees. Since 1968–69, these concerns have not taken the form of any activities as explicit as even exercising an oversight of negotiations. That is, most interest group representatives do not keep up with day-to-day issues in sanitationmen's bargaining, nor are they familiar with the specific provisions of the current terms and conditions of employment. They do have the impression, however, that these are progressing satisfactorily. This is based on feedback from the AFSCME leadership and union members. Consequently, the interest groups of 1968–69 have been inactive since then on the bargaining by the sanitationmen.

However, the potential for reactivating community interests in sanitationmen's bargaining puts constraints on the mayor and council. The concern, particularly that affecting the council, is not so much over the political power of the black community, but over the adverse publicity that the black community's political and economic sanctions can give to the image of the city and, hence, on its ability to attract new industry. This possibility motivates the business community to put pressure on elected officials to avoid situations like that of 1968.

The 1968 Settlement. Marshall and Van Adams, Collins, and Stanfield [6] have discussed the various influences on the 1968 strike situation. Marshall and Van Adams, in particular, documented third party influences. They attributed the following six "elements leading to a solution" [7] :

1. Unified Negro support of the strike.
2. Articulate Negro Leadership.
3. Coercive pressures from the Negro community (the economic boycott).
4. Support of organized labor and national civil rights leaders.
5. Communication through mediation and neutral third parties.
6. A factor which can be described as the "Memphis image."

Since the present case study included many of the same persons who were interviewed by Marshall and Van Adams, it is not surprising to find that these discussants tended to reconfirm the six influences. However, more emphasis can be given to the business community which is the third party most interested in the "Memphis image." Also, there was some disagreement over the depth of interest of organized labor and the national AFSCME, prior to the King assassination. One person closely involved pointed out that Walter Reuther didn't give his $1,000 check to support the strikers until after the King assassination. Another asserted that only after the death of Dr. King was AFSCME willing to concern itself with the situation.

As pointed out earlier, although the King assassination doubtless was the catalyst to the final settlement, many key participants and observers believed that the strike ultimately would have been settled without his appearances or the intervention from Washington provoked by President Johnson's reaction. The former president of the city council and the local mediator were of the opinion that an agreement would have been worked out. The council's ex-president said that the strike had been distinctly settled three times *before* the assassination; but each time the mayor would not accept the settlement. Apparently, it took telephone calls from Washington to the mayor and the governor to get the former to acquiesce. The view that Dr. King's death put pressure on the mayor is shared by a key Local 1733 official and many of the ministers. The mayor himself pointed out that "when the President of the United States asks you to do something, you do it."

Negotiations in 1969. The 1968 Agreement was only for one year. It was renegotiated in 1969. Marshall and Van Adams also have summarized third party inputs into the 1969 negotiations:

> Many of the factors leading to the 1968 agreement were present in 1969. They were interlaced, however, with a new set of factors which combined with the old to bring about a settlement. The presence of Negro leaders, the involvement of the Negro community, and the threat of coercive pressures were again available to the union. Pressure from the white business community for settlement also was felt by the city. This was supplemented by concern from a new group of white citizens [Concerned Women of East Memphis] and the white press [8].

The Concerned Women of East Memphis were upset over local civil rights and the city's image following the 1968 strike. They cooperated with AFSCME's strategy to "spread the misery" of low paid, black city employees by dramatically calling poor people's working conditions to the attention of the white middle and upper middle classes. Harrassment of merchants in the quasi-suburban shopping centers was intended to duplicate the pressures of the 1968 boycott on downtown white merchants. The Concerned Women were from the most politically and socially prominent families, including the Crumps. They proposed a visit en masse to the black ghetto in lieu of a threat by certain AFSCME officials to import the ghetto's rats to East Memphis. This was accepted and about 75 Concerned (White) Women turned out in busloads to "tour" the ghetto, to the accompaniment of the press.

They capped their visit by a meeting at city hall where 300 appeared to demand that the city council deal fairly with the workers' demands. They got a place on the agenda and made a statement. Due to the internal politics of the group, the statement's tone was more laudatory of the council's efforts to avert a crisis than it was demanding. The council members were said to have treated this appearance cavalierly. This infuriated the moderates among the women, who held a heated press conference in the lobby. They complained, in effect, that the council did not even have the courtesy to thank them for their support. This got good press coverage. The president of the Concerned Women thought that her group was very influential in this situation. The AFSCME official agreed. But no one else brought it up when asked to identify influential groups in sanitationmen–AFSCME city bargaining.

Strike Threats. The mere threat of a city public employees' strike is potentially very influential. This is due largely to fears of another 1968 situation, as discussed above. It was the threat of another 1968 type of confrontation that mobilized the Concerned Women. It was also a key factor in the interest of the new executive director of the Chamber of Commerce. Notably, it was not the strike itself and its attendant inconvenience from lost services that most influenced the white community in Memphis. This may explain why the original strike in 1968 lasted so long.[i] Lack of white community sympathy for the plight of black city employees seems to have been stronger than the inconvenience caused by the strike. In fact, initially the business community reportedly bombarded the mayor with telegrams of support for holding out.

The Press. The press has not reported much about the sanitationmen's bargaining, as such, since it covered the activities of the Concerned Women in 1969. Subsequent coverage has been devoted almost entirely to hospital authority workers' bargaining. Hospital workers' bargaining conflicts between a conservative management and a militant black union were strongly reminiscent of the 1968 sanitationmen's situation with the mayor. Like this activist group, the 1975 influence of the press on sanitationmen's bargaining was more latent than active. The papers could publicize conflicts between the sanitationmen and the city, especially those which could provoke a strike. However, the only such conflict which occurred was the threat by the city in 1972 to contract out. In both 1972 and 1975 the sanitationmen's leaders threatened *sympathy* strikes with the AFSCME hospital workers. But these did not materialize.

The press is influential in the classic sense of having the potential to mobilize public opinion against either the strikers (as reportedly was done in 1968) or the government (as was done following the Concerned Women's demonstrations). The two daily papers are perceived to be very influential in this respect. Their coverage is perceived to focus public attention and thereby to dictate the issues. One black minister with media experience quoted a local adage that "The Mississippi Delta is where the Bible is respected, but the [Memphis] *Commercial Appeal* is read."

[i]From early January through early April 1968.

SUMMARY

The negotiating climate for Memphis's sanitationmen was very different in 1975 from 1968. The union had been successful in gaining de facto recognition from the mayor and eventually a form of de jure recognition through a city council resolution directing all departments and divisions to "meet and confer." With union survival no longer an issue in 1975, the black community, particularly the influential ministerial community, no longer had to take a direct interest in the day-to-day relations between the city and the sanitationmen.

Latent interest in the continuation of Local 1733's collective negotiations relationship is strong, but there is a difference in perception of the role of the union between the black community's leadership and that of the union. Whether Local 1733 should be primarily a civil rights movement or a labor movement is at the heart of this difference. The ministerial and black community's leadership is still very keen to have the union stay in the forefront of black political and social interests, as evidenced by their position during the 1975 mayoral campaign. But the union's leadership seems more interested in the economic gains of its own members than in risking these on the alter of strong political support for black community economic and social causes.

Where the two sets of interests coincide, the old solidarity of 1968 is evident. This is mainly in the recognition and survival of Local 1733 as a symbol of black political progress and social equality. Where they differ is over the demands by the union for increases in wages and benefits that would exceed the black community's ability and willingness to pay in terms of both higher taxes under a regressive tax structure and the political costs of supporting a strike by workers who already are perceived by both the black and white communities as being fairly paid.

Although the membership did, Local 1733's leadership did *not* support the black community's candidate for mayor in 1975. Whether the black community, whose support of the 1968 economic boycott was crucial, would mobilize readily to come to the political defense of sanitation workers is an open question in many observers' minds. Local 1733's leadership seems confident that it would. Many of the ministerial leaders and others who were active in 1968, however, express doubts that this support would be automatic. They regard 1968 as a unique situation in which black workers obviously were being discriminated against by the city through denial of just grievance resolution and tolerable working conditions, as a result of the mayor's intransigent refusal to bargain.

Chapter 5

Public Access to Berkeley's Teacher Negotiations

THE DISCLOSURE LAW

In 1974 the League of Women Voters of California helped pass the "Vasconsellos" amendment to the 1965 Winton Act governing teacher "meet and confer" negotiations in California. It required that "all initial proposals" by certified employee organizations[a] that fall within the scope of "meeting and conferring"[b] be presented to the school board at a public meeting and become part of the public record. Following this disclosure, a minimum of seven days is required before meetings can be held between the school board and the union in order "to enable the public to become informed and to express itself regarding the proposals, as well as regarding other possible subjects of meeting and conferring." The school board is further required to, "in open meeting, adopt policies which shall comprise (its) initial proposals." Moreover, the board is required to discuss any *new* subject of negotiations within 24 hours

[a] Teachers and administrators holding teaching certificates.

[b] At the time of the study, the California Education Code (Winton Act) required only "meet and confer" negotiations. These differ from formal collective bargaining in that the school board, technically, was merely consulting with its employees on certain policy matters. A board retained the option of a unilateral decision regarding those policies. No written, formal agreements were required. However, a board could make a formal contract in writing, with its employees, if it chose. The scope of meeting and conferring included "all matters relating to employment conditions and employer-employee relations," including "the definition of educational objectives, the determination of the content of courses and curricula, the selection of textbooks and other aspects of the instructional program."

of the time they are raised, and make public its position on the new subject, if any.

A new law (the Rodda Act) was passed in the summer of 1975, effective July 1, 1976. It permits exclusive representation and organizational security, and requires negotiations culminating in a written contract and grievance arbitration. Although all matters within the scope of representation are specifically excluded from coverage by the California open meetings law (Brown Act), the Rodda Act has a "public notice" section patterned after the original Vasconsellos amendment.

The Winton Act (which the Rodda Act replaced) gave teachers the right to discuss all school board policies and make recommendations; but all such policy decisions were reserved to the board. Employees could form and join unions and select representatives of their own choice. There was no right to exclusive representation. Where there was more than one existing employee organization, teachers were required to meet with the school board through a "Certificated Employees Council (CEC) of up to nine members." The Council was to include proportional representation of the members of each teachers organization.

The Vasconsellos amendment, effective in January 1975, provided the following points of public access to teacher and other certificated personnel negotiations. These were retained with minor modifications by the Rodda Act.

1. All initial proposals of the employee organizations must be presented to the school board at a public meeting. The Rodda Act also specified that public school employers would have to make their initial proposals public, too, instead of just responding to employee proposals, as under 3, below.
2. Following the presentation of the initial proposals, no meeting or conferring can occur for at least seven days in order to allow the public time to become informed on the proposals and to express itself publicly. The Rodda Act specifically requires the school board to hold a public meeting to hear the public's response. It also changed the seven-day period to "a reasonable time."
3. After the public has had a chance to respond, the public school employer must adopt policies that comprise the initial proposals of the board, in an open meeting.
4. Once the negotiations have begun, any new proposal by either the employees or the board that was not presented at a public meeting must be disclosed to the public within 24 hours.

This does not require a public meeting for a response; but, the announcement must be made through public media such as the press and posted in public places. Any board position or roll call vote taken on the proposal also has to be made a matter of public record within 24 hours.

IMPLEMENTATION POLICIES

Initial Proposals

The amendment's author, Assemblyman John Vasconsellos, said the law's purpose was to involve the public in the governing process by making information about negotiations available, and to provide the public an opportunity to address the negotiating proposals. He did not intend to alter the "meet and confer" process itself nor tamper with any of the provisions of the Winton Act [1].

He clarified several points of the law, subsequent to its enactment. As to what constitutes proposals, he indicated that more than a simple "laundry list" of items is to be discussed by both sides. The word proposal should be given its broadest definition. He also intended that the presentation of initial proposals would be more than a mere formality, with at least a verbal explanation by the employee organization [2].

According to the California legislative counsel, initial proposals must be made public at a public meeting of the full governing board of a school district itself, not just a meeting of the negotiators. The counsel's office specified that "the initial proposal of the school board regarding salaries, salary schedules, and compensation paid in the form of fringe benefits, must be made public."[c]

The League of Women Voters of California suggested in their recommendations for implementation of the Vasconsellos amendment the creation of a citizens' advisory committee to advise the school board. In addition, they would have the presentation of employee proposals included as a regular agenda item by the board, which would have to supply copies to the public. Although the Vasconsellos amendment did not require it, the League recommended that the board schedule a public meeting at which the public could respond to the employee proposals. This meeting, in effect, would be an advisory meeting to the board [3].

The California School Boards Association (CSBA) advised its member boards to take plenty of time to "notify the (Certificated

[c]The office of the legislative counsel is attached to the California state legislature. It does legal research for the members and provides legal opinions at their request (Letter of April 7, 1975 to J. Vasconsellos).

Employees Council) that the board will receive employee proposals on one of several dates." The board should "include the employee presentation as a published agenda item." The boards were advised to limit their actions at this point to the receipt of the employee proposals and to schedule a date for public response [4]. The California Teachers Association (CTA) said that only the *subjects* that are being negotiated have to be made public [5].

School Board's Response

The California School Boards Association indicated that the school board's response to the initial proposals represents only a temporary policy [6]. This permits the flexibility necessary for negotiations. The League [7] and Assemblyman Vasconsellos supported this view [8], as did the California Teachers Association [9]. According to the CSBA, the board, technically, does not adopt its final position until a subsequent meeting ("under a listed agenda item, adopt its final positions at a public session . . . and make them available in printed form within 24 hours").

> Preferably it will take as much time as is necessary to thoroughly analyze the budget and program implications of the proposals and to make these available to the public and employees. If one additional board meeting can be held in the interim before the board's response is given, it will more adequately comply with the law's intent for the public to have an opportunity to respond [10].

The California Teachers Association argued that "there is no requirement that the board's counterproposals on these subjects be made prior to commencement of negotiations. There is no requirement that counterproposals by either party be made public" [11].

New Proposals

Vasconsellos defined a "new proposal" as one not mentioned previously. A shift in a position would not be a new subject of negotiations requiring 24-hour notice [12]. The League of Women Voters shared this view. They advised that any new subjects proposed by either party should be printed and available to the public within 24 hours. They should be distributed "for public pickup at a known and designated place in the school district" [13].

The legislative counsel pointed out that all proposals which are not initial proposals do not require a public meeting. These new proposals can be entered into the public record through distribution within 24 hours [14]. The California School Boards Association also advised that new subjects be printed for distribution within 24 hours and that "agreement on any matter . . . must be a matter of public record within 24 hours" and that "printed copies [be made] available for public pickup" [15].

The California Teachers Association took a much narrower view. It argued that the law "governs only the initial proposal incorporating the first introduction of the subject matter. There is no requirement that any counterproposals be published or made a matter of public record." The CTA also claimed that "board action is not required" on the disclosure of new subjects of bargaining [16]. The law does say that only if the board takes a formal position must it be public, not that the board must take a position.

As to the School Boards Association's recommendations on public disclosure of areas of agreement as they are reached, the CTA said that "Nothing . . . governs actions reached during meeting and conferring. . . . There is no requirement in this law that requires such agreements to be made prior to the presentation of the total package of agreements" [17].

SELECTION OF BERKELEY

Berkeley was chosen because the school board had made a serious attempt to implement both the letter and the spirit of the Vasconsellos amendment. The board of education of the Berkeley Unified School District went a step further than the letter of the disclosure law by creating the Citizens' Advisory Committee on Negotiations. As a body unilaterally sleected by the board, it had purely an advisory status. Nevertheless, this group not only acted as a fact finding and research body, but ultimately the parties allowed its members to attend the negotiations and to observe the caucuses of both sides.

After the field work for this study was completed in July 1975, the teachers struck the board in September. During this strike, the Citizens' Advisory Committee observed both the negotiations and the fact finding hearings and one of the committee members represented the board of education on the fact finding panel. The role of the Citizens' Advisory Committee in the 1975 Berkeley board of education negotiations, then, was an ideal "critical incident" to investigate the representation of the public interest in public sector labor relations. The California law is unique and the role of the committee adds a deeper dimension not identified in the other case studies.

Chronology of Negotiations

Originally, the teacher representatives tried to avoid the requirements of the new law. Their coalition, the Certificated Employees

Council, submitted its proposals in late December 1974. They expected the board of education to submit its proposals simultaneously. Instead, the board simply received the council's proposals, not making them public until January 2, 1975. This brought the parties under the jurisdiction of the new disclosure law.

The board issued a press release on the law's requirements, and in compliance with the new law, had the teachers' proposals distributed for public inspection. The public was invited to reply in writing or formally to request a hearing at the next special board meeting on negotiations the following week. At that meeting, the president of the Parent Teachers Association's council labeled the teachers' demand for the equivalent of a 25 percent salary increase "ridiculous." The black community, through a representative of the Concerned Black Parents of Berkeley, raised the question of "tripartite" negotiations. He asked for community representation at the bargaining table as equal partners in the negotiating process.

On January 21, the board adopted a resolution providing for a board-appointed citizens' advisory committee "to review the proposals of the board and Certificated Employees Council and to meet with the board, when requested, to advise it in the process of negotiations." This fell short of the "equal partner status" sought by members of the black community. But, it was at least a step towards direct citizen input into board negotiations policies. The board also decided that it would comply with the new disclosure requirements by announcing any new subjects raised in negotiations through a press release within 24 hours of the introduction of the new item.

The board's initial proposals did not include any definite salary commitments, because the board did not have a clear enough picture of the 1975–76 budget. At its January 28 meeting, the board revealed that the school district was $2.6 million in debt. The failure to discover this deficit earlier was attributed to bookkeeping procedures that were complicated by five years of relatively heavy federal funding.

On February 18, the board proposed "no salary increases," unless money would be saved elsewhere. This proposal was coupled with a "no layoffs" proposal. During subsequent meetings, the board offered a 5 percent pay increase, contingent upon available funds and the teachers scaled down their original 25 percent equivalent to 10 percent.

On March 6, members of the Public Employees Union Local No. 1, an independent union of school aides and other classified nonteaching employees, began a six-day strike. On the day that the strike was settled, 500 members of the Berkeley Federation of Teachers (BFT) voted nine to one to strike on April 3—just twelve days before the board of education elections on April 15.

On March 23 the League of Women Voters released a study of Berkeley teacher pay which indicated that city taxing and spending was among the highest in the state and that Berkeley teachers were among the highest paid. The Berkeley Teachers Association took out newspaper ads urging a reduction of administrative costs to pay for higher teacher salaries.

The next day, the superintendent sent a letter to all parents describing the board's budget crisis and negotiations position. It included a Citizens' Advisory Committee recommendation against any salary increases. It also proposed some program cuts designed to balance the budget even without salary increases. These drew public protests, both from white middle class parents defending educational enrichment programs and minority parents demanding just as hotly the continuation of remedial programs. As the Federation's strike deadline approached, the BFT voted to continue negotiations. The Certificated Employees Council reported that they had reached agreement with the board on all other issues except teacher salaries. Council members agreed with the board that there were no hidden sources of money this time. The board and the council finally agreed to no raise on April 8, just a week before election day, April 15. They also agreed that an increase of up to 6.5 percent would be given later, if new funds became available. But this eventuality was regarded as extremely unlikely.

To implement its "no layoffs" policy, the board proposed that art, music, special reading, and science be taught by classroom teachers instead of specialists. The press reported that about 800 people showed up at the May 6 board meeting to protest what they believed to be *cuts* in the special programs. Although these cuts were necessitated by the settlement, it is questionable to what extent the protesters saw this link. Complicating matters even further, at the end of June, the board discovered that its deficit amounted to $3.7 million, not $2.6 million on which basis they had negotiated. Because of this increased deficit, the board announced that it was reopening the negotiations to discuss a pay *reduction* of 15 percent as well as other extensive changes in the agreement.

In effect, the earlier negotiations were undone by new budgetary information. Because the Winton Act did not provide for collective bargaining, as such, the board believed that it retained the right to reconsider the terms and conditions of employment previously "negotiated." So, it reactivated the Citizens' Advisory Committee on Negotiations and appointed still another citizens' committee to examine the budget. The board asked the teachers to re-enter negotiations in view of the changed financial situation, but the teachers refused. The Certificated Employees' Council organizations struck on September 3, staying out until October 6. During the strike, the Citizens' Advisory Committee became involved again and, in fact, became one of the issues of the strike. The recommendations of a tripartite fact finding panel eventually were accepted by both sides. They simply bypassed the Citizens' Advisory Committee in accepting a solution.

For study purposes, these subsequent events do not affect the original negotiations as a "critical incident," to be studied in its own context. They do, however, shed light on some of the weaknesses of the original process of third party access.

INDEPENDENT VARIABLES

Government Structure

The Winton Act (1965) amendments to the State Education Code gave certificated school employees the right to form, join, and be represented by organizations of their own choice "to afford them a voice in educational policy." The employer was only required to "meet and confer" with such employee organizations. Traditional collective bargaining envisions a good faith attempt on the part of the union and employer to negotiate on all matters within its scope and to produce a written contract that obligates both sides to adhere to what they negotiated. "Meet and confer" contemplates only formal discussions. Ultimately, it is the school board which decides unilaterally the policy of the school district regarding all educational matters, including the terms and conditions of employment. In test cases, the California courts upheld the principle that agreements between California school boards and employee organizations did not have the status of contracts.[d]

The board of education of the Berkeley unified school district has five members. They are elected in stages, during odd-numbered years, to four-year terms; two are elected at one time and three at another. Members run at large in nonpartisan elections. After each election, the board members choose a president.

Attitudes Towards Organized Labor

School board members all were reportedly "pro labor" in their outlook. This does not mean that they were regarded as particularly "pro teachers' demands." Historically, the Berkeley community has

[d]The Rodda Act specifically changed this to provide for collective bargaining and exclusive recognition.

been "liberal" since the deposition of Republican party city government in the early 1960s. The population is heavily white collar and blue collar unionized workers, in addition to University of California faculty and students.

Although no local poll data was available for Berkeley, itself, a statewide sample commissioned that spring by the California Teachers Association revealed that 69 percent of the respondents thought public employees should have the right to collective bargaining and 75 percent agreed that teachers, specifically, should have this right. Moreover, 54 percent thought that public employees should have the right to strike and 59 percent thought that teachers should have the right to strike, "if every collective bargaining procedure has been tried and exhausted and an absolute stalemate has been reached."

Yet, ironically, 58 percent agreed that if negotiations break down and cooling-off and fact finding is exhausted, "the dispute should be settled by compulsory arbitration with no right to strike." Closer to the notion of the representation of the public interest, 55 percent agreed "that officials who are elected by the people to establish public policy would be put under unfair pressure by a strike or the threat of a strike which would shut down public services," and 50 percent agreed that elected officials "would be limited in their ability to really represent the taxpayers if they were pressured by the threat of a strike or by an actual strike which shut down public services" [18].

Political Activities of Labor

An examination of campaign contributions to the 1975 Berkeley board campaign did not reveal any substantial contributions from teachers or teachers' organizations. One teacher was listed among the contributors of $50 or more to one of the defeated candidates. The top vote-getting candidate did get small contributions from 22 school district employees.

The study found mixed attitudes towards labor's political influence. Opinions differed between the participants in the negotiations (board members and union representatives), who denied any influence, and representatives of the minority community who asserted that labor, especially the teachers, was influential. The California Teachers Association claims to have elected 58.1 percent of the 229 school board candidates whom they supported and financed statewide in 1975 [19]. A potential for 1,000 campaign workers consisting of the teachers who work in Berkeley is greater than the number of votes represented by the teachers who actually live in Berkeley. But, there was no evidence of any organized vote-getting drive by any teachers.

Locally, neither the Berkeley Federation of Teachers nor the Berkeley Teachers Association officially endorsed, campaigned, or financed any of the candidates in the 1975 Berkeley school board election. Their attitude was that their support of board candidates in previous years taught them that they could not count on the loyalty of their candidates once they were elected. Only one-third of the Berkeley Federation of Teachers' membership voted to endorse board candidates, for example. The AFL–CIO COPE organization was said to have helped some of the candidates, but this did not appear in the official campaign reports. The Federation is affiliated with the AFL–CIO, which provided strike sanction earlier in 1975. But few observers were willing to speculate on the degree of harmony between private sector labor and the teachers.

The representative of the Berkeley Teachers Association (the Berkeley Federation of Teachers' chief rival) claimed that the AFL–CIO really was against public sector collective bargaining and cited as evidence their withdrawal of support for pending state public sector collective bargaining legislation.[e] The Berkeley Teachers Association's president considered the AFL–CIO's strike sanctions in support of the Berkeley Federation of Teachers as merely pro forma. However, the Berkeley Federation of Teachers' representative cited the sanction as evidence of private sector labor's strong support. She also asserted that the Teamsters and Building Trades unions were "very supportive of teachers." The Association leadership tried to start a recall drive against the board members during the negotiations, but couldn't muster the necessary signatures. No vote of the membership was ever taken; but the leadership considered resuming this drive in the light of the subsequent budgetary disclosures and the announced intention of the board to renegotiate its agreement for 1975–76.

The 1975 bargaining and board election occurred simultaneously, and the interviews revealed mixed attitudes towards the possibility of a direct relationship between the two. The current board president, who previously acted as negotiator for the board, was quoted as stating that she wanted the negotiations to be concluded before the election. Members of the Citizens' Advisory Committee thought that the board did not accept all its recommendations against *any* increases

---

[e] In a news release of June 20, 1975, the CTA president angrily accused the executive secretary-treasurer of the California Federation of Labor (AFL–CIO) as having killed the statewide collective bargaining bill over an amendment "to permit nonvoting student representatives to participate in bargaining talks at the higher education level." He went on to charge that the AFL–CIO's "withdrawal of support in committee tells us that the nonpublic employee affiliated labor leaders in the AFL–CIO don't really want collective bargaining for public employees."

because of the impending election. In fact, negotiations were concluded just seven days before election day itself. The Citizens' Advisory Committee chairperson felt that if the agreement hadn't been signed so early, the more accurate figures of the budget deficit would have come to light. Unlike urban big cities, there was no assertion that either private sector labor of the teachers' organization "controlled" the board of education through political-electoral influence.

"Meeting and Conferring" Structure

Management. Prior to 1974, the Berkeley board of education's negotiations were conducted directly by a board member. In 1974, the director of certificated personnel was designated the board's chief negotiator. The director of certificated personnel is under the assistant superintendent for business and administrative services. He functions parallel to the director of classified personnel. The latter administers the separate merit system for the 650 nonteaching, noncertificated employees. The two systems are mutually independent.

The director of certificated personnel was a former high school principal. He was highly regarded personally by all observers and participants. However, he was not a labor negotiator by profession. The board sent him to a two-week training program last year. Union officials complained that this training seems to have made him self-conscious as a negotiator. One said that it took her a while to figure out the change in tone between the 1974 and 1975 negotiations until she decided that he must have felt that he had to practice some of the conventional bargaining strategies he had learned in the training program. She thought that such strategies had slowed down the negotiations. The board also hired a negotiations consulting firm whose advice, the leadership of the teachers felt, contributed to an adversary relationship that was noticeably stronger in 1975 than in the preceding negotiations.

At the time of the study the board was looking for a full time chief negotiator, because the director of certificated personnel declined to be involved in renegotiating the 1975 agreement. He felt that doing so would make him appear to have been lacking good faith during the previous negotiations.

Board negotiating positions are developed by the director of certificated personnel, largely from suggestions by principals and in response to Certificated Employees Council demands. A meeting of school principals was called in late 1974 to develop the 1975 package. The superintendent reviewed this package which was submitted to the board around the first of the year. The superintendent deals directly with the management employee representatives of the 80 to 90-member management council. He also got directly involved in the negotiations with Local No. 1, following their strike, but not with the Certificated Employees Council. Technically, negotiations with the board resulted in policy recommendations, not collective bargaining agreements. In previous years, negotiations and subsequent agreements have been on an *annual* basis. In July 1975, it appeared that, in view of the deepening financial crisis, there would be *two* sets of negotiations.

Employees. The Berkeley Board of Education negotiates with two kinds of employees: certificated (teachers and administrators), and classified (all nonteaching personnel). There are approximately 1,050 certificated personnel. The California Federation of Teachers and California Teachers Association each represent about 500 members. The Berkeley Pupil Personnel Association represents the remaining 50 or so who are counselors, guidance teachers, and school psychologists. The Winton Act did not provide for exclusive representation, but the law required rival units to negotiate in a nine-member coalition. Membership was apportioned according to the proportion of the certificated employees represented by each organization.

The negotiating group was designated as the Certificated Employees Council (CEC). The Federation and Association each have four of the nine members and the Pupil Personnel Association one. Given the intense organizational rivalry between the Federation and Association, the Professional Personnel held the swing vote on the Council. Previously, the Association had five votes and the Federation four. The Pupil Personnel group supported the Federation on the basic issue of who was to be the negotiator for the certificated employees. The California Teachers Association brought in an experienced professional negotiator from the National Education Association, as they had done two years previously. But the California Federation of Teachers and Pupil Personnel voted five-to-four to use a Federation vice president. The Association's spokesperson said that the Association lost control of the negotiations this year. She thought that an outside professional negotiator would have been better able to cope with the board's hired negotiating consultants who "used every legal loophole to (get) us."

Since nonteaching personnel were not covered by the disclosure amendment, their labor relations were not studied.[f] The three mem-

---

[f] Approximately 650 school district nonteaching employees are represented by Local No. 1, (200) (Independent) and by the California School Employees

ber organizations of the Certificated Employees Council polled their memberships for negotiations issues. In 1975, apparently, they did not screen their members' demands very carefully. The result was an initial package that was regarded by both sides as detrimental to the certificated employees' position. Some observers felt that the lack of priority setting by the certificated employees reflected weak internal leadership. This was said to be the result of the competition between organizations, in that each side was trying to please all of its members by including all of their negotiations demands in the initial package. Moreover, the package was said to have been rushed in order to submit it before the new Vasconsellos law was to take effect on January 1, 1975. The attendant publicity about the initial proposals proved embarrassing to the council members, who subsequently regretted that they didn't take more time to prepare a package that would have looked more reasonable to the public.

IDENTIFICATION OF INTEREST GROUPS

Groups and individuals interested in Berkeley teacher negotiations were almost exclusively what might be termed the "education activist" community; that is, they were the same people who scrutinize and try to influence educational decision making across a broad spectrum of educational issues. Unlike the general public, these people seemed to perceive more acutely the relationship between teacher negotiations and the other substantive educational issues in which they felt they had a stake. They analyzed the potential impact of tradeoffs in any teacher negotiations and tried to estimate the possible consequences. In this sense, these groups and their members practiced a pure model of political participation that is based on the perception of salience of governmental decisions (negotiations) to group or individual goals (tradeoffs with programmatic and other public interest educational goals).

The key activist groups in the 1975 teacher negotiations were (1) the League of Women Voters of Berkeley, (2) Parent Teachers Association Council, (3) National Association for the Advancement of Colored People, (4) Concerned Black Parents of Berkeley, and (5) Asian Alliance. These organizations had formal or informal representation on the Citizens' Advisory Committee on negotiations. Most of their inputs in the negotiations were funneled through the Citizens' Advisory Committee, or, to a lesser extent, the Citizens' Budget

---

Association, Public Employees Union (450) (Independent). These include clerical employees, custodians, food service workers, community aides, bus drivers, instructional aides, and student supervisors. Since there was no exclusive representation in 1975, employees were free to join either of these two groups.

and Finance Committee. The Chamber of Commerce was conspicuous by its lack of activity or interest in board of education affairs.[g]

Because there was no teachers' strike during the first phase of 1975 negotiations that was studied, it is not possible to estimate the extent to which such a strike might have triggered the interests of the community in reopening the schools at any cost—say, for the convenience of parents who work or who just didn't want to have their children around the house. This happened, for example, on a large scale in the 1972—73 Philadelphia teachers' strike and in the 1975 Milwaukee teachers' strike. This did not happen in Berkeley until the fourth week of the fall 1975 Berkeley teachers' strike.

In the case of the first phase of the Berkeley teacher negotiations, the concerns were more general. The key participants from the PTA and minority communities, as well as the League of Women Voters, Citizens' Advisory Committee and Citizens' Budget and Finance Committee all had children in the schools. In this sense, each had a self-interested goal pertaining to their own children. In a broader sense, however, the League and the two citizens' committees were stressing goals that transcended the immediate self-interest of their own membership. The League in particular was active at the state level in securing the legislation that contributed to the creation of the Citizens' Advisory Committee and made access possible.

The Citizens' Advisory Committee, for its part, stressed citizen interest in a balanced budget—in order to retain local control of the schools, as among the most important of its goals. The Citizens' Budget and Finance Committee stressed the more classic taxpayer interests. None was interested in settling the dispute according to the short run goal of giving the teachers everything that they wanted in order to assure the maintenance of services. Of course, they were not really able to make such a choice, in the absence of identifiable budgetary resources. But they could have urged deferral of the problem to the county or state level of government, as some interests subsequently urged when it became evident that even the April 15 agreement would have to be renegotiated downwards in terms of its costs.

The sharpest differences of goals and interests was along the pervasive "fault" that is growing between the minority and white middle class communities. The League and the Citizens' Budget and Finance Committee are dominated by white, middle class representatives. The president of the PTA council is black, but a majority of their board

---

[g]Most members live outside Berkeley. They have no direct interest in the schools. Politically they are said to have been alienated from the liberal Democratic politics which have dominated the city over the past two decades.

is white. The minority community representatives shared the goal of "no salary increases," but for different purposes from those of the white middle class. The white middle class interests wanted fiscal responsibility and retention of the governance of the schools without having them lapse into county control for lack of a balanced budget, *together with* retention of educational enrichment programs. Black community interests did not stress the governance issue, but definitely wanted resources diverted to remedial education and "basic" education. Since most of the teachers are white and middle class, and half of the students are nonwhite, there is a certain lack of sympathy for teacher demands among the minority communities. This probably is not unique to the minorities, as indications are that community attitudes towards teachers in general are low. Yet, a member of the Citizens' Advisory Committee and League of Women Voters reported that parental support for the teachers was high during the 1975 strike, based on the proportion of children who stayed home from school. Only one-third went to school.

The League of Women Voters of Berkeley

The League's primary goal was the implementation of the new law to assure public disclosure of initial proposals and subsequent introduction of new subjects. This was coordinated with the League of Women Voters of California, which was monitoring statewide implementation and providing local Leagues with policy advice as to how to do so. They believe that their success in enacting the Vasconsellos amendment paved the way for acceptance of the idea of providing for public access to negotiations issues. The Rodda Act was drafted to be expanded to include all public employees, should collective bargaining rights be extended in California beyond teachers.

The League's long standing interest in school affairs is based on the belief that a good educational system helps to insure a democratic society. So, they look at the educational system as a governmental process and are not strictly concerned solely with the services of the schools. Adequacy of school funding is a primary League concern, however. In 1972–73, League members studied the state role in education, extending from the original budgetary concerns to all levels of educational policy making and to the roles of policy-makers. The study was concerned with the potential impact of citizen participation on the educational policy making process. The League did not study negotiations, as such. But, when they looked at the influences on policy making and allocation of educational resources, members were struck by the implications of teacher negotiations. It was evident that teacher negotiations affected the citizen participation process, largely by excluding third parties—that is, persons who were not parties to the negotiations between teachers organizations and school boards.

Concurrently, the issue of collective bargaining for all public employees in the state was before the state legislature. League policy makers concluded from their study of the educational policy making process that, if citizens had virtually no effective access to this process under then current "meet and confer" legislation, they were not likely to do any better under prospective broader collective bargaining legislation. So, the concept of citizen access to public sector labor relations decision making became a high priority item for the California League.

The League's leadership believed that it was the only organization concerned with this issue; therefore, they felt that if they wanted to affect the legislation, they had to draft their own proposals and find a sponsor. In the past, the League usually had taken positions on somebody else's legislation; in this case, John Vasconsellos, State Assemblyman from the Santa Clara–San Jose area, agreed to sponsor the League's amendment to the Winton Act. It was drafted by the state legislative counsel's office and introduced in February 1974.

The League lobbied for this law heavily. According to a League spokeswoman, the major problem was in getting the legislators themselves to see the connection between governmental policies and collective bargaining with employees. The more liberal legislators, especially those with experience in private or public labor relations, felt that negotiations were best done in private. They held the opinion that negotiations were not clearly related to public policy. The conservatives were searching for ways to diminish the employees' role in negotiations. The League had to walk a fine line: it was criticized by both employees and management for its stand in favor of public disclosure of negotiations subjects and official positions taken by public bodies on negotiations.

The League's spokesperson said that the League tried to make it clear that it has no position on the format for negotiations, either collective bargaining or meet and confer. The League's bill was based on a concept which it did not consider controversial, namely, that citizens should have access to information regarding the proposals negotiated by public bodies with their employees. They were not pushing for direct access to the decision making process; for League members consulted with both administrators' and employees' groups.

Originally, they thought that these groups supported the amendment, but when it was in committee, these groups opposed it. The California School Boards Association supported the bill but did not work for it. The employee groups, apparently confident that it would not pass, were opposed but did not consider it a high priority matter. The League was acting as a public interest group, rather than a special interest group.[h] The goal of public access extended to all possible participants, not just to League members. The role of League members as parents was indirectly served; but the goals were not formulated strictly in terms of the effects of decision making on school children. Goals of taxpayers and other community interests would be served by the League's activities as well as those of parents and pupils.

Parent Teachers Association Council

The Berkeley PTA Council consists of 60 members representing 1,330 PTA members citywide. Half are black and the other half are white and Asian. Few teachers are said to belong. Most members are parents of school children. The Parent Teachers Association members were said to have interpreted the Certificated Employee Council contract proposals as a desire by teachers to spend more of their time outside of the classroom. They claim there were only three out of six hours of a teacher's day that would have been spent in the classroom. So, they opposed more preparation time and release time, and increased salaries, but supported smaller class size. In addition, they sought "teacher accountability." The current PTA Council president reported that the PTA was split over the controversy regarding "basic skills versus educational enrichment."

Citizens' Budget and Finance Committee

The Citizens' Budget and Finance Committee is a vestige of a 100-member master plan committee created by the board in 1969 to advise it on fiscal matters. In 1975, it was an 18-member group appointed by the board. Members may nominate themselves, or they may be nominated by a group. Included are the League of Women Voters, Asian Task Force, and a black parents' group, as well as some school district employees. There are no PTA members; however, all but two of the members have children in the Berkeley schools. Most of the members may be described as middle class; all are college educated. The chairperson of the committee describes it as a "taxpayers'" group. Since it is still a creature of the board, not independent of it, the committee does not really fit the description of a taxpayers' interest group.

---

[h] See Chapter 2 on Milwaukee for a discussion of the distinction between a public interest and a special interest group.

Management rights, including the ability to transfer teachers in order to save money and to control curriculum development (and therefore costs) were primary goals of the committee. Others were: Teacher accountability, no reduction of teachers' hours, no reduction in class size, and no increases in fringe benefits, release time, preparation time, or substitutes. Increased teachers salaries were "not the highest priority." They opposed the "no layoff" policy, not because it was explicitly against affirmative action, but because many members thought that affirmative action policies still could be maintained with selective layoffs. More positions than the minimum could be vacated so that some rehiring could take place in order to compensate for the initial layoffs.

Citizens' Advisory Committee on Negotiations

The board of education appointed the Citizens' Advisory Committee on Negotiations. Though somewhat representative of the community at large, or at least of major educational interest groups, the committee was clearly a creature of the board and its chief role was conceived by the board members to be restricted to giving them advice.

The committee had seven members, two of which were officially designated as PTA representatives and one from the Citizens' Budget and Finance Committee. Each of the four board members at the time appointed an additional member. Through board appointments additional representation was gained by the PTA, NAACP and Concerned Black Parents, Asian Alliance, and League of Women Voters.

A major consideration of this committee was the detrimental effect that firing the most recently hired—according to state law— would have on the affirmative action gains made by the district in recent years. The members finally reached a unanimous position on no salary increases, instead. It was said that, once the fear of minority layoffs was removed, relations among the members became harmonious. Members remained "surprisingly united" on other issues, both financial and educational.

On most other issues, the committee was reported as more conservative than the board by virtually all observers and participants. They wanted greater teacher accountability, stricter teacher evaluation, dismissal of incompetent teachers, reduction in the amount of preparation time allowed teachers, increased allocations for maintenance and building needs, and retention by the board of the right to transfer teachers to fill vacancies caused by attrition. Citizens' Advisory Committee members believed that they represented a viewpoint that was distinct from that of the board—namely, that of the consumer.

Unorganized Public

No public opinion data on the disclosure law or Berkeley negotiations was available by which to compare the attitudes of the unorganized public with the interests groups actively involved in trying to influence negotiations.[i] Participants and observers reported little direct feedback from people outside their own groups. Certainly, the black community spokesmen and women had a sense of representing the black community's goals regarding excessive teacher compensation and benefits in the light of no visible progress towards functional literacy of their children. The Asian community was reportedly more complacent with the system, though in opposition to the blacks' demand for more "basic," remedial education. But the white middle and upper middle class, nevertheless, appeared to dominate the school system in terms of citizens' committees and board representation, teachers, and educational program priorities.

DEFINITIONS OF THE PUBLIC INTEREST

An implicit definition of the public interest in "affirmative action" personnel policies of the board of education consistently emerged from the discussions with participants and observers. This definition was embodied in the "no layoff" policy of the Citizens' Advisory Committee, the board, and the Certificated Employees Council. This policy became the crux of the 1975−76 agreement, according to virtually everyone interviewed, regardless of whether or not the person agreed with that policy.

The explicit definitions of the public interest volunteered in the course of the interviews did *not* reflect this universal recognition of the affirmative action policy. Most people did not have a clear conception of a public interest. When asked to relate that concept to the specific situation in which they were involved, they cited broad prescriptive or normative generalizations rather than citing any specific examples. In fact, "affirmative action" was commented upon *negatively* by three of the five people who did refer to it explicitly in the context of the public interest. They argued that the schools had a primary mission that was *not* a manpower responsibility and that the schools should not have to stretch their limited resources to accomplish secondary manpower program missions.

The plurality of respondents mentioned the "ability to pay" as the public interest. This is consistent with the foremost issue of the

---

[i]The Opinion Research of California poll found that 88 percent of the Californians sampled agreed that "public employees and employees in private industry ought to receive comparable pay for comparable work." See Table C.4.e.

negotiations: the schools' budgetary crisis. Next often mentioned was "quality education." Management rights notions received the next highest number of references. Only four people raised the concept of due process, or citizen access to the decision making process and the need for accurate information. These were, understandably representatives of the three groups most active in implementing this aspect of the public interest: the Citizens' Advisory Committee, the Citizens' Budget and Finance Committee, and the League of Women Voters. The representative of the NAACP also cited the notion of access.

Next to affirmative action, the public interest in "fiscal solvency" or budgetary responsibility, was implicitly the most important public interest issue. Ability of the board to remain solvent and self-governing was discussed by almost everyone, even though not always explicitly in response to the notion of the public interest. If the board of education cannot produce a balanced budget, legally, the next step is for the county government to take over the operation of the schools.

The preservation of management's rights to transfer employees and to decide program priorities followed in importance. This is related to the notion of fiscal responsibility or governmental sovereignty through ability to control the expenditure of money. It is also at the heart of the controversies surrounding the implementation of the affirmative action policy. Minorities opposed teacher pay increases because these would involve layoffs of teachers recently hired under affirmative action programs.

With the June 1975 discovery that budget deficits were even greater than those originally forecast even the "no layoff" policy had to be reassessed. The board president remarked that affirmative action had been accommodated (through the no layoff policy) partly out of anticipation of community reaction against its dilution. Apparently perceptions of the climate changed as a result of the new budgetary pressures, according to such participants as the spokesperson for the Berkeley Teachers Association. In this new climate of increased budget deficits, the affirmative action no layoff policy of continued employment of recently hired, largely minority employees was weakened in the face of demands by major parent factions. These factions represented minority pupils, upper middle class "enrichment program" beneficiaries, and handicapped pupils. They maintained a stubborn resistance to any cuts in special program administration that were intended by the board to save the money necessary to prevent layoffs of more recently hired classroom teachers.

Program cuts are largely the result of reassignment of professional, certificated staff occupying administrative positions to teaching vacancies resulting from natural attrition. The staff available for such reassignment are largely involved in administration, teaching and special education programs. Also, consolidation of schools in order to save money would result in the closing of some small schools located in upper middle class neighborhoods. The legal problems involved in layoffs were not solved, either. The board of education was trying to accommodate conflicting notions of the public interest that place contradictory demands upon the resources available to operationalize these interests.

Unfortunately, the board was still in a dilemma in terms of satisfying the public interest in minority groups' needs. Program administration cuts and supplies' cuts were about the only places that were identified for budgetary savings, in lieu of teaching staff layoffs, and in addition to natural attrition. Conflicts over program cuts also ran deep along class and ethnic lines. The white middle and upper middle class did not want accelerated programs cut. At the same time, minorities were clamoring for additional remedial programs. "Representation" on the board was split three-to-two, with three white upper middle class members (an attorney, a professor of education finance, and a PhD candidate in education), one black woman (a credit union assistant director), and an Asian (a probation officer).

The board president remarked that the board probably should have laid people off and paid the remaining employees more. "We lost sight of the focus of providing education to children, which blurred into providing employment for adults."

DEPENDENT VARIABLES

Access
The Berkeley board of education's labor relations decision making process is marked by both a wide range of potential structural access points, that is, those that are available through practice and board policy, as well as an extensive use by interest groups of them. By contrast, the degree of political activity is low.

Management. The superintendent keeps in touch with the educational activist groups, all of which regularly attend all board meetings and "workshops"[j] on virtually all educational policy matters, including negotiations. The Berkeley board of education has a long history

---

[j]Workshops are unofficial public meetings of the Board unrestrained by formal rules of order and where no formal votes are taken.

of creating citizens' committees and task forces to inquire into various aspects of educational policy making under consideration by the board. Prior to the Citizens' Advisory Committee, the Citizens' Budget and Finance Committee was the only such permanent standing committee. But there were several ad hoc committees for the major policy matters.

Still, the black community had been pressing for further access. Groups such as the Concerned Black Parents saw access as a racial issue. The minority community was dissatisfied with the schools and wanted access to the negotiations' decision making which they perceived ultimately affected programs. Jealousy of the majority (68 percent) of white teachers in a system with only 44 percent white pupils also undoubtedly was a factor. While minority workers were being laid off in the local economy at a higher rate than whites (due to a combination of their being more dependent on jobs vulnerable to economic slowdown and having less seniority in more stable occupations), white-dominated teachers' organizations were perceived as demanding an increase of 25 percent in wages and further reductions in classroom time. The two white board members at the time, who tended to share the teachers' middle to upper middle class educational values, were defensive of the board's prerogatives to conduct negotiations without outside interference. The Asian community, which was represented by the Asian board member, tended to hold an ambivalent view. On the one hand, their cultural and educational values are shared with the white middle class; on the other hand there is an emotional identification with minority groups.

While black leaders focused on access for these reasons, the Berkeley League of Women Voters was pursuing a more generalized goal of access to the board's labor relations decision making process. After succeeding in their lobbying efforts for the new disclosure law, they followed up by publicizing its disclosure requirements and new opportunities for access, and by monitoring its implementation. Partly as a result of League publicity, groups of citizens, PTA members, Concerned Black Parents, and the NAACP were aware of the new possibilities for access to negotiations. With the new law, the League's efforts, and the black demands, there was a new climate for community access.

At the January 7, 1975 board meeting, the NAACP representative demanded that the negotiations be conducted on a tripartite basis, with public representatives having full veto power. The three non-black board members adamantly opposed the suggestion. As a means of compromise, one of them suggested a Citizens' Advisory Committee on Negotiations, limited to an advisory role to the board. This wasn't particularly palatable to themselves, either, but the board president said that she originally saw the notion of the Citizens' Advisory Committee as "a palliative."

With the board's history of setting up task forces, workshops, and citizen committees, the Citizens' Advisory Committee was not a radical innovation; but in creating it, the Berkeley board of education went a long step beyond the requirements of implementing the new law which had no requirements for any such structure. Formally, only the PTA Council and Citizens' Budget and Finance Committee members were allocated membership on the Citizens' Advisory Committee; informally, the League of Women Voters, NAACP, Concerned Black Parents, and Asian Alliance were also represented. Thus all the educational activist groups were appointed to the newly formed negotiations policy advisory committee.

Under the board's interpretation of the new disclosure requirements, copies of the initial proposals of both the Certificated Employees Council and the board were placed on public display in all school offices, public libraries, and the board of education headquarters. In compliance with the law's requirement of public consideration and vote on negotiation proposals, the board formally adopted its policies at the January 14 meeting. As a means of keeping the public informed about the progress of negotiations, the board published and distributed a newsletter on each session, similar to its reports of board meetings. The board asked the Certificated Employees Council to participate in this newsletter, but this offer was refused.

These materials were mailed to 179 church groups, 150 community organizations (including the ten deans at the University of California, Berkeley), plus the Lions, Kiwanis, and Rotary clubs. Thus the board's version of negotiations, at least, was made public prior to and during negotiations, and in advance of formal ratification. In previous negotiations, representatives of the PTA and NAACP each had been given copies of the Certificated Employees Council's proposal, but the NAACP representative complained that there was never any follow-up by the board in seeking his position.

Critics of the board's new procedures asserted that it violated the spirit of the law by holding all decision making sessions, except for formal ratification, in closed, or "executive" session. The California League of Women Voters believed that these executive sessions were in violation of the state's open meetings law (Brown Act), which requires that all discussion of non-personnel matters be held in public.[k] The distinction is drawn between the actual negotiations be-

---

[k]The League of Women Voters interpreted the Brown Act to "require that *all* discussions of negotiations matters, except wages and fringes, be held in public."

tween the Certificated Employees Council and the board, which apparently are exempt, and the board's own internal policy making deliberations regarding negotiations matters impacting upon management as well as personnel issues.

The board's president, on the other hand, argued that the board discussed at length the restrictions of the Brown Act and, after consulting with its attorney, concluded that the board as a whole could *not* negotiate in private or executive sessions. Only two members, or less than a quorum, could negotiate in private. However, it could *discuss with its negotiator* in executive session all items properly the subjects of "meet and confer" sessions for the purposes of determining the board's position, as well as for developing strategy for negotiating sessions.

Budgetary Process. Heretofore, the budgetary process had followed the conclusion of negotiations. The budget must be adopted by August 1 of each year. Negotiations were concluded on April 6. Theoretically, the impact of the negotiations could be accommodated by the budget. Thus, the cost of labor negotiations generally are known before, during, and after the budget making. Also, the disclosure of labor and related costs takes place prior to, during, and after negotiations.

The biggest problem with the budgetary process in 1975 was that accurate data were not available to anyone. The chairperson of the Citizens' Budget and Finance Committee complained that her group did not have access to budgetary information. Except for their member on the Citizens' Advisory Committee, the Budget Committee was effectively excluded from the negotiations. She claims that the Budget Committee nevertheless "sent clues" to the board regarding the magnitude of the deficit, but that there was nothing that they could prove. It was hoped that the board would investigate.

The Berkeley Teachers Association also claims to have tried to get accurate budgetary information during the negotiations in order to double check on the board's claims of insufficient resources to fund a salary increase. The Association brought in a financial expert from the California Teachers Association. He was permitted to examine the books. His conclusion was that he was not shown enough information by the board on which to make a rational judgment. The board claimed that that was all the information they had.

In retrospect, the Citizens' Advisory Committee also believed that its own investigations were impeded by reliance on the board business manager's budgetary figures. The committee had no professional staff of its own, and there was no professional accountant among its members. Members relied on their own efforts and heavily on information supplied by the board's finance officer.

Legislative Process. The board's legislative process for negotiations policy making consisted of a special meeting on January 2 to present the Certificated Employees Council proposals, a response by the community members on January 7, and a formal presentation of the board's proposals (without salary proposals) on January 14 at which time these proposals were formally adopted. The Citizens' Advisory Committee was formally created at this meeting. Members were appointed on January 28. On February 18 the board presented its salary proposal, but there is no record of a formal vote on this matter. There is no record of any other *formal* board actions prior to the announcement of the agreement on April 8 and a formal vote adopting it on April 15. There were numerous public discussions of negotiations, but all board deliberations and decision making on this subject were done in executive session.

Mandatory Disclosure. Participants and observers agreed that the new requirements for disclosure were not an end in themselves; rather, they stimulated public interest in the negotiations and caused the board to create the Citizens' Advisory Committee as a means of implementing the disclosure requirements. It should be noted again that this committee was neither envisioned by the framers of the disclosure requirements, nor by the legislation itself.

There was a split between the participants and the interest groups regarding mandatory disclosure. The two white board members were opposed to the concept. The board president thought that it "encourages a form of public posturing." The unions had tried to get their proposals in before the January 1 implementation of the new law, but were thwarted by the board. When the board disclosed the teachers' proposals, the attendant publicity was very embarrassing to the Certificated Employees Council members, although they said that they "had no problem" with the concept of public disclosure of negotiation positions. The board president supported this view. She argued that the disclosure requirements had put the teachers on the defensive, and that this was not conducive to negotiations.

The other white board member said that the new law was an attempt to placate a small and vocal minority. In his view, minority rhetoric seems to have been that the public's right to know what public officials are doing is the solution to all problems. He thinks that the disclosure law exacerbated conflict in the negotiations. It caused the unions to make even more outrageous demands—for the consumption of their members—than they had previously. This argument is countered by the fact that the teachers neither wanted nor thought that their original demands would be made public when they submitted them before the 1975 deadline. The Asian board member said that initially he was ambivalent.

Only the black board member unequivocally supported disclosure. The board's chief negotiator also favored it, with reservations. But, he felt that the law was not well written; that its language was nebulous. He said that the public should be informed of the substance of negotiations and hear the issues, but the law should not impose formal procedures, as these, that can inhibit negotiations.

Interest group support for the law was strong, except from the NAACP, whose representative felt that the law was "academic." Nothing happened in 1975, in his opinion, which hadn't happened before. According to him, no real disclosure had been made, as evidenced by the subsequent budgetary revelations. He also pointed out that it is too difficult to recognize a "new subject" of negotiations, as the law requires, for the language to be effective. Despite the public availability of the proposals, the NAACP representative didn't think that anybody who attended the board meetings had any idea as to what was being negotiated.

Some interest group representatives noted that the parties' proposals had been available to them in one way or another in preceding years. A longstanding journalistic observer believes this to be untrue. She said that very few people knew that the proposals were published: "I had followed the board for years and did not know." The Citizens' Advisory Committee's chairperson said that without the law "we never would have known what the original proposals contained." Most third parties were pleased with the publicity resulting from the formal disclosure requirements in 1975, but there is not much evidence that this publicity actually produced greater inputs from the general public beyond those of the groups mentioned.

Originally, according to the Citizens' Advisory Committee's chairperson, the board did not want the committee to have any more information than the board had, presumably in order to reduce the possibility of conflict and, hence, the usefulness of the group as a purely advisory, not policy making body. In fact, the committee members did try to do research on their own. But the budgetary information at least, they were dependent upon the board's finance officer. The committee members satisfied themselves that they had adequate budgetary information; but their perception as laypersons was limited, consequently, "we satisfied ourselves in that we knew of no more questions to ask."

The Budget Committee member of the Citizens' Advisory Committee compared the two groups in terms of the information gathering channels available to each. The former rarely met more than once a month, while the latter was meeting several times a week. The Citizens' Advisory Committee had access to all board information and board staff analysis, as well as the opportunity to meet with the negotiator. The Budget Committee did not have such information, partly because its members did not want to bog the board staff down in responding to inquiries at the expense of trying to do their own work. In the negotiator's opinion, the Budget Committee had some weak people who were chosen for the purpose of "balancing" the membership. Nor did they have the formal and informal communications channels back to educational activitst groups, which the Citizens' Advisory Committee had.

In July 1975, after the June budget deficit revelations, the board appointed yet another citizens' advisory group. Termed the Citizens' Fiscal Review Committee, a group of fourteen members was charged with going back over the fiscal situation of the board. Presumably, this committee possessed the financial expertise to produce a definitive statement. It was the idea of the newly elected board member, who teaches educational finance at the University of California. The committee membership came officially from the PTA Council, Citizens' Advisory Committee, Citizens Budget and Finance Committee, each of the five employee groups (Professional Personnel, Classified, and Administrative group), the Dean of the University of California's School of Business Administration, and five board appointees. The Citizens' Advisory Committee also was reconvened. However, its members were reluctant to get involved again without some assurance of access to accurate budgetary information. The Fiscal Review Committee was supposed to conclude its investigation rapidly in order to provide such information.

Open Negotiations. The Citizens' Advisory Committee was the only third party with any access to the actual negotiating sessions. Although it was created partly in response to the demand for tripartite community representation, the board had conceived of the committee strictly in terms of its playing an advisory role. According to its chairwoman, the Citizens' Advisory Committee had requested observer status early in February. This was refused by the board, which said that the committee then would be unable to "advise" without being "tainted by having attended the negotiations sessions." It was also said that the board was concerned about offending the Certificated Employees Council by bringing in outsiders.

Apparently the representatives of the teachers didn't want the Citizens' Advisory Committee to observe the negotiations, either. All the participants who responded were opposed to public negotiations or transcripts. This attitude is the familiar one against negotiating in a fishbowl. The chief negotiator reportedly thought that the Citizens' Advisory presence did restrain the teachers' negotiators. Committee members reportedly felt that remarks occasionally were made for their benefit. There was even "a violent outburst against misguided citizens groups getting involved in things they didn't know anything about." The notion also was raised that open negotiations make it impossible for the negotiating parties to set priorities; that they must protect their dealings from the observation of their *own* constituencies. Any announcement or disclosure of negotiating priorities always risks alienating a portion of their constituents; yet in order to negotiate effectively, issues must be narrowed by both sides. Negotiators felt that a final package that represented a balancing of constituents' interests is preferred to piecemeal revelations.

In mid-negotiations, the Citizens' Advisory Committee adopted a position of no salary increases. Talk of a teachers' strike grew and board members began to contend that it would enhance the board's own credibility for the Citizens' Advisory Committee to observe negotiating sessions. The teachers still objected. But, without any announcement to the board's negotiator, they brought in a representative of the noncertificated employees (Local 1) to observe. The board's immediate counterdemand for observer status for the Citizens' Advisory Committee was successful. The committee attended negotiating sessions from early March onward. Initially, Citizens' Advisory Committee members caucused with the board's negotiating team. Feeling that the citizens would get only one side of the issues, the Certificated Employees Council invited them to send a delegation to its caucuses also.

On March 6 the committee met with the Certificated Employees Council. Reportedly the council's lawyer explained his client's position on how unyielding the board was on the need for a salary increase. He thought that the council would have to take its case to the community. Committee members said they interrupted frequently to cite what they thought were inaccuracies and exaggerations. In the exchange of views that followed this presentation, the Citizens' Advisory Committee members said that they felt that the council was trying very hard to impress its ideas on the citizens, but that the council had no interest in hearing any ideas from the committee. The council appeared surprised to discover that they took a harder line than the board on some issues and that committee members had done their homework "too well to be taken in by propaganda."

Citizens' Advisory Committee members reported that the council was not very conversant with the board's budget. They said the council members definitely were not interested in making comparisons with other districts (since Berkeley is already among the highest paid in the state). Committee members thought that they were better prepared to ask some questions than were the representatives of the Certificated Employees Council. They said that the council took the stance that they simply did not believe the budget figures. In previous years there had always been "windfall" money to bail out the district. The citizens were forced to agree that the budgeting and accounting system made it very difficult for laypersons to trace where money was actually spent. In retrospect, the committee members admitted that they were misled by the budget figures.[1] Unfortunately, these were the only figures accessible to it, in view of the lack of accounting and professional staff help.

By late March all issues but the salary question were settled. As the teachers' caucuses became more heated, the Citizens' Advisory Committee members were "gently" excluded. Members of the committee attended all negotiating sessions, sometimes in shifts. They expressed frustration over the slowness of the process (30 sessions of five to eight hours each). One commentator felt that "problems often arose through misunderstanding and insensitivity of each side to the other's position, caused by fatigue and emotional strain of long hours at the bargaining table."

Committee members felt that the teachers were handing out flyers that "grossly misrepresented the state of negotiations." This provoked the Citizens' Advisory Committee to write its own public statement. They requested and received permission to read it at a mass meeting of the teachers at which the teachers voted overwhelmingly to strike on April 3rd. Again, the committee member reporting felt that the leaders of the Certificated Employees Council reported inaccurately to their own members also in front of television cameras. The committee member felt that their own statement received scant press coverage alongside the strike headlines. This is borne out by an analysis of press coverage. The Citizens' Advisory Committee also distributed their statement to community groups and put a copy in every teacher's school mail box.

It should be pointed out that the one group that can be classified as a public interest group—the Berkeley League of Women Voters—

[1]There is no implication that there was any dishonesty in the budget figures. Reportedly, the board itself was not aware that the figures were inaccurate. In fact, some of the discrepancy was caused by a huge error in the business manager's projections of the next year's income. His public disclosure of this, together with his resignation, was a bombshell for everyone, including the board.

had only informal access, through its informal participation on the Citizens' Advisory Committee. As noted, the committee was the only third party with any access to the actual negotiations sessions, and there is great question whether the committee itself, created as it was to be an arm of the board, was an appropriate vehicle for access.

Nevertheless, the new access available to the middle class educational activist community as well as the minority communities to the negotiations decision making process doubtless provided a sense of community participation and satisfaction with the outcome. Most thought that the public interest had been served in the negotiations. Caveats were mostly that the budgetary information had been misleading. But this was not so much the fault of the concept of access as it was a failure to attempt to exploit access thoroughly enough to get independent analytical assistance.

During the fall 1975 Berkeley teacher's strike, the Citizens' Advisory Committee encouraged the board to hold open negotiations. These occurred only once; the teachers refused to do it again. During the strike, committee members were present at all negotiating sessions, except one about which they weren't notified, and at all board caucuses and executive sessions. By this time, their credibility with the teachers, who regarded them as an arm of the board, had expired.

Public Referendum. Only four out of seventeen respondents in Berkeley favored a public referendum on negotiations agreements. The principal argument against such a procedure is that it undermines representative government by taking power away from elected officials. The teachers' organizations and the board members were equally adamant against a referendum: the former because they did not want to be subjected to public whims (it is preferable for them to cultivate elected officials) and the latter because they did not want their own sovereignty undermined by popular sovereignty.[m]

Proponents of a public referendum argue that this is the most direct way for the public—which pays the bills—to have a voice in policy. California state law does require that a referendum be held on any increases in the Berkeley school tax rate. Since the built-in inflation escalator in the present law is only about four percent per year, this is insufficient even to keep up with inflation. A referendum certainly would be linked to the negotiations process. Nobody thought that it would be possible to get such a referendum approved in 1975.

[m] However, 69 percent of the Californians interviewed by the Opinion Research Poll agreed that if either "an arbitrator or an elected board of public officials gives a pay raise or otherwise approves an agreement with public workers which results in an increase in the cost of government, such an agreement should not take effect until it has been approved by the voters." See Table C.4.d., Q3.

Tripartite Bargaining. The impetus for the Citizens' Advisory Committee came from a well organized black community, which demanded a role at the bargaining table. Black respondents were as unanimous in support of tripartite bargaining as all participants in the negotiations were unanimously against it. ·

The argument in support of tripartite bargaining is that it would give a select, informed segment of the citizenry real "clout" in negotiations. The problem is one of "representation." Who would serve as citizen representatives; how would they be selected? The Citizens' Advisory Committee generally became regarded as a creature of the board, even though the individual members asserted their independence. Nobody identified a mechanism for assuring the selection of a citizens' third party that would be any more or less representative than the board itself.

The unions, of course, react negatively to what they regard as a further stacking of the negotiations in favor of the board, whom they contend already "represents" the public. The board, as with a referendum, does not want to see its own power diluted by having to share decision making with another body. The citizen *advisory* concept was much better received. It is significant that a key member of the Berkeley League of Women Voters also supported tripartite bargaining, as did the chairperson of the Citizens' Budget and Finance Committee and the Citizens' Advisory Committee on Negotiations.

Influence

A broad spectrum of community interests were influential in the Berkeley board of education negotiations with the Certificated Employees Council. Both the white and minority communities were represented on the Citizens' Advisory Committee, which was the most influential of third party access to the negotiations decision making process. Although black and Asian interest groups were not very influential *as such*, they had representatives on the committee who were influential. Taxpayer interests were represented through the representatives of Citizens' Budget and Finance Committee and the Berkeley League of Women Voters. All the Citizens' Advisory Committee members also had children in the schools, so they had a feeling for "parent" interests as well.

The principal defect of the committee was its inability to grasp fully the dimensions of the budgetary crisis and the fact that it was conceptualized as an advisory group to the management, not to the parties, thus further underscoring its institutional weaknesses. As a purely "advisory" arm of the board, it was limited to a dependence on the board's own resources for information. This helped the committee to gain an understanding of the board's decision making process, but it did not enable it to override the board in the court of public opinion, as it had no better evidence than the board.

Student interest representation and influence apparently was token. The student member of the Citizens' Advisory Committee said that she reported only to her school principal and board members. Unlike the other interest group representatives, she did not have regular communication with an interest group constituency. Also, unlike other committee members, she never was an interest group "representative," having been picked by her principal on request by a board member for a student representative.

Most of the direct influence was channeled through the Citizens' Advisory Committee. The committee itself was partly a result of the *indirect* influence of the League of Women Voters of California in getting the law passed in the first place and of the Berkeley League's publicity about the new law, including notifying the board of education about the new provisions. The Berkeley League was not identified as an interest group that was *organizationally* active in the actual 1975 negotiations, although its education chairperson participated informally in the Citizens' Advisory Committee.

Some persons knowledgeable and active in education in the black community contend that the Berkeley League of Women Voters got too much credit for stimulating public participation. The citizen participation mode, they argued, existed in the Berkeley education community long before the new law. They also say that, in fact, it was black leadership that first raised the issue of direct participation in bargaining (with its demand for tripartite bargaining), and that the League had not intended direct public participation even with the new law, but only citizen access to information. Thus, the black educational activist community should be accorded at least as much influence as the (white dominated) League of Women Voters.

The creation of the Citizens' Advisory Committee went beyond the letter of the law, but fell short of the tripartite citizen representation demanded by the black community. Although the board did not follow the Citizens' Advisory Committee's recommendations to the letter, most respondents thought that it had a very influential impact on the board. Except for the spokespersons for the Berkeley Federation of Teachers and the Berkeley Teachers Association, who insisted that it was merely a tool of the board, the other respondents gave the committee's members credit for exercising independent judgment. Nobody denied that they were even more "conservative" than the board on the issues of no salary increases and retention of management prerogatives.

This conservatism reflected the minority community interests more than the board alone (which was dominated by the two white members) probably did. Certainly the conservative minority influence through two black and one Asian community representative was supplemented by the budgetary conservatism of the Citizens' Budget and Finance Committee representative and probably also by the League of Women Voters' representative. The remaining student representative said that she was torn by having to recommend cuts in programs which she had participated in. So, she might have been comparatively "liberal."

Observers, who agree that the Citizens' Advisory Committee was more representative of the minority community's interests than the board, believe that it was the committee which urged the "no lay-offs" policy and its corollary of no salary increases. But a long time journalistic observer believes that all four board members were already opposed to layoffs and that the advisory committee merely reinforced their views. In any case, it appears that the ultimate influence was its independent stance. The board's motivation in creating the Citizens' Advisory Committee and eventually allowing it to observe negotiations was to lend credibility to the board's own "tough" negotiating stance, necessitated by the budgetary crisis. When the committee proved to be even "tougher" than the board is likely to have been without it, this put considerable pressure on the board to embrace the committee's position.

Naturally, the interests of the Certificated Employees Council weren't represented in this arrangement. They did, however, call for the inclusion of their own members in any future advisory committee. But this demand raises the question of the independence of such a body and its ability to represent interests apart from the labor-management parties to bilateral negotiations. Even the board had created the committee with the expectation that it would be an arm of the board. Its intellectual independence was limited by its dependence on board budgetary information; but on management issues it was critical of the board for having given so much to the teachers in previous negotiations. Ultimately, the committee represented a conservative community view. This might also have been a "majority" view. In the absence of any public opinion polls, there is no way to verify this hypothesis. Certainly the committee did reflect the educational activist community, because it consisted of key members of the major groups interested in educational affairs.

Besides regarding the committee as "very influential," the board members came to support it very strongly, despite any policy differences. Since the committee did not have any independent power, the board did not have to accede—and didn't—to all its recommendations. The fact that the citizens were urging the board not to grant *any* pay increases probably helped to slow down negotiations as much as anything else. This was despite the desire of the board president to conclude them as far as possible in advance of the election. Negotiations over most other matters not affected by salaries were concluded in early March. The board's resistance to giving in on the salary issue, buttressed by the citizens' committee position, provoked the teachers' strike movement of mid March.

Ultimately, the board tried to satisfy both Citizens' Advisory Committee and minority group interests in no layoffs and the teachers in agreeing to a 6.5 percent pay increase, contingent upon available funds from possible savings. Politically, the board was unable to produce any savings, since none of the program interested communities would tolerate any cuts. Thus, the board had hoped to use the Citizens' Advisory Committee to influence the general public by lending credibility to the board's own assertions of a tight budget. Objective budget realities, together with the differences in "representation" between the Citizens' Advisory Committee and the board, helped the committee to have an influence on the board that was more fiscally conservative than the board itself was inclined to be, in the light of the forthcoming election. When the full depth of indebtedness was discovered, the board members, superintendent, and chief negotiator became strongly supportive of the concept of the Citizens' Advisory Committee, since they would need it even more to legitimize reopening negotiations.

The board members all supported the idea of the institutionalizing the Citizens' Advisory Commitee concept. As a condition for reconvening, members tried to use their leverage with the board to gain more formal powers. The committee's chairperson didn't believe that her group was very influential because the board did agree to pay salary increases against the committee's recommendations— albeit this was to be a contingent increase depending upon future revenues. Other groups were influential indirectly, through formal or informal membership on the Citizens' Advisory Committee or on the Citizens' Budget and Finance Committee.

Hardly anyone thought that the AFL—CIO or other private sector unions had been at all active or influential in the 1975 negotiations. The local Chamber of Commerce had never been active in school affairs, but their president believed that the school system has been hopelessly mismanaged and that members would not support any tax increases for the schools. The Chamber is likely to become active in local school matters in the future.

The Press

The press was regarded as both accurate and influential. The employee organization representatives, especially, thought that the play given to their demand for a 25 percent increase had overemphasized a single aspect of the negotiations. Unfortunately, they felt that this had turned the community against the demands. The Certificated Employees Council did state that its initial salary demands would amount to the equivalent of a 25 percent increase. The reaction of the PTA ("ridiculous") was widely commented on by observers and participants, who also felt that the press had set the community against it. Minority community leaders in particular said that the announcement of these demands had produced a widespread outcry against them. Ironically, the minority community is least likely to read the Berkeley *Gazette*, which carried the PTA's comment.

The *Gazette* also gave substantial coverage to the League of Women Voters' analysis of the costs of the Berkeley school system in comparison with other districts. The teachers also felt that this coverage was detrimental. Since many of the statistics had been obtained from the California Teachers Association's own research service, the Berkeley Teachers Association asked them not to disclose any more such information to the League. Prior to the negotiations, the *Gazette* frequently reported on the new requirements for disclosure, as interpreted by the League of Women Voters and the board. This could have helped to create and reinforce the atmosphere that prevailed in favor of public access.

The influence of press coverage was thought to be largely because of the issues it covered. The participants and observers probably read the press more consistently than did most other citizens. They may have taken their cues as to what was important from the press, and they may have modified their behavior on the assumption that the rest of the community was paying attention to the same issues covered by the press. In this way the press was perceived to have influence. Except for reports that people in the minority community were greatly upset by the teachers' initial demands, and the turnout at board meetings to discuss the changes in program and teacher assignments necessary to implement the no layoff policy, and the 6.5 percent contingent salary increase, there is no evidence that press coverage directly affected the negotiators.

ROLE OF THE CITIZENS' ADVISORY COMMITTEE IN THE FALL 1975 BERKELEY TEACHERS' STRIKE[n]

Following the revelation of the budget deficit and the board of education's decision to change the policies agreed to on April 15, the board asked the Citizens' Advisory Committee to advise it again while they and the teachers (the board hoped) considered policy changes and necessary salary cuts. The committee lost several members who were on vacation or who had moved. The election of the fifth board member added another position to the committee. The reconvened Citizens' Advisory Committee consisted of four white, three black, and one Asian member (six females and two males).

Representatives of the Certificated Employees Council said they could not get a quorum until the end of August. Consequently, the board acted unilaterally to change policies and compensation in order to meet the August 10 legal deadline for its budget. The Citizens' Advisory Committee met informally in executive session with the board several times in July to discuss the proposed changes.

The teachers planned to strike as soon as the board changed the April 15 agreement by lowering salaries by 15 percent and cutting a major portion of the fringe benefits in order to meet a July 1 deadline for a "balanced publication budget." To avert a strike, the board restored some medical benefits and reduced the salary cuts to 2.5 percent. Within days of the start of the eventual strike, the board "found" the money to eliminate the salary reduction altogether. Shortly before school started in September, the Certificated Employees Council had asked the board for an "informational" meeting to explain how the board had made its decisions during the summer. But there was no way for any such "informational" meeting to substitute for "meet and confer" at this point, or to avert a strike. An overwhelming number of teachers voted on September 3 to strike the next day.

The Citizens' Advisory Committee issued a statement prior to the strike which emphasized that there was no money and reiterated its earlier position. Members of the committee observed the beginning of the negotiations the night the strike started. The parties agreed that they could have whomever they wanted present to advise them. The teachers had representatives of their state and national organizations; the board had members of the administration and of the Citi-

[n] Based on a commentary by two members of the Citizens' Advisory Committee on Negotiations, who were also members of the League of Women Voters of Berkeley.

zens' Advisory Committee on Negotiations. The Certificated Employees Council's negotiator asked Citizens' Advisory Committee members not to make statements to the press that were substantive in nature. Members agreed, with one member adding that the committee would make general statements relating to the problems of negotiations, but that statements would not be based on specific issues discussed at the table or attributed to specific individuals.

At least one member of the committee was present at all the negotiations sessions, except for one about which they had not been notified. The committee continued to meet with the board in executive sessions and to give their individual opinions. Due to time constraints and personal commitments of the members, the committee did not meet as a group during most of the strike.

Toward the middle of the strike, when board members were negotiating with the Certificated Employees Council directly, the board demanded that the teachers make some kind of specific proposals for changes. The teachers made a proposal twelve hours after the board's deadline. After the deadline had passed and while waiting for the teachers' proposal, the Citizens' Advisory Committee issued a statement to the press to substantiate the board's position that the council had made no move toward settlement. The statement called on the council to invite all teachers to observe the negotiations to determine whether the negotiators were acting in their best interests. The council reacted by claiming that the statement was a violation of the committee's commitment not to make substantive comments to the press. The board's negotiator argued that neither the board nor the committee was any longer bound to that agreement since, soon after the beginning of negotiations, everything that was discussed at the table had been made public by both sides through the press.

The teachers also were angered by the fact that the chairperson of the Citizens' Advisory Committee was teaching as a substitute during the strike. They took it as a direct insult to have a "scab" observing the negotiations and chairing the committee that was advising the board on negotiations. The council questioned the objectivity of the Citizens' Advisory Committee. Once the matter became an issue, the board stood firm in supporting the individual freedom of the committee members and maintained the original composition of the committee. This was done despite urging from within the committee itself that the continuance of the substitute as an observer was not politic, in view of the difficulty of the negotiations.

Ultimately, the strike was settled by a three-member panel created to provide fact finding with recommendations. The teachers went back to work on October 6, when they accepted the appointment of a tripartite fact finding panel. The panel recommended restoration of $450,000 of the $1 million cuts unilaterally made by the board. This restored almost one half of the April 15 settlement. The board, however, did not adopt the recommendations until November 18, due to the time it took for the teachers formally to approve the recommendations and a misunderstanding between the board and the teachers' organizations. One important role of the Citizens' Advisory Committee was to provide as a member of this panel a knowledgeable citizen who understood the entire history of the negotiations. However, that person was the *board's* representative on the panel. He was also a member of the Citizens' Budget and Finance Committee.

The Citizens' Advisory Committee observed all the panel's hearings. It made a statement to the panel favoring reductions in all nonessential expenses and making essential supplies available to the classroom. The statement also urged consideration of the budget implications of any settlement such as the effects on the next year's budget of the loss of state revenue from declining enrollment and reduced attendance during the strike. The committee also argued that, in attempting to restore the April 15 agreement, only money known to be available should be used. The committee also was against a proposed application for a loan from the state legislature, because this would obligate the district to make program cuts and increased layoffs the following years. The committee wanted the board to be able to maintain maximum flexibility in its assignment of personnel in order to minimize expenditures for substitutes and new hires.

The board did not ask the committee's advice regarding the acceptance of the fact finding panel's recommendations. Since the chairperson of the panel had made an effort to see that both sides agreed to its recommendations, the board argued that there was no need for the Citizens' Advisory Committee's advice. The board too, apparently, lost confidence in the citizens' committee and saw it as a detriment to the resolution of the dispute, or saw no further utility in using it.

After the strike was settled, the committee met to recommend its future function. The board did not solicit these recommendations. In fact, there was no attempt by the board to meet with the committee. The recommendations cited the need to "hold the confidence of the board, . . . have access to information, . . . and be representative of large segments of the community." No reference was made to "holding the confidence" of the teacher organizations. The committee members also recommended that all appointments be made by the board, based on community nominations at large, rather than from specific interest groups as had been done the first time. They thought that the term of membership should be one contract negotiating period and that appointments should be made sufficiently in advance of negotiations that the committee members could both educate themselves as to the issues and have an input into the board's initial proposals. They specified their duties and responsibilities as: (1) soliciting inputs from teachers, principals, parents, students, and community groups; (2) doing relevant research and making comparative studies; (3) communicating with teacher organizations; (4) meeting regularly with the board in executive session; (5) providing observers for all negotiating sessions; and (6) informing the public on the progress of negotiations.

During the strike, the committee members felt that their influence was less than during the first phase of negotiations. This was due in part to the marked difference in the character of the two sets of negotiations. According to a committee member, during the first, there was a detailed discussion of the issues and constructive bargaining on both sides; the second set of negotiations were really "nonnegotiations," in that the issues were not raised.

Psychological pressures of the strike hardened the positions of both sides. Negotiating sessions were irregular and were frequently interrupted for several days. There was reportedly more rhetoric than communication between the two sides. Committee members thought that the teachers wanted to avoid negotiating, to the end that the pressures of the strike would force the board to give in. Several delaying tactics reportedly were used by the Certificated Employees Council. First, they raised the issue of negotiating directly with board members rather than through their negotiator; second, they objected to the Citizens' Advisory Committee's public statements and the presence of a "scab."

The Citizens' Advisory Committee members seemed to feel that they had played a useful role in advising the board members, who relied on committee members to relay the sense of the different community attitudes which they represented. The board also relied on the committee to reassure it that it was doing the right thing. It was said to be very difficult for anyone to maintain an objective view of the situation because of the emotional pressures of the strike. Emotions throughout the community were high, with up to 75 to 80 percent of the children being kept at home, the presentation of a dynamic television film made by a Berkeley teacher and shown on the local station, almost continuous press coverage by the Berkeley *Gazette*, a daily "raspberry sheet" published by the teachers organizations and distributed widely throughout the district, and statements by various individuals about the chaos in the board's business office, all being contributory factors.

The board called for "public negotiations" early in the strike. This was rejected by the teachers. The board then invited members of the public to observe the negotiations. The teachers stipulated that anyone who observed had to be a member of the board's caucus, so the observers were limited to board supporters. Student leaders from Berkeley High School, whose student senate had already voted to support the teachers and had urged their fellow students not to cross the picket lines, requested that the Certificated Employees Council allow them to observe the negotiations. They were refused, so they asked the board, and thus became a part of the board's caucus.

Near the end of the strike, on the day which the teachers did not receive their paychecks, the teachers demanded public negotiations through the press. A conflict in the published time and the accommodations for seating found the teachers in the administration building and the board at the Community Theater. Finally, the rank and file teachers demanded that the council representatives go to the Community Theater, where public negotiations did take place for several hours. The next day, reportedly, a board member and three Certificated Employees Council alternates spent twelve hours discussing the "shape of the table" and could not agree on a place to hold the meeting; so, public negotiations were ended.

Newspaper coverage was judged by a League of Women Voters member of the Citizens' Advisory Committee to be "regular and factual under the circumstances" in that much of the literature put out by the teacher organizations was inaccurate. Those statements were printed, as well as the board's analysis. A major factor in the parents' support of teachers during the strike was a poorly-timed advertisement by the board in the *Gazette* early in the strike, entitled "Dry Your Eyes Berkeley." The ad attacked the teachers for having too many vacation days and high pay. This reportedly upset parents and citizens because the board was in fact trying to decrease compensation for the teachers who thereby gained parent and citizen sympathy. She thought that the most effective media coverage was a television film which was produced by a teacher strictly from the teachers' point of view. When challenged for equal time, the station that showed the film created an interview format for two board members to give the point of view of the board, including statements and questions by citizens. This was said not to be nearly as effective as the film of rallies, children, parents, and picket lines.

According to the former board president[o] the fact finding panel's

---

[o]The presidency of the board changed following the April election.

recommendations "were substantially influenced" by the arguments of the Citizens' Advisory and Budget and Finance Committee representatives. She noted that these recommendations gave the teachers "only somewhat over $100,000 more" than the board had offered on the first day of the strike.

SUMMARY

The 1975 Berkeley teacher negotiations were characterized by a high level of interest and participation by the educational activist community. To the extent that there was a general public interest, it was represented by the Berkeley League of Women Voters and the new law, which provided the impetus to increased access by third parties who were neither labor nor management. Black demands for direct participation were also part of the pressure for access. Ultimately, community influence was channeled through the board's new Citizens' Advisory Committee on Negotiations.

A crucial factor in the 1975 negotiations was a deficit in the school budget of $2.6 million (later more accurately calculated as $3.7 million). Simultaneously, minority demands and prevalent social attitudes among Berkeley's predominantly white, middle class, University dominated population reinforced the pressure for continuing affirmative action manpower policies and equal education opportunities in school programs. Constraints mandated by the state education code, together with recent state legislation restricting the ability of the already heavily taxed jurisdictions to increase school taxes *without* submitting the issue to public referendum, exacerbated the existing budget difficulties and strained the district's ability to maintain its affirmative action program. The continued employment of the recently hired became a weakened priority when major parent factions resisted any program cuts that might be refunded to maintain staff levels without layoffs.

The Citizens' Advisory Committee was caught up in and reflected these community pressures. Although originally conceived as a creature of the board, the committee took a harder line than the board against teacher salary increases and layoffs. The committee eventually gained access not only to the negotiating sessions but to board and union caucuses as well. It was the only third party with direct access to the negotiations. Other groups, including the one public interest group (the Berkeley League of Women Voters), had only indirect access through formal or informal representation on the Citizens' Advisory Committee.

The committee's influence was greater during the spring negotiations, when it put constraints on the board's salary concessions, than during the subsequent strike that fall. The committee was clearly an arm of the board the second time around. The fact that its chairperson was also working as a substitute teacher during the strike completely alienated the unions. Apart from one of the committee members who was also a member of the fact finding panel, the committee had no role in the final acceptance by both the board and teachers.

Despite the severe drawbacks in the implementation of the Citizens' Advisory Committee, the concept of a citizens' group to advise the board and observe the negotiations was generally regarded as promising. Even the teachers' organizations did not dispute the *principle* of citizen access to information. The new access available to the middle class educational activist community as well as to the minority communities doubtless provided a sense of community participation, if not complete satisfaction with the outcome. Most thought that the public interest had been served in the negotiations. The principal weakness of the advisory committee was its dependence on the board of education for budgetary information to a larger degree than proved functional. But this can be considered not so much the fault of the concept of access as it was a failure to exploit access thoroughly enough to get independent staff assistance. Whether the members of the board of education represented the public interest or whether they represented that of elected officials in their own political survival was another question. There was little evidence that the board members were politically beholden to school district employees, although some members may have shared many of their values.

The decision making process of the Berkeley board of education traditionally has been open to public participation. The atmosphere of political pluralism surrounding school board decision making, while far from approximating pure democracy, nevertheless differs dramatically from big city urban politics. Neither the private sector AFL–CIO, nor independent unions, nor the Berkeley Chamber of Commerce, for example, were anywhere to be found in the analysis of the interest groups that were influential in the 1975 negotiations— or in any other aspects of school policy making, for that matter. The relative autonomy of the board of education from the city made it easier to study than one whose economic and governing fortunes are deeply intertwined with city politics.

Financially, the plight of the Berkeley board of education is somewhat less drastic than that of Philadelphia in terms of its ratio of debt to obligation. But the legal and political problems associated with a deficit appeared to be more stringent in Berkeley. Thus, despite its recent history of liberal, progressive politics, Berkeley school affairs at least appeared to be suffering from many of the same problems as a big eastern city such as Philadelphia.[P]

PWith the adoption of the 1976−77 budget, the board ultimately laid-off 60 certificated employees, 60 percent of whom were minority group members.

Chapter 6

Findings

GOALS

A principal goal of the case studies was to suggest possibilities for the further identification of the relationship between the independent variables of governmental labor relations settings, and the dependent variables of interests, access, and influence. Any conclusions to be drawn from these findings are necessarily tentative. The object was not to try to rigorously test hypotheses, rather it was to begin to identify the nature of these relationships in more precise detail than was previously available.

Definitions of the public interest are discussed in terms of the assumptions of the study, the findings in the literature search, and the attitudes and opinions of practitioners, interests, and observers interviewed during the case studies. The representation of the public interest is dealt with in the discussion of the motivation of interests and responses to public sector labor relations situations, followed by judgments as to whether the public interest actually is represented and by whom it ought to be represented. A summary identification of interests is then presented.

"Access" is summarized according to the structural and behavioral or political access points that were found to have been used in the jurisdications in the case studies. (A model containing these points is shown in Appendix A.) "Influence" is discussed in terms of the interviewees' own self-estimates and in the assessments by others of interest group influence. The press is treated as a separate category of influence.

DEFINITIONS OF THE PUBLIC INTEREST

For study purposes, the public interest was defined as access to—and influence upon—the governmental labor relations decision making process by third parties or "interests," who were not parties to the bilateral negotiations between labor and management but who perceived themselves to be affected by the outcome of such negotiations. During the course of the study, this definition was modified to include the concept of access to information regarding the subjects and positions of bargaining as a prerequisite to holding the parties to bilateral negotiations accountable for their decisions. This added notion of access to information takes account of the greater political, rather than structural, access observed in the case studies.

The search of the expository and legal writings described in Chapter 1 revealed eleven broad categories of both implicit and explicit definitions of the public interest. These ranged from definitions used to argue in favor of banning all public employee unions and, especially, strike activity, to those in support of the full spectrum of employee relations activities. They included: continuity of services, inconvenience of interrupted services, essential services, public safety, governmental sovereignty, efficiency of government, constraints on employers and employees, constitutional rights of employees, equitable settlements, stable collective bargaining, and preservation of the merit system.

Over 150 persons were interviewed for the five case studies of Milwaukee city and schools, Philadelphia, Berkeley, and Memphis. A catalogue of attitudes and opinions was abstracted from the notes of the discussions with 100 of the major decision makers, interest group representatives, and neutral observers. There is no attempt at representation of the types of respondents for each jurisdiction. Some types of respondents occasionally were not available or relevant in a particular jurisdication. However, the union, legislative, and interest group representatives were evenly distributed among the five jurisdictions.

Few of the persons interviewed in the case studies volunteered any conception of the public interest. So, almost all were asked to articulate the public interest in the particular public sector labor relations situation in which they were interested. Explicit definitions were not suggested to them; rather, they voiced their own views. Many could not abstract from their particular policy concern to a more general level of the broader public interest in the question. For example, a large proportion of the persons concerned with teacher negotiations and threatened or actual work stoppages simply wanted the children back in school so that they could "get an education." The notion of a broader public interest such as that which would be involved in balancing the immediate desire to reopen the schools and that of the relative costs and benefits to the general public was not considered.

Nevertheless, nearly all the responses could be categorized according to the definitions identified in the literature search. Table 6—1 consolidates these responses under six broad categories, encompassing most of the eleven original categories abstracted from the literature search. None of the definitions was cited by anything approaching a majority of all the persons interviewed. The highest rate was 35 percent of all persons whose responses were catalogued. Another significant response category not covered by the literature search was the concept of pay comparability between the public and private sectors. This notion also appears frequently in legislation as a criterion for arbitration decisions.

The other responses share a common problem in that they do not provide a clearly observable standard for judging whether a particular public sector labor relations decision is in the public interest. Such vague notions of the public interest help to confuse the debate over representing the public interest, because they do not provide a widely enough shared standard to which to hold the parties accountable. The definitions of the public interest volunteered by the respondents in the case studies include, in order of frequency: employee equity (35 percent), access or "due process" (33 percent), service delivery (33 percent), pay comparability (31 percent), ability to pay (28 percent), and management rights (18 percent).

Employee Equity

The largest proportion of respondents (35 percent) mentioned employee equity or fair treatment of employees as in the public interest. Although 52 percent of all respondents thought that community attitudes towards public employee unions were negative (see Table 6—2), a higher proportion was concerned about employee equity than any other topic. Interest group members had the highest rate of concern for employee equity (52 percent). Union representatives did not mention these concerns with any greater frequency than the average for all respondents (36 and 35 percent, respectively).

Access or "Due Process"

Access to the decision making process, or "due process" received the next highest frequency of mention (33 percent). Newspaper employees cited this notion with the highest frequency (64 percent), followed by formal third parties (50 percent). Only 34 percent of

Table 6–1. Summary of Definitions of the Public Interest

Key: No = Total Number of persons

% = Percent citing definition

Definition	Legislators No	Legislators %	Council No	Council %	School Board No	School Board %	Negotiators No	Negotiators %	Other Management No	Other Management %	Unions No	Unions %	Municipal No	Municipal %
Employee equity or fair treatment[a]	12	25	6	17	6	33	5	0	6	17	11	36	5	40
Access to decision making, "due process," or information[b]	16	13	7	0	9	22	4	0	4	25	11	9	4	25
Quality of services, continuity of services, maintaining essential services, quality of employees	19	47	10	40	9	56	5	60	6	0	13	23	5	0
Pay comparability between private and public sector jobs[a]	12	42	6	67	6	17	5	40	6	50	11	27	5	20
Costs and efficiency of government, ability to pay	19	42	10	20	9	67	5	60	6	33	13	23	5	0
Preservation of management rights[b]	16	19	7	29	9	11	4	75	4	50	11	0	4	0

Table 6-1. continued

Key: No = Total Number of persons
% = Percent citing definition

Definition	Teachers		AFL-CIO Council		Interest Groups		Legal 3rd Parties		Newspapers		Total	
RESPONDENTS	No	%	No	%	No	%	No	%	No	%	No	%
Employee equity or fair treatment[a]	4	50	2	0	31	52	5	40	7	14	77	35
Access to decision making, "due process," or information[b]	5	0	2	0	29	34	4	50	11	64	72	33
Quality of services, continuity of services, maintaining essential services, quality of employees	5	60	3	0	41	39	5	0	11	18	100	33
Pay comparability between private and public sector jobs[a]	4	0	2	100	31	23	5	40	7	14	77	31
Costs and efficiency of government, ability to pay	5	40	3	33	41	20	5	60	11	9	100	28
Preservation of management rights[b]	5	0	2	0	29	14	4	50	11	0	79	18

[a]Philadelphia excluded.
[b]Memphis excluded.

Table 6–2.   Public Apathetic Towards Public Employee Labor Relations Decision Making

	Number		Agree		Partly Agree		Disagree	
	Total	Respond	% Total	% Respond	% Total	% Respond	% Total	% Respond
Legislators	19	15	47	60	5	7	26	33
Council	10	7	60	86	—	—	10	14
School board	9	8	33	38	11	12	44	50
Negotiators	5	5	80	80	—	—	20	20
Other management	6	3	50	100	—	—	—	—
Unions	13	6	15	33	—	—	27	67
Municipal	5	2	—	—	—	—	40	100
Teachers	5	4	40	50	—	—	40	50
AFL–CIO Councils	3	0	—	—	—	—	—	—
Interest groups	41	23	36	65	5	9	15	26
Formal third parties	5	3	60	100	—	—	—	—
Newspapers	11	4	27	75	—	—	9	25
Total	100	59	39	66	3	5	17	29

interest group representatives cited it. Still fewer union, legislative, and management representatives were in favor, at 9, 13, and 25 percent, respectively. Notions of access to information regarding the subjects and parties' positions in bargaining are included in this summary. However, having access to information is not the same as having direct access to the decision making process itself. Information may be used for political access, that is to hold the parties to bilateral negotiations accountable for their actions. But direct access to the structure of the decision making process in terms of having input into these decisions is qualitatively different.

Service Delivery

Concern with service delivery also was cited by 33 percent of the respondents. This got the highest mention in terms of numbers, as it was raised in every jurisdiction. Negotiators and teachers showed the highest rates of concern at 60 percent. Legislators, especially school board members, also showed substantial levels of concern (47 percent). Below that were interest groups at 39 percent. Unions and newspaper employees had the least concern, 23 and 18 percent.

Pay Comparability

The most concrete or "operational" definition of the public interest offered was pay comparability between the private and public sectors. This was mentioned by 31 percent of the persons in the jurisdictions where it was raised. Again, it seems to be favored most strongly by legislators (42 percent) and management (50 percent).

Ability to Pay

Costs and efficiency of government, together with government's "ability to pay" the costs of negotiated agreements, were of concern to 28 percent of the respondents. Formal third parties, negotiators, and legislators cited this concept most frequently. Interest group members and newspaper people, again, had a relatively low level of concern (20 and 9 percent).

Management Rights

Preservation of management rights was an issue frequently at the heart of the controversies surrounding government labor relations decision making, yet it was not cited very often in the specific context of the definition of the public interest. Only 18 percent of the respondents in the jurisdictions where it was mentioned at all defined the public interest in terms of "management rights." Only three out of sixteen legislators and four out of 29 interest group members mentioned it.

REPRESENTING THE PUBLIC INTEREST

Three categories of responses were used to analyze the representation of the public interest. These include the motivation or stimulation of interest perception and activity, private and public sector labor union political activities, and attitudes towards and perceptions of accountability of the parties to the bilateral negotiations.

Interest Motivation

Attempts by interest groups or individual interested citizens to influence public sector labor relations is a form of political activity, regardless of the goals or methods involved. Therefore, the political science literature that describes interest motivation and participation is applicable to public sector labor relations.

Political motivation is a function of the perception by an individual of the saliency of a governmental decision. The perceived impact of the decision is a motivation for political action. Political participation, however, also depends upon the resources at an individual's disposal for bargaining with those who will make the governmental decisions. Resources for bargaining with governmental officials most commonly involve the perception of the potential effect an individual may have on the election or reelection of the governmental decision maker, or in the case of civil servants or appointed policy makers, upon the elected officials to whom they are responsible or upon whom they depend.

These resources involve votes, but they are not limited to one vote per individual. Individuals can increase their political influence by combining into groups both for the purpose of organizing block votes and to mobilize economic resources necessary to pay for campaigns, especially to pay for advertising designed to influence voters who are not part of the particular interest group interested in backing a candidate for election or reelection. Interest groups can also provide services to candidates and elected or appointed officials. For the former they can provide manpower for election campaigns, such as canvassers; for the latter they can provide factual information and propaganda from their own staffs to augment those of the elected or appointed officials.

As Table 6-2 indicates, public apathy towards governmental labor relations policies, outside of crisis situations, was perceived to be widespread. This indicates a low level of the perception of the saliency of such decisions. Since in most instances outside Berkeley these policies were made virtually in absolute secrecy, where little if any public attention was drawn to them, public awareness of both their existence and impact probably is low. As the Philadelphia teachers' and Memphis sanitationmen's strikes illustrate, these kinds of critical incidents dramatize the saliency of the decisions and can lead to increased participation by certain interests.

In all the jurisdictions, there was an equally high degree of agreement about this perception of public apathy to public sector labor relations decision making. According to the table, 66 percent of the 39 persons who discussed this question agreed that the public was apathetic. Another 5 percent agreed with reservations. Only 29 percent disagreed. Many expressed the view that the general public was "interested" in public employee labor relations only during a crisis, or during critical incidents like the 1968 Memphis sanitationmen's strike or the 1972–73 Philadelphia teachers' strike.

Views of public apathy were more mixed in Berkeley, which had completed negotiations without a strike at the time of the case study. The strongest perceptions of public apathy were expressed in Memphis, where the 1968 strike had receded into the background, and in Milwaukee, where there were no recent "critical incidents." The 1973 Milwaukee public employee general strike elicited almost no public reaction. Teachers' strikes have received far more attention in Milwaukee.

Interviewees also discussed whether or not they received any feedback from their own interest group members or from the public at large concerning governmental labor relations decision making. Despite the general perceptions of "apathy," 47 percent of the 36 persons who discussed this topic said that they had received feedback, as shown in Table 6–3. However, some of this feedback was related to critical incidents. By contrast, 52 percent said that they never received any feedback, critical incidents notwithstanding. This negative view reinforced the notion of widespread citizen apathy.

In Memphis, sanitationmen's bargaining has avoided a major critical incident since 1969. Strike threats there have implicit racial overtones, and this complicates the interpretation of citizen motivation. During the 1968 strike the community was in great turmoil. Again, this was more because of the racial question than the interruption of sanitation services. Memphis decision makers and interest group leaders did not find the thought of another garbage strike particularly abhorrent in terms of having to dispose of their own refuse. Their fear was over the potential impact of such a strike upon race relations, especially if a strike is accompanied by another black boycott of white merchants.

The 1975 Berkeley teachers' strike generated only one additional interest group in that community's set of educational activists. This

Table 6—3.   Person Interviewed Regularly Receives Feedback from (Group Members) or General Public on Public Employee Labor Relations Issues

	Number		Agree		Partly Agree		Disagree	
	Total	Respond	% Total	% Respond	% Total	% Respond	% Total	% Respond
Legislators	15	7	33	71	—	—	13	29
Council	10	5	30	60	—	—	20	40
School board	5	2	40	100	—	—	—	—
Negotiators	4	4	50	50	—	—	50	50
Other management	5	1	—	—	—	—	20	100
Unions	10	7	50	71	—	—	20	29
Municipal	5	4	60	75	—	—	20	25
Teachers	2	2	50	50	—	—	50	50
AFL–CIO Councils	3	1	33	100	—	—	—	—
Interest groups	31	11	6	18	—	—	29	82
Formal third parties	5	2	20	50	—	—	20	50
Newspapers	9	4	22	50	—	—	22	50
Total	70	36	24	47	—	—	27	52

Note: Berkeley is excluded.

was a parent group, which supported the teachers during the second round of negotiations.

In all these cases, 52 percent of the participants, interests, and observers never received any feedback even during the strike or other critical incidents. Coupled with the fact that the Harris Poll of September 4, 1975 shows that 50 percent of the public believes that federal, state, and local employees have the right to strike, the *preoccupation with the question of public employee strikes in public debates and among decision makers may be exaggerated.*

UNION POLITICAL POWER

Nevertheless, community attitudes towards public employee unions were perceived to be more negative than positive. As Table 6–4 indicates, 53 percent of those who discussed the issue (60 out of 100) disagreed that these attitudes were positive. Only 23 percent thought that they were positive, and another 25 percent agreed, with reservations. Whether the individuals making these observations were merely projecting their own prejudices on the general public is not known.

Public opinion poll data was not available for cross checking. Attitudes were perceived to be most strongly against the teachers' union in Philadelphia, as a result of a prolonged and bitter teachers' strike. Perhaps the greatest consensus was reached on the notion that unions generally and public employee unions in particular exert influence on local elected officials with whom these unions negotiate. Fully 64 percent agreed with this notion; another 15 percent agreed with reservations. In Milwaukee, 22 out of 23 persons agreed that labor was influential in local politics (see Tables 6–5 and 6–6).

Despite the widespread perception that labor is influential in local politics, 57 percent of those with whom the idea was discussed disagreed that there was any relationship between a local public sector labor relations situation and a local election. Plausible suggestions were made that the Philadelphia teachers' strike produced the apparent split between the majority leadership in the city council and the mayor; that the mayor of Memphis declined to seek reelection as a result of the business community's reaction to the 1968 sanitationmen's strike; and that the 1975 contract settlement by the Berkeley board of education was timed to precede the school board elections. But such views were not shared by a majority of the discussants in any of these jurisdictions. The relationship between collective bargaining and public policy—and hence issues—is thought to be so

Table 6–4. Community Attitudes Positive Towards Unions, Especially Public Employee (or Teacher) Unions

	Number		Agree		Partly Agree		Disagree	
	Total	Respond	% Total	% Respond	% Total	% Respond	% Total	% Respond
Legislators	19	9	5	11	—	—	42	89
Council	10	3	—	—	—	—	30	100
School board	9	6	11	17	—	—	55	83
Negotiators	5	1	—	—	—	100	—	—
Other management	6	6	83	83	—	—	17	17
Unions	13	7	23	43	23	43	8	14
Municipal	5	3	40	67	—	—	20	33
Teachers	5	3	—	—	50	100	—	—
AFL–CIO Councils	3	1	33	100	—	—	—	—
Interest groups	41	32	10	13	20	25	29	63
Formal third parties	5	2	—	—	—	—	40	100
Newspapers	11	3	9	33	18	67	—	—
Total	100	60	14	23	15	25	32	53

Table 6–5. Labor (Especially Public Employee Unions) Influential in Local Politics

	Number		Agree		Partly Agree		Disagree	
	Total	Respond	% Total	% Respond	% Total	% Respond	% Total	% Respond
Legislators	19	13	32	46	11	15	26	38
Council	10	6	50	83	—	—	10	17
School board	9	7	11	14	22	29	44	57
Negotiators	5	3	40	66	20	33	—	—
Other management	6	5	75	80	—	—	17	20
Unions	13	9	38	56	17	11	23	33
Municipal	5	3	40	67	—	—	20	33
Teachers	5	4	20	25	20	25	40	50
AFL–CIO Councils	3	2	67	100	—	—	—	—
Interest groups	41	31	32	68	12	16	12	16
Formal third parties	5	4	80	100	—	—	—	—
Newspapers	11	8	42	63	17	25	8	13
Total	100	73	47	64	11	15	15	21

Table 6–6.   Relationship Between Local Election and Public Employee Labor Relations Situation

	Number		Agree		Partly Agree		Disagree	
	Total	Respond	% Total	% Respond	% Total	% Respond	% Total	% Respond
Legislators	19	9	10	22	10	22	26	56
Council	10	3	—	—	—	—	30	100
School board	9	6	22	33	22	33	22	33
Negotiators	5	0	—	—	—	—	—	—
Other management	6	2	17	50	—	—	17	50
Unions	13	5	8	20	8	20	23	60
Municipal	5	1	—	—	—	—	20	100
Teachers	5	4	—	—	—	—	—	—
AFL–CIO Councils	3	0	—	—	—	—	—	—
Interest groups	41	25	20	32	10	16	32	52
Formal third parties	5	2	—	—	—	—	40	100
Newspapers	11	6	17	33	—	—	33	67
Total	100	49	14	29	7	14	28	57

little perceived by the Milwaukee electorate that virtually no one agreed with the statement.

There seems to be a predominant feeling that private sector union members often think of themselves more as taxpayers than as union comrades of organized public sector employees. As the data in Table 6–7 indicate, 59 percent of the discussants disagreed that private sector unions were in harmony with their public sector counterparts. Thirty-four percent agreed, with another 7 percent expressing agreement with reservation. The relationship in Philadelphia was the most ambiguous, depending upon whether one thought that the general strike threat—in support of the teachers' strike—could have been implemented by the private sector union leadership.

ACCOUNTABILITY

Sixty-five of the 100 persons cited in Table 6–8 below or 90 percent of all those with whom the subject was discussed, believed that elected officials *should* represent the public interest in public sector labor relations. The disagreement came from some union representatives who felt that the unions themselves represented the public interest, and some interest group leaders who felt that community groups ought to represent the public interest. The absolute majority of responses, however, shows a strong support for the conventional norms of political legitimacy in a democratic society. This strong reliance on the democratic process was apparent in the general acquiescence in labor relations decision making, particularly in Milwaukee and Memphis in 1975.

In both cities there was little involvement by persons who are not parties to the bilateral negotiations between labor and city officials. Still, in both cities, officials are constrained by the potential for interest group activity. So, there appear to be tacit limits. In all cases elected officials and unions preferred to bargain without public participation or observation. However, in Berkeley, the presence of the Citizens' Advisory Committee as observers tended to strengthen the board's hand.

"Professionalism" of bargaining was strongest in Milwaukee and Memphis. It was fairly strong in Berkeley and Philadelphia. However, neither of these jurisdictions had a management chief negotiator with the length and depth of experience found in Milwaukee and Memphis. The Milwaukee schools' negotiator was also new to his job; but he was assisted by the former negotiator who had been the board's negotiator since the inception of collective bargaining with teachers. In all cases, including Berkeley in the early stages of bargaining, the

Table 6—7. Private Sector Unions Locally in Harmony with Public Employee Unions

	Number		Agree		Partly Agree		Disagree	
	Total	Respond	% Total	% Respond	% Total	% Respond	% Total	% Respond
Legislators	19	4	—	—	—	—	21	100
Council	10	1	—	—	—	—	10	100
School board	9	3	—	—	—	—	33	100
Negotiators	5	1	—	—	—	—	20	100
Other management	6	1	—	—	—	—	17	100
Unions	13	9	38	56	8	11	23	33
Municipal	5	3	20	33	—	—	40	67
Teachers	5	3	40	67	33	33	—	—
AFL—CIO Councils	3	3	67	67	33	33	—	—
Interest groups	41	12	7	25	2	8	20	67
Formal third parties	5	1	20	100	—	—	—	—
Newspapers	11	1	8	100	—	—	—	—
Total	100	29	10	34	2	7	17	59

Table 6–8. Elected Officials Should Represent the Public Interest in Public Sector Labor Relations Decision Making

	Number		Agree		Partly Agree		Disagree	
	Total	Respond	% Total	% Respond	% Total	% Respond	% Total	% Respond
Legislators	19	15	79	100	—	—	—	—
Council	10	7	70	100	—	—	—	—
School board	9	8	88	100	—	—	—	—
Negotiators	5	5	100	100	—	—	—	—
Other management	6	6	100	100	—	—	—	—
Unions	13	11	62	73	—	—	23	27
Municipal	5	3	60	67	—	—	20	33
Teachers	5	5	60	60	—	—	40	40
AFL–CIO Councils	3	2	40	100	—	—	—	—
Interest groups	41	27	56	85	—	—	10	37
Formal third parties	5	3	60	100	—	—	—	—
Newspapers	11	5	42	100	—	—	—	—
Total	100	72	65	90	—	—	7	10

negotiators were able to control access and thereby exclude citizens from observation and participation. It was not until after the union brought in an observer that the Berkeley board of education allowed the Citizens' Advisory Committee to participate as a quid pro quo.

Despite the fact that bargaining was effectively controlled by the most visible public official in Milwaukee, Philadelphia, and Memphis, there appeared to be little public interest in assigning responsiblity to the mayors of these cities for the costs of bargaining. This may be because the costs were not yet perceived as salient. Or it could be that the mayors were able to avoid the responsibility for bargaining by publicly keeping a low profile during bargaining.

The tendency of legislators to defer to the mayor on bargaining may be a function of political leadership. Bargaining decisions could be highly controversial. This was the case in Memphis in 1968—the mayor got most of the credit and blame for what happened. In Philadelphia, during 1972—73 teachers' strike, the political pressure was on the city council, since the mayor was perceived as immovable on the issue of no additional school funding. In Milwaukee, the bargaining technically is under the aegis of the common council; but the political leadership was exercised by the mayor.

Milwaukee and Memphis were perceived as still solvent at the time of the case studies. Acquiescence in the closed system of public sector labor relations decision making appeared greater in these two cities than in financially troubled Berkeley and Philadelphia. So, there may be a correlation between the perception of a budgetary crisis and interest activity in labor relations decision making. Subsequently, the possibility of a default by the city of New York and voter adoption of a city charter amendment to disclose public employee labor contracts supports this elementary hypotheses. At the time of the case study of Memphis, elected officials were keenly aware of New York's situation. The remark was frequently made that Memphis would have to avoid New York's plight by paying closer attention to its labor contracts.

Fifty-two percent of the 69 persons who considered the matter disagreed that elected officials did, in fact, represent the public interest in public sector labor relations. However, 38 percent agreed and another 10 percent agreed with reservations, for a total of 48 percent. The closeness of these two positions requires a closer look at the positions of the various groups questioned. The greatest agreement was among negotiators (100 percent) and elected officials themselves, while the greatest disagreement was among union representatives (77 percent) and interest groups (75 percent). Neutral observers also disagreed that elected officials represented the public interest. Two of the three formal third parties (67 percent) and six of the eight news-paper people (75 percent) disagreed that elected officials actually did represent the public interest (see Table 6—9).

Qualitatively, elements of the more idealistic approaches to the representation of the public interest may be seen in this notion that the elected official, not an interest group or political activist, is char-ged with the responsibility for balancing the conflicting interests of society for the common good. That 52 percent of these persons also disagreed that their current elected officials did in fact "represent the public interest" in governmental labor relations, suggest the applica-tion to elected officials of a critical standard of behavior regarding their labor relations policies.

INTEREST IDENTIFICATION

"Interest" in the public sector collective bargaining process appears to be limited to the established, policy activist community. In Mil-waukee, this is the taxpayers and public interest group community; in Philadelphia and Berkeley school matters it is the educational activist community; in Memphis it is the civil rights community.

General public interest may be stimulated by critical incidents when these are perceived as salient. The case studies indicate that for most citizens, this appears to be a work stoppage which threatens to hamper a service on which they believe themselves to be depen-dent. The prospect of a tax hike, as the result of collective bargaining costs, did not appear to get the same amount of attention as a threat-ened work stoppage. But even a strike threat, by itself, was not enough to elicit a strong response. The 1973 strike by 12,000 Mil-waukee city and county employees generated little public response. Only school strikes, where parents are directly affected when they can't go to work or where they pay close attention to their childrens' education, elicited strong public reaction. No one knows what would have happened in Philadelphia in 1973, had the AFL—CIO persuaded all of its locals to strike in sympathy with the teachers. But a lot of observers were skeptical: they thought that the threat of violence in such a situation was more persuasive than the cessation of services.

Public Interest Groups

A public interest group was distinguished from a special interest in that a public interest group seeks as its primary purpose, goals that benefit a larger public than its own members. The Citizens' Govern-mental Research Bureau in Milwaukee and the League of Women Voters in California came closest to meeting that definition. The

Table 6–9.   Elected Officials Do in Fact Represent the Public Interest in Local Public Sector Labor Relations Decision Making

	Number		Agree		Partly Agree		Disagree	
	Total	Respond	% Total	% Respond	% Total	% Respond	% Total	% Respond
Legislators	19	15	50	60	6	7	28	33
Council	10	7	30	43	—	—	40	57
School board	9	8	67	75	11	13	11	13
Negotiators	5	5	100	100	—	—	—	—
Other management	6	5	50	60	13	20	13	20
Unions	13	9	15	22	—	—	31	77
Municipal	5	4	20	25	—	—	60	75
Teachers	5	4	20	25	—	—	60	75
AFL–CIO Councils	3	1	—	—	—	—	33	100
Interest groups	41	24	10	17	5	8	43	75
Formal third parties	5	3	20	33	—	—	40	67
Newspapers	11	8	17	25	—	—	50	75
Total	100	69	27	38	7	10	36	52

Concerned Women of Memphis also fit, to the extent that their upper middle class membership allied itself with AFSCME on behalf of the sanitationmen's struggle for civil rights.

The Citizens' Governmental Research Bureau, by seeking public access to the city's and board of education's decision making process, was acting on behalf of a broader public interest than that of its own businessman constituency. The League of Women Voters of California, in lobbying for the passage and implementation of the teacher negotiations disclosure law, did the same. In both these cases the benefits would go beyond the groups' own members. Also, both organizations were created for a public service function, a major component of which is to open up the political system to all citizens, not just to members. Yet both organizations were essentially "middle class" and in some sense elitist and liberal institutions, thus qualifying their representativeness of the public at large.

The original Citizens' Advisory Committee on Negotiations in Berkeley functioned as a public interest group in the sense that it had representation by more than parent organizations. But it was created and appointed by management as an advisor to the employer. In the second round of negotiations, in the fall of 1975, its position was further compromised by the fact that its chairperson worked as a substitute teacher during the teachers' strike. This made it more clearly a management committee, particularly in the eyes of the unions. They were infuriated. The committee's independence also was compromised by the fact that the board of education would not permit it to issue press releases.

Special Interest Groups

Special interest groups observed in the case studies are of two basic types. The first type is concerned with revenues. These are largely taxpayer groups. They want to reduce expenditures foremost, without much consideration given to the impact upon service delivery. The other type includes the service-consumer interests. These groups want to maintain or increase services. This goal usually entails increased costs. An example would be a parents' group which supported teacher demands for higher wages or smaller class size. These two kinds of special interests represent a basic conflict between service delivery and costs. This conflict is not easily reconciled. One way to accommodate both sides may be to have them represented by a more inclusive public interest group that includes the goals of maximizing services within the bounds of efficiency and minimal resources.

The problem of the public interest is illustrated by these two types of special interest groups. They seem to predominate in the literary discussion of public sector labor relations. In the case studies, there were few interest groups that represented the goals of maximizing service delivery or cost efficiency. Some writers have defined the public interest as getting the most public service for the least cost. Other considerations also may apply, which include the effects upon employees of this kind of an attitude towards costs. Many writers (and our interviewees) would modify the demand for the lowest possible wages and benefits by adopting the additional goal of securing employee justice, defined as public employee wages and working conditions comparable to those enjoyed by the rest of the taxpaying public. Five key special interest group types emerged from the study: parents, civil rights groups, private sector unions, business groups, and taxpayers.

Parents. Parent groups were most active in school affairs in Milwaukee, Philadelphia, and, to a lesser degree, Berkeley. In Milwaukee the Council of PTAs was about the only group apart from the Citizens' Governmental Research Bureau active in school affairs. In Philadelphia, parents' groups—both black and white—were the most vocal forces at city hall.

Parent groups, like the public generally, appear to acquiesce in the outcome of public sector labor relations decisions unless these clearly threaten to interrupt services or raise taxes. The concern with interruption of services, particularly in the case of schools, appears to be stronger than any taxpayer interest. The educational activist groups tend to clamor for a reopening of the schools, even at increased costs. The potential impact on taxation is not judged by the educational activist community as being as salient as the fact that their children are not in school. This applies to both the middle and lower middle class whites as well as black parents.

Most of the Berkeley educational activist community appeared to feel that the teachers ought to be satisfied for the present with their existing wages and benefits. The greatest pressures were on the school administration to freeze hiring and restructure the work loads of qualified teachers who were employed in administrative positions.

Civil Rights. The continuing linkage between the civil rights movement and the sanitationmen's union in Memphis is explained by the history of the sanitationmen's 1968 strike. Certainly this was the clearest case of third parties working to influence the public sector labor relations decision making through the union rather than through management. The bonds between the two groups were forged in the original struggle against the city. The civil rights groups' representatives who maintain contact with the sanitationmen's union do so largely on a personal basis, because of their mutual experiences during a painful and emotional confrontation with the establishment. Because of these historical bonds, civil rights groups feel that their interests are represented through the union rather than through elected officials. As a result, the civil rights movement supports the workers rather than a broader public interest in other aspects of public sector labor relations.

Civil rights interest groups also were involved heavily in the 1972–73 Philadelphia teachers' strike. The Urban Coalition led a coalition of civil rights and parent groups in major public demonstrations and lobbying efforts. In Berkeley, too, the Citizens' Advisory Committee was, in part, created as a response to the demands by representatives of the black community, especially the National Association for the Advancement of Colored People, for direct community involvement in tripartite negotiations. In Milwaukee, on the other hand, civil rights groups such as the Urban League were interested in the issues of public sector collective bargaining but had made no attempt to influence the negotiating process.

This study supports the thesis that black interest in educational issues comes largely from a growing dissatisfaction with the academic progress of their children. This is blamed on the white community partly in terms of the emphasis on "special" curricula for so-called "gifted" children, perceived to be the children from privileged families. This is widely regarded in the black community, which is demanding remedial programs, as a sign of cultural discrimination. Teachers are also blamed for the lagging progress of black students. Black parents accuse teachers of being more interested in their own pay and fringe benefits than in the function of being a teacher. Moreover, it is also felt that the white teachers are not able to relate culturally to black children.

Collective bargaining is at the heart of these concerns because teachers in Milwaukee, Philadelphia, and Berkeley bargain on both educational policies and economic questions affecting curriculum funding. These issues affect the educational program over which the disagreement has arisen.

Private Sector Unions. Although there was a feeling that the private sector unions were not in harmony with those in the public sector, the AFL–CIO Councils in both Philadelphia and Memphis were active on behalf of public sector workers at least in the crucial stages of critical incidents in those two jurisdications. The private sector union in Memphis provided organizational help to the Memphis sanitationmen, and the AFL−CIO in Philadelphia threatened a general strike of the entire city on behalf of the teachers there. In Milwaukee, the AFL−CIO Council leadership expressed solidarity with the public sector unions. In Berkeley, the AFL−CIO Labor Council endorsed the threatened teachers' strike but was not identified as active in any other way in the 1975 or preceding negotiations.

Business.   Chambers of Commerce and other businessmens' groups were not particularly active in any of the jurisdictions in trying to influence governmental labor relations directly. The Citizens' Governmental Research Bureau and the Public Expenditure Survey of Wisconsin, however, are professional research staff operations funded by business. Businessmen in Memphis in both the 1968 strike and threatened strike in 1969 certainly were the target of civil rights organizations boycotts. In this sense they became vitally "interested" in the labor relations situation in which the civil rights organizations were interested.

Taxpayers.   The Citizens' Governmental Research Bureau and Public Expenditure Survey of Wisconsin, together with the Milwaukee Property Owners' Association and the Wisconsin Citizens for Legal Reform basically are taxpayers' associations. The Citizens' Governmental Research Bureau also may be described as a public interest group in terms of its general appeal for citizen access, rather than a limited appeal for governmental cost cutting. The Citizens' Committee on Public Education in Philadelphia also is representative of taxpayers as well as broader community interests in education.

No taxpayer groups were active as such in Memphis, Berkeley, or Philadelphia. The Citizens' Advisory Committee on Negotiations in Berkeley did have a component of taxpayer interests, even though the interest groups of which it was composed were not taxpayer groups, except perhaps for the representative of the Citizens' Budget and Finance Committee, which had a budgetary interest. Judged by the minimal organized taxpayer activity, taxpayer perceptions of the saliency of teacher negotiations did not surface in any significant degree in any city studied. Nevertheless, the mayor of Philadelphia did perceive a connection between his concept of taxpayer interests and the teacher negotiations. That he was reelected by a landslide in November 1975 may be testimony in part to the accuracy of this perception. At the time of the 1972−73 strike, he was opposed by virtually the entire educational activist community as well as by the board of education and by the key leaders of his own party in the city council.

STRUCTURAL ACCESS

Tables 6—10, and 6—11 represent a model of access points to the governmental labor relations decision making process. They summarize the availability of potential access points and their use by major interest groups in Milwaukee, Philadelphia, Memphis, and Berkeley. The tables are divided into two parts: structural and political. Structural access points (Table 6—10) represent institutionalized procedures for direct participation. Changes in access to these points generally require legislative or formal policy changes. Political access points (Table 6—11) represent all informal procedures and contacts with decision makers which, theoretically, are available to all citizens in a democratic society.

The first two vertical columns in Table 6—10 indicate whether a structural access point is mandated by law (Column 1) or whether it is simply a practice (Column 2). The letters indicate in which jurisdictions the access is exercised. Absence of a legal or formal access requirement does not mean that informal access is not possible or that informal access is not used.

The fractions in Columns 3—7 in both tables indicate the actual use of the potential access points by major interests in each jurisdiction. The denominator is the total number of interests identified as active and the numerator is the number which actually use the access point. Columns 8 and 9 summarize the use over the five jurisdictions by the 33 interests involved. Column 8 is the numerical use and Column 9 is the percentage of use arrived at by dividing Column 8 by 33. Columns 1 and 2 are omitted from the description of political access points in Table 6—11, since these, by definition, are informal contacts by citizens with their governmental officials.

On the whole, the availability and use of access points is very low. The *range* of interest participation and access observed in the case studies is more important than any measures of its volume or intensity.

Quantitatively, there were more instances of the political approach to interest group access. These notions are held in particular by the negotiators (labor and management) and legislators (councilmen and school board members). This is the interpretation of the representation of the public interest as a situation of shared bargaining power among pluralistic interests. These interests trade off support among one another and with elected officials. Their principal access is to the

Table 6–10.   Availability and Use of Structural Access Points

Access Points—Structural	Required by Law	Practice	Proportion of Interest Groups Using, by Jurisdiction					Total Use	
			M	MS	P	B	E	No.	Percent
Column No.	1	2	3	4	5	6	7	8	9
1. Management Process									
Appointment of citizens to policy positions	P[1]	B			7/8	5/6		12	36
Formal consultations by negotiators with citizens		B	1/4			4/6		5	15
Public hearings held on negotiations		P/B			5/8	3/6		8	24
Citizens allowed to speak at public hearings		P/B			5/8	3/6		8	24
Citizens participate in negotiations, observe, concur		B[2]			1/8	1/6		2	6
Disclosure requirements on negotiations positions									
Before negotiations	B				1/8	6/6		7	21
During negotiations	B				1/8	5/6		6	18
Prior to ratification	B					4/6		4	12
After ratification		P/B				3/6		3	9
During impasses						3/6		3	9
Contracts published	P	P/B			2/8			2	6
2. Budgetary Process									
Knowledge of labor costs: Before budget adopted	E	B			1/8	3/6		4	12

	Code		/4	/3	/8	/6	/12		
During budget consideration		B			1/8	2/6		3	9
After budget adopted		B				3/6		3	9
Public hearings held on budget	M/MS/P/B/E		2/4	3/3	4/8	4/6		13	39
Public allowed to speak at public hearings	P/E		1/4	1/3	4/8	3/6		9	27
3. Legislative Process									
Public hearings before negotiations	B			1/3	1/8	5/6		7	21
During negotiations	MS					4/6		4	12
After negotiations						5/6		5	15
Public allowed to speak at hearings	B				1/8	5/6		6	18
Legislature ratifies contracts	MS/B/E	M				4/6		4	12
4. Judicial Process									
Bring suit				1/3	2/8			3	9
Friend of court					1/8			1	3
5. Referenda									
On taxes	B/E						8/12	8	24
On contracts								0	0
6. Arbitration-Mediation									
Citizens participate in panel selection								0	0
Citizens members of panel								0	0
Fact finders make recommendation public	P		2/4		3/8	1/6		6	18

Key: M=City of Milwaukee; MS=Milwaukee Schools; P=Philadelphia Schools; B=Berkeley Schools; E=City of Memphis
[1] Nominations for School Board   [2] Done informally in Berkeley

Table 6–11. Availability and Use of Political Access Points

Access Points—Political	Proportion of Interest Groups Using, Jurisdiction					Total Use	
Column No.	3	4	5	6	7	No.	Percent
	M	MS	P	B	E	8	9
1. Officials Consulted							
Chief executive	1/4	2/3	5/8	5/6		13	39
Chief negotiator				4/6		4	12
Legislature—president		1/3	4/8	5/6		10	30
Legislature—committee chairwoman		1/3	3/8			4	12
2. Electoral Process							
Endorse candidates	2/4	2/3				4	12
Finance candidates	2/4	1/3				3	9
Campaign		1/3		1/6		2	6
Run for office			2/8	1/6	4/12	7	21
3. Lobbying							
Contact officials by letter	2/4	1/3	4/8	2/6		9	27
Contact in person	2/4	3/3	4/8	5/6	2/12	16	48
Volunteer work	1/4		2/8	1/6		4	12
4. Indirect							
Publish position papers	2/4	1/3	2/8	4/6	1/12	9	27
Press coverage	2/4	2/3	2/8	2/6		9	27
Advertise positions			1/8			1	3

Key: M=City of Milwaukee; MS=Milwaukee Schools; P=Philadelphia Schools; B=Berkeley Schools; E=City of Memphis ballot box and their bargaining power is the perception of the elected officials or their appointees of the importance of an interested individual or group in their own election or reelection.

The case studies lend weight to the view that the determinants of interest participation, access, and influence on the public sector labor relations decision making process largely are political, rather than structural or institutional. Structural access points, or those which involve direct, institutional procedures for providing information to the public and soliciting advice from the public, are very limited in practice.

Only the California teacher negotiations legislation provides direct access beyond the most cursory legislative budgetary hearings. Even where the legislative process might technically be open to citizen participation, there was little demand for public hearings on negotiations and the existing machinery was not used to generate any public input. Partly because of the disclosure law, access in Berkeley teacher bargaining was largely structural, as opposed to political. Influence was pursued through participation in public meetings and membership on policy advisory committees, rather than through public demonstrations or organized electoral behavior.

Outside of Berkeley, there is relatively little demand for structural access. This is especially true of Memphis, where the interest groups fear that attempts for structural access would backfire by opening up sanitationmen bargaining to influence by the reactionary forces of the community. In Milwaukee, the Citizens' Governmental Research Bureau has pursued structural access, to the point even of asking for interest group representation on fact finding and arbitration panels. The Council of Parent-Teachers Associations in Milwaukee has also sought open negotiations. The Citizens' Committee on Public Education in Philadelphia is the strongest advocate of structural access there. Still, they are pressing for budgetary influence, not for participation in collective bargaining.

The League of Women Voters of California was the most successful advocate of structural access, through passage of the disclosure amendments to the teacher negotiations legislation. Even the League did not advocate direct participation in negotiations, in the sense of tripartite bargaining. But it did call for—and, in Berkeley, got—citizen advisory committees established to advise school boards on bargaining policy. The Citizens' Advisory Committee on Negotiations was a chief beneficiary of the League's new policy. Its members were admitted to the actual negotiations in both the first and second rounds of 1975 negotiations. No other group studied approached this degree of structural access.

There is virtually no direct structural access to the labor relations decision making process in Memphis city government. Access in 1975 as well as in 1968 seems to be through the union (AFSCME) rather than through elected officials. Key elected officials, except for the mayor seem to take a hands-off attitude.

Levels of demand for access may be correlated with the sophistication of the interest group. In Milwaukee, the Citizens' Governmental Research Bureau and Council of PTAs sought structural access to decision making, as did the Citizens' Committee for Public Education in Philadelphia and the League of Women Voters of California. Except for the Council of PTAs, all these groups had been active in local civic affairs for a long time. Only the PTA Council is a limited issue organization. By contrast, the single issue organizations, especially the civil rights organizations in Memphis, sought political rather than structural access. None of the civil rights organizations had been around as long as these three. The various units of the Chamber of Commerce are of long standing; but these also are "establishment" organizations as opposed to social policy reformers or single issue activists.

Management

Management activities refer to those persons, including negotiators, who administer labor relations policies. *Budgetary Process* refers to budgetary proceedings. *Legislative Process* is that of the formal deliberations and adoption of resolutions and legislation, or ratification of contracts.

Appointment of Citizens to Policy Positions. The executive director of the Citizens' Governmental Research Bureau in Milwaukee has tried to have citizens who are not labor relations professionals appointed to fact finding and arbitration panels, with no success. Appointment of citizens to policy positions is related only indirectly to bargaining in Philadelphia, through a citizens' committee which nominates members of the board of education for appointment by the mayor. In Berkeley, citizens' committees have formal status in negotiations, including the Citizens' Advisory Committee and Citizens' Budget and Finance Committee. They were created by the board of education, which also appoints the committees' members. The total of 36 percent use of appointment to policy committees shown in Table 6-10, Column 7, is high, considering the indirect role of citizens in Philadelphia.

Formal Consultations by Negotiators with Citizens. Direct consultations by negotiators with citizens or interest groups is formalized only in Berkeley. Two-thirds (4/6) of the interest groups there took advantage of this procedure. One did so in Milwaukee, on an informal basis. This is a total of 15 percent of all the interest groups studied.

Public Hearings on Negotiations. Public hearings on labor negotiations or negotiations policy were held in Philadelphia in the context of the budget process and the teachers' strike. But, this is not a regular occurrence. The Berkeley board of education, however, did adopt a formal policy of public hearings on initial positions and responses by citizens, even though the original disclosure law only required that these matters be made public, not necessarily at a formal board meeting. In both jurisdictions citizens were allowed to speak at the hearings, rather than to remain passive observers as in Milwaukee. Use of public hearings in both these jurisdictions was only by about half the interests involved. The Memphis city council had no public procedures.

Citizen Participation in Negotiations. In the middle of the Berkeley negotiations, certain designated citizens were allowed to observe; these were the members of the Citizens' Advisory Committee. In Philadelphia, the Urban Coalition reported observer access to the negotiations during the 1972−73 strike. No group was a direct participant in any of the jurisdictions in the sense of their concurrence being required before an agreement could be adopted. A member of the ministerial alliance in Memphis participated in the 1968 negotiations, but he was eased out by the other parties at the crucial moment over differences in the interpretation of what constituted "recognition" of the union.

Disclosure Requirements. Disclosure requirements were mandated by the California teacher "meet and confer" law. At the time of the study, employee representatives were required to submit their initial proposals to the board of education at a public meeting. The public was then given at least seven days to respond. The board then had to adopt its initial position at a public meeting. Any new subject of negotiations also had to be made public within 24 hours. School boards were not explicitly required by the law to adopt contracts in public, but any position taken on an employee proposal was subject to the public disclosure requirements. In other cities, no formal disclosure of the contents of bargaining was made until after the unions ratified the contract.

Contracts Published. In Berkeley, the agreement with the teachers' unions by the board of education was legally the adoption of a formal policy, not a notice of a contract. The policies or agreements are routinely published in both Berkeley and Philadelphia for public consumption. The Milwaukee board of education and city government and Memphis also print their contracts. In Milwaukee and Memphis, publication is largely for the use of city officials. There is no formal requirement that contracts be published for the general public; however, the public may request copies.

Budgetary Process

All five jurisdictions were required by law to hold hearings on their budgets. Presumably, the issue of labor costs would arise at this time. But for all practical purposes, they did not arise in Milwaukee city, Milwaukee schools, and schools in Philadelphia, since the negotiations were not synchronized with the budget making process. In these three jurisdictions, budgets generally are adopted before negotiations are completed, thus there is no way of knowing actual labor costs. In Memphis, the 1975 budget was the principal constraint on labor negotiations, so its effects were known ahead of time. The Berkeley board of education's budgetary process also was sufficiently open in format as to permit public debate of the labor costs.

Budgetary hearings provided the second-highest participation level for all access points. Thirty-nine percent of all interest groups attended. Their participation in terms of speaking was lower (27 percent) as shown in Table 6—10, Column 9. Despite the fact that labor costs are difficult to discuss as such at budgetary hearings, the hearings constitute the only legally required access point in Milwaukee and Milwaukee schools, Memphis, and, for all practical purposes, Philadelphia schools.

Legislative Process

Legislative Access Through Budgetary Process. No city council legislative committee participated directly in public employee negotiations in Milwaukee schools, Philadelphia, or Memphis, despite the fact that in each of these jurisdictions the city councils have direct legal responsibilities for funding contracts. In Milwaukee, the common council must approve the school budget. In Philadelphia, the city council must appropriate the funds for the schools, and in Memphis, the city council must appropriate the funds for the city employees under contracts negotiated by the executive branch. As noted above, the budget process in Milwaukee and in Philadelphia is out of synchronization with the bargaining process; consequently, bargaining influences the next year's budget, not the current one.

Role of Legislatures in Bargaining. In the case of Milwaukee the distinction between the executive, or management, and the common council's role is blurred because the negotiators are technically employed by the council, not the mayor. Nevertheless, the negotiators' activities can be classified as "management," while the council's deliberations and votes are "legislative."

Only in Milwaukee was there a mechanism for formally coordinating key common council members with the city's bargaining process. The labor policy committee includes key executive branch representatives such as the mayor, the personnel director, comptroller, treasurer, city attorney, and director of the office of budget and management, along with the common council president and five members of the committee on finance. Technically, bargaining in Milwaukee is under the auspices of the common council. In practice, it is done by a professional labor relations office and the mayor.

In Philadelphia, access to management was mostly through elected officials, particularly the city council and notably *not* the mayor— despite the fact that he was perceived as being the dominant political force. The city council president was excluded from participating in the 1973 negotiations, after his break with the mayor on school funding. The budget and finance and the education committee chairmen seemed to eschew any desire to be involved in negotiations, even though the council was directly responsible for funding the agreement between the board of education and its teachers.

In Memphis, labor relations policy decision making is done by the mayor and his chief administrative officer. The chairman of the city council's finance committee was "consulted" on the 1975 wage offer, as were other influential council members. But there were no opportunities for public inputs to the council on this issue, beyond the councilmen's own perception of constituency preferences. They held no public hearings and got no voluntary inputs from citizens on the 1975 city contracts. In Memphis the distinction between the mayor, who negotiates for management, and the city council is clear. The three school boards studied, however, play both legislative and executive roles, similar to the Milwaukee city council. In these cases, "management" refers to the activities of the chief negotiator's office, while "legislature" refers to the deliberations and policy adoption by the members of the board of education themselves.

Public Hearings by Legislative Bodies

In none of the three jurisdictions with direct city council responsibility were any public hearings held or other public input solicited on bargaining by the respective legislatures.

Milwaukee Board of Education bargaining policy discussions and decisions all are in "executive session." No public hearings are held on contract ratification. The vote is taken in public on the contract, after the teachers have ratified it. The public is not allowed to speak at formal board meetings. They may only observe. Board committees are supposed to receive public feedback at their public meetings throughout the year. But there is no formal procedures for gaining public inputs at contract ratification time.

The Philadelphia board of education held numerous public meetings throughout the 1972–73 strike. One negotiating session was even held on television. These were mostly meetings to inform the public, not formal hearings for the purpose of eliciting citizen inputs into policy making.

The California disclosure law in effect at the time of the Berkeley case study required that the employees and school board employer disclose their positions at a public meeting and that the public have a chance to reply publicly, before negotiations. The latest California law requires that this public response be made at a formal meeting of the board of education. The Berkeley board of education held public meetings on the 1975 negotiations and during the subsequent strike.

Contract Ratification

Contracts in Milwaukee must be ratified by the Milwaukee school board. The Milwaukee common council ratifies city employee contracts also, but is not required to do so by law. In Philadelphia, the city council must vote the money to fund the teachers' contract, but has no role in contract adoption as such. The board of education is solely responsible for ratifying the teachers' contract. It does not do this in public. The Berkeley board of education was required by the California disclosure law to adopt its formal position on negotiations in public. This amounted to ratification, since the formal policy vote was not taken until the entire contents of the teachers' agreement had been negotiated. The Memphis city council ratifies all city contracts, despite the absence of a bargaining law.

Judicial Process

Groups in Milwaukee and Philadelphia have attempted to use the courts to influence public sector labor relations policies. Individuals in Milwaukee went to court to seek injunctions of public employees disputes and the Parents' Union brought suit in Philadelphia to restrain the bargaining over management rights in teacher contracts.

Referenda

Berkeley and Memphis have referenda requirements for increasing funding for the schools or city government. In 1975, the issue of police and teacher pay was the subject of a referendum in Memphis, which lost. In Berkeley, the consensus was that any referendum to increase school funding would fail.

Arbitration-Mediation

Citizen Participation in Panel Selection. The executive director of the Citizens' Governmental Research Bureau in Milwaukee has requested citizen participation in the Wisconsin Employment Relations Board's mediation and arbitration proceedings, but this has not occurred. During the 1975 Berkeley teachers' strike, a member of the Citizens' Advisory Committee served as the board of education's representative on the fact finding panel. The rest of the committee members observed all of the panel hearings and testified before it. In Pennsylvania, fact finders are required by law to make their recommendations public. Only one of the interest groups in Philadelphia claimed to have observed the fact finding hearings that took place during the 1972–73 teachers' strike.

Open Negotiations

Several kinds of public access mechanisms were discussed in the case studies. However, only the concept of open negotiations[a] was discussed frequently enough to get a sense of attitudes on this notion. Open negotiations connote some form of public attendance, a record of proceedings, or televised coverage. As shown in Table 6–12, half the persons with whom this notion was discussed disagreed with it. Taking the groups which agreed or disagreed with it, unions (88 percent) and elected officials (63 percent) were most strongly opposed. Agreeing with it were 83 percent of newspaper employees (plus 5 percent who had reservations), interest groups (55 percent), and other management officials (50 percent). Two out of three negotiators supported the idea, albeit one with reservations. Probably the most surprising finding is that 40 percent of the interest group members opposed open negotiations.

"Sunshine" Laws

Wisconsin, Pennsylvania, California, and Tennessee all have open meetings or antisecrecy acts designed to require the deliberations of legislative bodies to be held in public. However, in none of these had government officials felt the laws applied to their labor negotiations. Nor had there been any legal challenges to this interpretation. Consequently, labor relations policy making decisions by school boards

[a]"Open negotiations" and "sunshine laws" are not shown in the model in Table 6–10 because they were not used in any of the jurisdications studied.

Table 6–12.   Favor Open Negotiations for Public Employees in Some Form (Public Attendance, Record of Proceedings, or Television Coverage)

	Number		Agree		Partly Agree		Disagree	
	Total	Respond	% Total	% Respond	% Total	% Respond	% Total	% Respond
Legislators	16	16	31	31	6	6	63	63
Council	8	7	25	29	13	14	50	57
School board	9	9	33	33	—	—	67	67
Negotiators	5	3	20	33	20	33	20	33
Other management	4	2	25	50	25	50	—	—
Unions	11	9	9	11	—	—	72	88
Municipal	4	4	25	25	—	—	75	75
Teachers	5	3	—	—	—	—	60	100
AFL–CIO Councils	2	2	—	—	—	—	100	100
Interest groups	29	20	38	55	3	5	28	40
Formal third parties	4	2	—	—	25	50	25	50
Newspapers	11	6	45	83	—	—	8	17
Total	80	58	30	41	6	9	36	50

Note: Memphis excluded.

and city councils were all arrived at essentially in private. Even in Berkeley, where the disclosure law requires the initial positions to be on record, the board of education held virtually all its deliberations in closed "executive session."

POLITICAL ACCESS

In impasse situations and similar critical incidents threatening an interruption of services, the demand for access was largely political. Structural access may take longer to implement than political access, because enabling legislation or changes in institutional practices may be required that cannot be immediately effective. Structural access is more important in theory, in the sense of institutionalizing access to make it available to all persons or groups who wish to use it. Political access was more important in practice because, in the absence of much structural access, political access was the only alternative for the interested third parties.

Both Milwaukee and Philadelphia had little structural access and strong unions. Memphis also had virtually no structural access, but its private and public employee unions were not perceived as nearly as powerful as those in Milwaukee and Philadelphia. There is also the potential for political opposition to structural access in Memphis by the civil rights movement itself, which is larger in numbers than the public employees' union.

The case studies suggest an inverse correlation between perceived union power and the availability of structural access to the public sector labor relations decision making process. Lack of structural access in strong union jurisdictions may be the result of the desire of elected officials not to offend the unions by enlarging the channels of citizen influence. Union spokespersons tended to oppose increased structural access because they perceived any potential citizen access point as a threat. Citizens who tried to use access points are perceived as being against possible union achievements through bargaining.

Even without union political pressures against access, elected officials might be just as reluctant to dilute their own power by widening the channels for direct citizen input. Still, they may be more likely to resist citizen pressures where the union is powerful, than where they perceive their own reelection to be potentially influenced by those citizens demanding increased structural access. Elected officials may reluctantly agree to greater citizen participation (as they did in Berkeley) where there is less countervailing union opposition to such access, on the grounds that the citizens demanding increased structural access represent a potent electoral force.

Thus the stronger the perception of union political influence by policy making officials, the fewer opportunities they are likely to provide for third party access to the public sector labor relations decision making process. This can force public interests into political channels. If they succeed there, they then may be able to countermand union pressures against structural access.

Officials Consulted

Political access points appear to have been used with only slightly greater frequency than the structural. Table 6−11 indicated that 39 percent of the interest groups said that they had contacted the chief executive about a labor relations matter, 30 percent said that they had contacted a legislative body's president. Negotiators had very little one-to-one contact with interest groups. Only 12 percent had spoken directly with a negotiator.

Electoral Process

Political activities involving endorsing, financing, and campaigning for candidates ranked lowest among all political activities. This seems largely because most of the interest groups are tax exempt and therefore not permitted to engage directly in political activities. Leaders of 21 percent of the interest groups had run for political office as individuals, however.

Lobbying

Lobbying activities were more frequent. The highest single percentage of the interest groups (48) reported they had contacted elected officials in person at one time or another over government labor relations. This frequency of contact is very close to reports by officials (47 percent) who said they got feedback on government labor relations issues. (See Table 6−3). Notably, only 18 percent of interest group leaders who responded said they got feedback from their own members. Since 66 percent of the respondents also thought there was public apathy on the issue (Table 6−2), contacts probably were from the leadership of organized groups who had little direct input from their own rank and file members.

Indirect Access

Twenty-seven percent of the interest groups published position papers in an attempt to influence public opinion. This is not entirely the same 27 percent that got press coverage, although some of the interests did rely on press coverage of their reports on public employee bargaining. Others got coverage by virtue of their demonstrations. Only one of the groups had ever taken out paid advertising on a public sector labor relations matter.

INFLUENCE

Influence is a nebulous concept to measure in the context of third party interests in the outcome of governmental labor relations decisions. Two forms of assessment were used. The first was the interest group's own estimate of its "influence" in the situation under study. The second was the estimate by the other participants and observers of that group's influence. By both measures, the total percentages of interests perceived as active were higher in favor of influence (39 and 51) than noninfluence (30 and 40). This is shown in Tables 6—13 and 6—14.

Thirty-nine percent of all interest group members rated themselves as "influential," compared with 30 percent who did not. More of those involved with the Milwaukee and Philadelphia schools (67 and 60 percent, respectively), however, did not think themselves influential as compared with those who did (33 and 40 percent). More interest group members in Berkeley, Memphis, and Milwaukee city rated themselves influential than those who did not.

Ratings by *others* of interest group influence were stronger in the aggregate than the groups' self-ratings. Fifty-one percent of the ratings were positive with another 10 percent positive with reservations. Only 40 percent of the interests evaluated were said not to be influential. Milwaukee had the strongest negative rating of interest influence: 68 percent of the responses by 35 participants, interests, and observers. Philadelphia was next with 47 percent negative. But 40

Table 6—13. Self-Influence Ratings

Jurisdiction	Total No. Interests	Influential		Not Influential	
		No.	Percent	No.	Percent
Milwaukee	9	2	22	1	11
Milwaukee schools[a]	3	1	33	2	67
Philadelphia schools	10	4	40	6	60
Berkeley[b]	10	5	50	3	30
Memphis	12	5	42	1	8
Total	44[c]	17	39	13	30

[a]Overlapping with Milwaukee city.
[b]Includes more than one representative for some interest groups.
[c]Some groups did not judge their own influence.

Table 6—14.   Ratings by Others of Influence

Jurisdiction	Total No.		Influential		Influential with Reservation		Not Influential	
	Raters	Ratings[a]	No.	Percent	No.	Percent	No.	Percent
Milwaukee city and schools	35	76	14	18	10	13	52	68
Philadelphia	21	53	21	40	7	13	25	47
Berkeley	20	83	60	72	5	6	18	22
Memphis	20	45	34	75	4	9	7	16
Total	106	257	130	51	26	10	102	40

[a] Each respondent rated more than one interest group.

percent of the Philadelphia ratings were positive, with another 13 percent positive with reservations. Berkeley and Memphis interests got high ratings for influence of 72 and 75 percent.

Newspapers also were rated as influential on the governmental labor relations situations studied. Seventy-five percent of the 51 persons rating them agreed that they were influential and another 14 percent agreed with reservations. Only 12 percent disagreed that the local newspapers were influential. (This is shown in Table 6–15.)

In Milwaukee, the principal mode of interest influence was to supply information to the negotiators regarding the comparative costs and budgetary impact of prospective settlements. Indirectly, the same information, when made public through the press, was perceived by the negotiators to influence members of the public. The perception of the public officials who were involved in the decision making process was that the public, to a certain degree, would act upon this information in the next election. This constrained both the union demands and the city's settlements.

In Philadelphia, the interest groups did not so much supply information as publicly to question the board of education on its fiscal and educational policies, in the hope that their questions would strike a responsive chord among the voters. They also lobbied the city council and the board of education members heavily, as a form of demonstrating to these officials their ability to mobilize voters and campaign resources. The demonstrations got press attention, too. The press carried their messages to interested citizens who were not interest group members, thereby widening the scope of potential interested voters.

The AFL–CIO Labor Council's method was to threaten even greater and more immediate political consequences for the mayor, through the call for a general strike of *all* organized labor in the city. This tactic appears to have been more effective than the other interest group activities. It merely demonstrates that the labor movement is a more potent social and electoral force in Philadelphia than the educational activists and that part of the civil rights community that tried to influence the outcome of the 1972–73 teachers' strike.

The political resources of the civil rights movement in Memphis were focused on the economic boycott of that segment of the community (the Memphis business community) which was perceived to be the most influential politically in terms of its support of candidates. The violence which was also part of the demonstration influenced the Memphis business community in another way. Its detrimental effect on the reputation of the city and its ability to attract outside investment was perceived strongly by local officials.

Table 6–15.   Newspapers Influential in Public Employee Labor Relations Decision Making

	Number		Agree		Partly Agree		Disagree	
	Total	Respond	% Total	% Respond	% Total	% Respond	% Total	% Respond
Legislators	19	10	53	70	10	10	20	20
Council	10	5	30	60	10	20	10	20
School board	9	5	44	80	—	—	11	20
Negotiators	5	2	40	100	—	—	—	—
Other management	6	3	50	100	—	—	—	—
Unions	13	10	31	—	15	—	31	—
Municipal	5	4	40	50	20	25	20	25
Teachers	5	5	20	20	20	20	60	60
AFL–CIO Councils	3	1	33	100	—	—	—	—
Interest groups	41	23	49	87	7	13	—	—
Formal third parties	5	2	40	100	—	—	—	—
Newspapers	11	1	—	—	9	100	—	—
Total	100	51	38	75	7	14	6	12

The assassination of Dr. Martin Luther King, Jr. influenced the national political leadership—namely the President—to do something to end the threat of more violence. A solution to the violence had to involve the end of the boycott which, in turn, was dependent upon the recognition of the sanitationmen's union.

Berkeley has a history of citizen involvement in policy advisory committees to the board of education. The League of Women Voters of California got structural access through the disclosure amendment to the teacher negotiations legislation. However, the Berkeley League of Women Voters pressed for even more direct access through citizen advisory committees as recommended by the California League. Moreover, the black interest groups wanted equal influence over negotiations, as they made clear through their call for tripartite bargaining in which citizen representatives at the bargaining table would have the right to concur in or veto any proposed settlement. So, there was an element of politics in the creation of the Citizens' Advisory Committee. It was the sense of the members of the board of education of the need to accommodate strong community pressures especially in the face of an election. This is not necessarily translatable into a mere calculation of votes at the next election, given the Berkeley board's established practice of at least providing forums for citizen participation on policy advice.

The Press as a Special Type of Influence

As Table 6-15 shows, among every group there was a strong sense that the local newspapers were influential in governmental labor relations decision making. In Milwaukee, by their coverage of the position papers by the Citizens' Governmental Research Bureau and the Public Expenditure Survey of Wisconsin, the press tended to support these groups. Coverage of the Milwaukee Council of PTAs was limited to public demonstrations against the January 1975 teachers' strike.

In Philadelphia, the 1972–73 teachers' strike received considerable press attention. But there was little analysis of the long range costs and effects of prospective settlements. Interest group activity coverage, again, focused on the public demonstrations. Editorially, the papers shared the educational interest group demands for the Board to settle the strike and for the council and the mayor to accept the need for additional money to fund such a settlement.

In Memphis, observers of the 1968 strike situation generally were harsh in their criticism of the city's two papers as unfairly treating the sanitationmen's cause. By 1975, however, the press was no longer being accused of trying to influence public opinion against the sanitationmen. Negotiations as such received minimal coverage. Again, only threats of strikes and the implicit threat of violence had received much attention since 1968. This was most evident in the coverage of the 1969 strike threat and demonstrations by the Concerned Women of East Memphis on behalf of the sanitationmen's demand for better pay and working conditions.

The Berkeley press got high marks for thorough and accurate coverage of the 1975 teacher negotiations. As a small paper in a small community, the Berkeley *Gazette* probably was able to pay more attention to the issue of the schools, including negotiations, than a big city's press. There was not much else of local import to distract from the issue of teacher bargaining. Furthermore, as the seat of the University of California, Berkeley is an education-conscious community. More people probably are concerned with the schools in Berkeley than most other local governmental issues.

In Philadelphia and Memphis, press coverage of public sector labor relations may be best characterized as emphasizing critical incidents, especially strikes and strike threats and large scale political demonstrations by citizens, rather than providing an analysis of the impact of potential settlements. Even the Milwaukee press relied largely on analyses provided by interest groups. But this view may be distorted by the fact that the local press in Philadelphia was only reviewed in terms of its coverage of the 1972–73 teachers' strike and the press in Memphis for its coverage of the sanitationmen's bargaining.

The Milwaukee press was reviewed for its general coverage of public sector labor in 1973–75. The Berkeley press was analyzed only for its coverage of the first phase of the 1975 teacher negotiations, during which there were no critical incidents.

If strikes and threats of strikes are the most salient public sector labor relations issues in the public mind, it is not surprising that the newspapers emphasize them. However, they tend to do so, at least in the big cities where local news competition is strong, at the expense of other potentially salient interests such as the general taxpayer's interest in the cost and service delivery implications of various positions or possible settlements.

The emphasis on critical incidents seems to influence interest group methods of influence. They undertake public demonstrations in order to get press coverage. This supports Professor Paul A. Dawson's analysis of interest group tactics (see Chapter 1). He says that public interest groups, because they tend to be weaker politically than special interest groups, have to rely more on attempts to give the appearance of stimulating grass roots campaigns aimed at legislators. In Philadelphia and Memphis, even the special interest groups trying to influence the outcome of the strikes were comparatively weak by comparison with the mayor's respective constituencies.

Analyses of press influence are particularly vulnerable to the "chicken-egg" dilemma. Whether the editors perceive their readers' interest in critical incidents and respond to this interest, or whether the editors are interested only in critical incidents and feed these to their readers is an open question. Except in Berkeley, press coverage of public sector labor relations appeared no different from general press coverage of other government news. Emphasis was on the dramatic and those events, like demonstrations or threats of strikes, which can be conveyed simply to the reader.

Long range policy considerations were not covered nearly so thoroughly as critical incidents. Even in the Berkeley press, the positions of the Citizens' Advisory Committee on Negotiations received only passing comment in the first phase of the 1975 negotiations. Although the committee was forbidden by the board of education to issue press releases during the second phase, the one press release that they did issue was not even picked up by the local papers.

The technical issues of bargaining can seem obscure. Moreover, without any requirements for objective disclosure, the parties try to manipulate press coverage in their own interest by the kinds of information they leak "in confidence" to the reporters covering the negotiations. The parties try to use the press to influence public opinion, as do the interest groups that are not at the table. At the same time, the members of the press—both editors and reporters—insist that they do not intend to influence public opinion. Most wanted to be taken as neutrals. One editor in Milwaukee admitted the most common charge against the press coverage: that the papers are business oriented, as purveyors of advertising and by implication biased on the side of management in their coverage of labor relations.

The Milwaukee papers did give good coverage to the business-financed Cltizens' Governmental Research Bureau and Public Expenditure Survey of Wisconsin. Both of these groups' policy positions tend to be in favor of restricting the level of public employee settlements. In Philadelphia, however, the press generally sided with teachers and most interest groups in calling for increased taxes to pay for better schools. In Memphis, in 1968, the press could be said to have sided with the business community against the strikers. In 1975 there was far less of this attitude; however, the editorials were still cool towards the union.

The question arises as to whether the apparent preoccupation in public discussions of public sector labor with the "right to strike" issue is a function of the press coverage. It would take an extensive public opinion survey to know to what extent the public perceives strikes and threats of strikes as more salient than the costs of public employee settlements in terms of taxes and services. As noted earlier, the Harris Poll of September 4, 1975 indicates a majority of persons surveyed to be in favor of the right of public employees to strike (see Table 6–16). This would appear to weigh against the notion that the public is so fearful of strikes as to be concerned with them to the exclusion of all other related considerations.

Whatever the objectivity of the press coverage, or the extent to which it meets the needs of its readers concerning public sector labor relations decision making, there was little doubt among the parties that press coverage is influential. This could be a misperception of the impact of press coverage. There was no instance observed of press coverage having created a critical incident or having specifically affected one—except for the possibility that the Memphis press may have affected the response of the Memphis city council to the demonstration of the Concerned Women of East Memphis. That group's method of influence was strongly oriented towards press coverage of their inspection tour of the ghetto. In this case the method may have backfired, since the city council, possibly annoyed by the publicity, gave the group a hostile reception.

INFLUENCE OF STRUCTURAL AS COMPARED WITH POLITICAL ACCESS

The impact of access on the public sector labor relations decision making process by interests which attempted to influence it does not

Table 6–16. Public Attitudes Toward Public Employee Bargaining at the Federal, State, and Local Levels

Topic	Agree	Disagree	Not Sure
Right of public employees to belong to labor unions	59	29	12
Right of public employees to strike	50	41	9
Right to strike by: (of the 50% agreeing, above)			
School employees	53	41	6
Sanitation workers	53	41	6
Firemen	45	49	6
Police	45	50	5

Source: Louis Harris Poll, February 4, 1975

appear to have been significantly affected by whether the access was structural or political. Hypothetically, there could be a difference. Structural access appears more permanent, predictable, and more open to use by all citizens than political access. But the structural access observed in Milwaukee, Philadelphia, and Memphis was of such minor proportions that few conclusions can be drawn.

Political influence seems a prerequisite for structural access/influence, in that structural access is created by law or by the policies of those responsible for labor relations decision making. Once structural access has been created, however, it is open to all interests. Political access usually is monopolized by the interests actually using it. For example, the civil rights community in Memphis (which had demonstrated a certain degree of political power in getting recognition for the sanitationmen) was opposed to structural mechanisms for access to the labor relations decision making process mainly out of fear that their opponents would pursue these avenues to the detriment of the civil rights groups' interest in improved working conditions for the sanitationmen.

By contrast with Memphis, the political influence of the League of Women Voters of California was responsible for the disclosure amendment. This opened the door for a wide range of citizen participation, including parent groups in Berkeley whose interests didn't always coincide with those of the League of Women Voters of Berkeley. Simultaneously, in Berkeley, the political influence of the black community and the League of Women Voters persuaded the board of education to create the Citizens' Advisory Committee on Negotiations, in satisfying demands by both groups for implementation of the disclosure law, beyond the letter of the law.

In Milwaukee there was little demand for structural access by citizens. However, due to the organization of city government for bargaining, elected members of the common council had structural access to the bargaining decision making process through the committee on negotiations. Since the council, technically, is one of the parties to the bilateral negotiations, this structural access is different than it would be in Memphis or Philadelphia, where the executive branch bargains for the public employer. Moreover, in Philadelphia and Memphis, the legislators have tried to stay out of negotiations, even though they still have the responsibility for funding the agreements.

Certain kinds of structural access, such as tripartite bargaining at one extreme, can be more effective than certain kinds of political access, such as lobbying by an interest which is not perceived as very important to the official's own goals and interests. A decision making process that incorporated all the potential points for third party access (as described in the model in Appendix A) would be formidable. But the attitudes of the elected officials and their appointees still play an important role in policy implementation, even without structural access. These attitudes are always subject to political influence.

Influence of Structural Access

There did not appear to be any significant influence from structural access in Milwaukee, Milwaukee schools, Philadelphia schools or Memphis. Berkeley, by contrast, had two important structural mechanisms by which citizens could and did influence the 1975 negotiations: the disclosure law and the Citizens' Advisory Committee on Negotiations. But those persons in Berkeley who were not parties to the bilateral negotiations probably did not have any greater and may not have had even as much influence on the 1975 teacher negotiations as the Urban Coalition in Philadelphia or the civil rights movement in Memphis in 1968 had in their respective labor relations situations.

The original 1975 Berkeley settlement reportedly was reduced through the influence of the Citizens' Advisory Committee. The 1972–73 Philadelphia teachers' strike was ended when the Mayor apparently influenced by AFL–CIO threats of a general strike, allowed the Board of Education to settle. The political demonstrations led by the Urban Coalition already had helped to soften the city council. In Memphis the civil rights movement, led by the ministerial alliance, put the pressure on the business community which, in turn tried to influence the mayor. The final blow was said to have come from Washington, as a result of the political situation brought on by the original demonstrations.

Disclosure, as practiced in Berkeley's 1975 teacher negotiations, probably is not as effective in itself as is the publicity associated with it. Still, the disclosure mechanism in Berkeley is automatically available for subsequent negotiations, and the Citizens' Advisory Committee was still intact. But these are well established organizations in both cities, and thus provide a certain permanence for political access.

Influence of Political Access

The influence of political access by persons who were not parties to bilateral public employee negotiations was observed on a limited scale in Milwaukee. Nonlabor groups were not very influential. The Citizens' Governmental Research Bureau and Public Expenditure Survey did not engage in direct political activities. The Chamber of

Commerce had not tried to be politically influential with regard to public employee bargaining.

On the other hand, private sector labor unions were perceived as highly influential in the Milwaukee and Wisconsin political system. Citizen voter attitudes probably are strongly influenced by the private sector unions in support of public sector bargaining. Certainly, the elected officials appeared to believe this.

The Philadelphia city council was the target of most of the political activities of the interest groups which tried to influence the outcome of the 1972–73 teachers' strike. The council leadership was not willing to accommodate these interests until the strike had begun. In Philadelphia, there was no discernible evidence that the political activities of the interest groups prolonged the strike. All were against it. Most were pressuring the board of education and the city council hard to settle. A quick settlement meant that the board would have to agree to the teachers' demands. But the board lacked the fiscal power to do so, as the city council must raise and appropriate the funds for the school system. The board of education was forced to hold out against the teachers and the interest groups because it believed that it could not get the money from the city council to pay for any increased costs resulting from the settlement. The council, dominated by the mayor's political leadership, would not at first agree to such added funding.

This stalemate was not broken by the interest groups who were most active in the situation. They did manage to persuade the leadership of the city council and the board of education to agree to an increase. However, they never managed to persuade the mayor. When the private sector unions sensed that the teachers could lose the strike and a local judge began putting the strikers in jail, the AFL–CIO Council, together with other private sector unions, threatened the general strike. This action was said to have had the greatest influence on the mayor, who feared the violence that might ensue. He, in turn, reportedly allowed the board president to settle. The city council already was prepared to vote the additional funding.

The mayor of Philadelphia may have been rewarded for his stand in the 1972–73 teachers' strike by his overwhelming reelection in 1975. But by 1975 the strike, although it was remembered with bitterness by the participants and observers, was no longer a public issue. The mayor of Memphis, who had been responsible for bargaining since he was first elected in 1972 and who had developed a pro-labor image in the process, also was reelected by a large margin in 1975. However, the mayor at the time of the 1968 sanitationmen's strike did not run for reelection, probably because of the reaction of businessmen to his continued refusal to recognize the sanitation-men's union. This became the issue of the strike and prolonged the black boycott of Memphis's white merchants, thus alienating much of his political base.

The AFL—CIO's actions in Philadelphia were not directly related to the political activities of the Urban Coalition. The jailing of strik-ers provoked this. Nor was the President's response in Memphis brought on directly by the activities of the ministerial alliance. Dr. King's assassination was certainly not what the demonstrators had intended, though threats of violence reportedly were a strategy. It might be argued that in the Philadelphia and Memphis situations, interests who were not at the bargaining table, who were not even active participants in the situation, stepped in at the last minute to influence the outcome decisively.

In Memphis, in 1975, political influence on the mayor concerning bargaining seems to have come mostly from the sanitationmen's leadership in the AFSCME rather than from the civil rights interest groups which supported the sanitationmen in the 1968 strike situa-tion. In fact, these civil rights groups supported the black opposition candidate to the mayor in the 1975 election, as did the black mem-bership of the sanitationmen's union Local 1733 of AFSCME. Since the membership of Local 1733 did not support the Mayor's reelec-tion, its political leadership probably was overestimated when the study was conducted prior to the election. Only a couple of Memphis interest group representatives claimed to be in direct contact with the AFSCME leadership regarding bargaining and only one other was identified as having a direct contact. So, the evidence is that there was a comparatively low level of direct influence with AFSCME in 1975 as compared with 1968.

Chapter 7

Conclusions

NATURE OF THE PUBLIC INTEREST

The case studies reveal that, with one or two exceptions, those groups that got involved in the bargaining process represented special interests and not the public interest. They did not represent the general public even in those few cases where the group actually was a public interest group, in the broad sense of having concerns beyond the immediate special interest of the group. As noted, these interest groups generally were representative of middle class values. Hence, it is reasonable to conclude that special interests are more likely to seek access and influence.

This conclusion regarding the special interest nature of groups seeking access and influence does not undermine the concept of the public interest in the ability of individuals or groups to gain access to the decision making process and information by which to hold elected officials more accountable. It is consistent with the American tradition of interest group oriented government. The case studies also substantiate that critical incidents receive the most public attention. This results largely from the impression given by press coverage that tends to focus on dramatic events, rather than on longer range budgetary and service delivery implications of government labor relations. The press pays almost no attention to the possible structural access points which may exist for persons who are not parties to the bilateral negotiations to influence the decision making process. The Berkeley *Gazette* was an exception to the extent that it announced the disclosure requirements of the new California law.

The extent to which the general public is influenced by press coverage has not been measured. Maybe it is the policy makers themselves who perceive the influence by the press on public opinion. They might even project their own prejudices into their interpretation of public opinion, prejudices that lead to exaggerated estimates of public reaction to critical incidents. The situation in Milwaukee during the 1971 police "blue flu" and 1973 general strike by city and county employees did not provoke the kind of massive outcry for an immediate end to the strike as many would believe to be the case when public services are threatened with a cutoff. The impression was that these stoppages were hardly noticed.

In Milwaukee, where the 1975 Milwaukee teachers' strike elicited the greatest public response, the response was largely from the educational activist community, primarily the Council of PTAs. However, there was some activity by individual citizens who brought lawsuits. The 1972–73 Philadelphia teachers' strike got extensive press coverage. The educational activist and civil rights communities mounted large demonstrations aimed at influencing the city council and board of education. Yet, the mayor remained steadfastly against the aims of the interests that were trying to end the strike at the cost of higher taxes to pay for many of the increases the teachers were demanding. Opinion polls show that 56 percent of Philadelphians were against higher school taxes and the mayor was reelected by a landslide in 1975 [1].

The preoccupation with strikes also comes at the expense of other considerations affecting the representation of the public interest in government labor relations. The working definition of the public interest for study purposes was the identification and analysis of interests who were not parties to bilateral negotiations but who sought to influence the public sector labor relations decision making process by gaining structural or political access to it. The case studies indicate that such efforts were more political than structural.

Most of the interests which worked for structural access emphasized a limited notion of structural access. This is the notion of access to information about the decision making process (as well as the facts of the situation) in order that elected officials may be held accountable for their own decision making. Those who argued the need to open the public sector labor relations decision making process to greater public access generally did not describe it in terms of public negotiations or tripartite bargaining. Most of the major interest groups involved in the situations that were studied rejected these access mechanisms. However, many were convinced that decisions were made without sufficient public attention to the details that could affect longer range factors than critical incidents such as strikes. These details include questions of management rights, calculations of the costs and financing of settlements, the impact of settlements on service delivery, and the lack of public consideration of alternative settlements to those proposed by the parties to the bilateral negotiations.

Part of the explanation for the absence of informed public debate and lack of discussion of government labor relations decision making lies in the closed nature of this aspect of public policy making. With rare exceptions, practitioners seem to think it a virtue to carry on such decision making *in camera*. The unchallenged interpretation of the "open meetings" acts has been that they exempt labor relations decision making. The case studies reinforced what the literature search already indicated: that the attitudes of negotiators, mediators, and other professional "neutrals," as well as of most legislators, tend to support the notion of professionalism in public employee negotiations. This professionalism, by definition, excludes all persons who are not parties to the bilateral negotiations or professional third parties from any structural access to the decision making process.

Although the study found considerable dissatisfaction with the performance of elected officials in public sector labor relations, the high level of support (90 percent) among all persons interviewed who agreed that public officials *should* "represent the public interest," strongly reinforced the tenets of representative government. "Accountability" of elected officials generally was supported, while there was little support for usurping their power through supplementary mechanisms such as giving citizens the power to veto or to ratify agreements through direct participation in bargaining or referenda.

Accountability, however, requires access to information regarding the basis for decisions made by elected officials. What was the information on which they based their decisions? What were the constraints? What were the alternatives? The view of citizen access to information in order to hold elected officials more accountable, represents a slight modification of the notion of the public interest adopted for this study. Originally we defined the public interest in terms of access to and influence upon the decision making process itself. This definition included access to information, but also went beyond it. The case studies showed some support for our original definition, particularly in Milwaukee and Berkeley and to a lesser extent in Philadelphia. In these cities, persons who were not parties to bilateral negotiations wanted to influence decision making by gaining structural access. Primarily these groups were the Citizens' Governmental Research Bureau, Public Expenditure Survey of Wisconsin, Citizens' Advisory Committee on Negotiations, League of Women Voters of Berkeley and of California, and the Citizens' Committee for Public Education in Philadelphia.

The definition of the public interest as access to information was taken by these groups as a necessary but not sufficient condition for influence. At the same time, most persons interviewed on the question believed that elected officials ought to represent the public interest. Many more groups defined the public interest as access to information. The argument for the need of access to information regarding government decision making goes to the heart of classical representative government: that the citizenry needs to be able to have access to the same information on which public officials base their decisions in order to be able to hold them (the officials) accountable.

Unlike the original definition of the public interest posed for this study, this modification does not entail direct citizen participation in the decision making process itself. Citizens are limited to indirect political access, through their influence on the electoral process. In fact, this is the kind of behavior which the case studies revealed to be the most prevalent and the most influential. For example, the strength of private sector unions and favorable public attitudes towards unions generally in Milwaukee seemed to explain the high level of acquiescence in public sector labor relations decision making there. In Philadelphia the AFL–CIO Labor Council and other private sector unions used their political leverage on the mayor to break the log jam during the 1972–73 teachers' strike. In Memphis, the political activities of the civil rights community, combined with the pressures they put on the politically influential business community, forced the issue in 1968 and could do so again if the sanitationmen were perceived to be threatened to a degree that would hurt the black community. In California, political influence brought about the passage of the disclosure law, the primary purpose of which was to provide access to information, not access to the decision making process itself.

The need for information on bargaining remains critical in these circumstances. The problem of getting such information is complicated by the problem of confidentiality which affect the strategies of the negotiating process. Groups in Milwaukee and Philadelphia had a fairly high level of access to budgetary information without having much direct, structural access to the decision making process itself. The Citizens' Advisory Committee in Berkeley gained access to the actual negotiations and caucuses by agreement with the parties that it would not discuss the substance of the proceedings in public. The case studies suggest the utility of information in attempting to hold elected officials accountable. They do not clearly show the utility of structural access in influencing the outcome of decisions. The hearings that took place did not elicit much citizen participation. Those who spoke in Milwaukee and Philadelphia probably did not have much of an impact. The Berkeley board of education's hearings on teacher demands came closest to providing citizens with influence, because of the press coverage of those hearings.

Even with expanded access to information on governmental collective bargaining issues, there may be problems in using the information to hold elected officials accountable at election time. The ability to do so assumes a long enough attention span by the electorate to keep public sector labor relations decisions alive as electoral issues, as discussed in Chapter 1. Nevertheless, the concept of informed voters holding officials accountable is the classic view of representative democracy, a value which the case studies show is shared among practitioners, interests, and observers.

DISCLOSURE

The implications of the case studies for public sector labor relations policy development are that most participants, interests, and observers were not very interested in gaining structural access to the decision making process. That is, they did not want to become involved directly in the decision making process in terms of having a voice at the bargaining table. Third party interests and observers especially were more concerned with the accountability of decision makers, rather than with becoming decision makers themselves. Their concern was with political access to the elected officials responsible for public employee negotiations. As noted, this attitude reinforces the idea of representative government.

A major weakness with accountability is the low visibility at election time of the persons who actually may be responsible for bargaining decisions. Another is that the lapse of time between the bargaining decision and the election can obscure the relationship between policy making and election issues. The findings of the case studies point to disclosure and citizen advisory committees as potentially, though not conclusively, effective means to make elected officials more accountable for their public sector labor relations decisions.

With disclosure, management and labor cannot ignore the prospect that their initial demands will be made public. Therefore they may be forced to modify these from the onset to appeal to public opinion.

This was a principal lesson learned by the Certificated Employees Council in Berkeley, whose initial demands for a 25 percent salary increase got extensive and, to them, embarrassing press coverage. Disclosure can have an effect analogous to that ascribed to "final, best offer" arbitration, in the sense that each party is forced by circumstances to appear more "reasonable" to the arbitrator—in the case of disclosure, that arbitrator is public opinion.

Since under the process of disclosure the commencement of negotiations is more likely to receive press attention than under ordinary circumstances, the parties cannot ignore public opinion questions from the beginning. Without such exposure, public opinion is not likely to become "interested" unless there is an impasse that threatens service interruptions or an increase in taxes. It is conceivable that the possibility of an impasse can be reduced in cases where public attention has focused on negotiations from the beginning. By having to bear in mind public reaction, the parties to the bilateral negotiations may be forced to stay away from extreme positions.

The argument sometimes made, that disclosure results in "posturing," was not sustained by the Berkeley negotiations. Posturing is usually done to impress one's own constituency. In public sector bargaining, attempts to influence public opinion require the appearance of "moderation," because the public involved is so much larger than the constituencies of either the public employee unions or of the key legislators or management officials who may be involved in bargaining. Only where the constituency is both jurisdictionwide and has made its perferences known, can an elected official afford to take an extreme position. This was the case in Philadelphia, where the mayor took an "extreme" position by refusing to consider any increase in taxes to pay for schools. By the same token, only a union confident of its political power can do likewise. Otherwise, as in Berkeley, it risks alienating the general public.

In the case of Memphis, disclosure of negotiating positions, then, was not an issue. In 1968, everybody knew that, for Memphis, merely bargaining with the sanitationmen could be considered extreme. Interests friendly to the union had no wish to rock the boat by pressing for disclosure. Disclosure did not appear to be an issue in Philadelphia teachers bargaining the way it might be in Milwaukee. The "interested" educational activists got their information through their established channels from the beginning. Press coverage of the negotiations took place from the onset. The "extreme" position of the mayor also was known from the beginning, because it was part of his election platform.

In Milwaukee, on the other hand, negotiating positions and subsequent bargaining disclosures were dependent upon the voluntary disclosure by the parties to the press. No persons who were not parties to the bilateral negotiations seemed to have any inside channel to information either through the union or the management. If the Citizens' Governmental Research Bureau did have such information, confidentiality kept this from becoming a public issue. In practice, the Citizens' Advisory Committee on Negotiations, in Berkeley, with its eventual access to the actual negotiations and to budgetary information, was able to gain a more complete picture of the 1975 negotiations. That its analyses and recommendations were not covered in much detail by the press is another issue. That the Citizens' Advisory Committee was not able to identify the scope of the budget deficit that was revealed after the close of the first round of 1975 negotiations may be a fault of lack of staff, rather than of the legal ability to gain access to information.

The Citizens' Advisory Committee's experience also illustrates that much public information exists without having to rely on a disclosure law that covers initial bargaining information. But the average person is not likely either to be aware of what to look for or be able to cope with information obtained, without expert assistance. The costs in terms of both time and consultant fees are prohibitive for most people. An interest group can serve a public function in this regard: by amassing the resources and staff necessary to develop and disseminate factual information, it can help the public judge the bargaining stance of its elected officials and of the unions. The usefulness of independently developed facts depends upon the extent to which bargaining positions have been disclosed. The active cooperation of the parties to the negotiations also may be necessary. This is more likely to come from a climate of openness on bargaining policy, as in Berkeley, than from the attitude of extreme "professionalism" that characterized the bargaining in Milwaukee and Memphis.

Certainly there is an increased demand for "information" at the time of a crisis. At such periods, more information is disclosed, but at the discretion of the parties, and usually it is manipulative. Each side selectively feeds the press what it want the public to perceive about its own side. There is no mechanism for either the press or the general public to get the *whole* picture, from which to make a balanced interpretation. The California disclosure requirements for teacher negotiations provide a base of information which interested persons can use, either in terms of subsequent demands for access to information, or in interpreting what the parties divulge about the progress of negotiations.

Interest groups can use the situation in which public attention is drawn to bargaining to appeal to an interested public. Moreover, some interests in Berkeley did believe that the disclosure requirements enabled them to get access to information on the negotiations positions which they would not have obtained otherwise. This implies that disclosure can benefit interests which are not tied closely enough to one or the other of the parties to the bilateral negotiations to be able to get inside information from them. Dependence upon such leaks may entail promises of confidentiality, thereby restricting its distribution. The parties can try to control the interests in this way. When public release of this information on initial negotiating positions is required by law, the parties lose this means of control.

CITIZENS' ADVISORY COMMITTEE

It is hard to conceive of an ideal compromise between "professional" bargaining and citizen access to information. An important consideration is that access to information not be limited to knowledge of the negotiating sessions themselves. The California disclosure law at least provides access to the initial positions of the parties, to any subsequent subjects raised, and to the final policy positions, including the contract. In the form applied in Berkeley, elected officials and their designated negotiators retained their legal powers to negotiate, even in the face of demands for tripartite bargaining with citizens at the negotiating table.

One of the positive aspects of the Berkeley situation was that the law required the disclosure of initial positions. This gave the interested parties a chance to at least see where the negotiations would be headed. They also had the opportunity to make a public response. The responses were a limited kind of critical incident which the local press reported. Those reports influenced the bargainers, particularly the unions.

The Citizens' Advisory Committee provided a vehicle for representatives of some of the major educational activist groups to investigate budgetary and related information pertaining to the negotiations. Theoretically, these were all public documents. Practically, it took time and effort to peruse them, something most individual citizens and even interest groups would not be able to do. The committee also sat in on the first round of negotiations. Both sides were anxious to impress upon the committee the merits of their own cause. This gave committee members a better feeling for the nuances of the negotiations and helped them to better judge the issues.

The weaknesses of the Berkeley situation were that the disclosure requirements are only as good as the catalyst they provide to interested parties to pay attention to the negotiations and to try to dig deeper. The lack of any professional staff or consultants to the committee greatly impeded its ability to develop information, particularly budgetary information. Although committee members were aware of certain budgetary problems, they did not discover the magnitude of the actual deficit. This was because members relied on the budget office for their information. Since the budget office itself had not yet discovered the magnitude of the problem, the committee wasn't able to do so either.

The greatest weakness of the committee, as evidenced by the second round of negotiations, was the fact that it was wholly a creature of the board of education. Although appointments to the committee were made from the membership of the major interest groups, including the PTA, League of Women Voters, Citizens' Budget and Finance Committee, and representatives of the Asian Alliance and the black community, the reality that they were all appointed by management, plus the fact that its chairperson was a substitute teacher for the board during the fall 1975 teachers' strike destroyed any credibility the committee might have had in the eyes of the unions. One member even represented the board of education on the fact finding panel. Finally, the committee did not seek much publicity. It did make recommendations, but these got little press coverage. It did not publish a report or supportive materials, as did the Citizens' Governmental Research Bureau and Public Expenditure Survey of Wisconsin.

A more effective kind of citizens' advisory committee would have been one that strove for more objectivity in both its representation and its public image. An equal number of members might have been nominated by both management and labor, with a "neutral" chair selected by both sides. As a safeguard against creating a committee that would exclude the interests of those other than management or labor, there could be a further stipulation against any of the members being or having been employees or officials of any government, union, or personnel function of any private enterprise.

Representation could be further accorded to community groups which have demonstrated an interest in the policy area with which the particular employee negotiations were concerned. Conceivably, members could even be selected at random from voter lists, as juries are chosen. If "ordinary" citizens can understand the complexities of criminal and civil court trials, they ought to be able to understand public sector bargaining.

The counterargument—that persons with public employment or management experience are necessary to understand the issues in bargaining—can be met through committee staff and consultant support. Berkeley illustrates the problem of including persons who already represent one side or the other. They may· become advocates for those interests, rather than for a broader public interest. The public interest could be represented by bringing persons with backgrounds that at least are as minimally representative as possible of the interests of the parties to the bilateral negotiations. No cross-section of the public could be selected, any more than juries are true cross-sections; but juries do attempt to exclude persons who are prejudiced either for or against either the defendant or the plaintiff.

A citizens' advisory committee amounts to a form of mandatory fact finding, with optional recommendations, starting from the onset of negotiations. Fact finders don't usually become involved in labor disputes until there is an impasse. A citizens' advisory committee would neither inhibit nor preclude the operation of any other legal machinery for dispute settlement or impasse resolution. That is not its function. Its function is to represent the public interest from the beginning of a labor relations situation.

Conceivably, the greater information and analysis of the bargaining situation developed by such a committee might reduce the possibility of an impasse, since both sides would realize that the general public was not ignorant of the situation that produced the impasse. Or, if an impasse did occur, the public would be in a better position to judge its merits, thereby constraining one or both sides to the dispute from prolonging it. At least the public might be in a better position to judge the stance of elected officials or their representatives in holding out or giving in at the time of an impasse.

To carry the judicial analogy one step further, the citizens' advisory committee would be a kind of jury, which judged the merits of a public employee labor relations situation and rendered its verdict, together with its backup arguments, to the public at large. It is not suggested at this time that it have any legal powers in the actual negotiations. Its function would be to inform the public, or interested publics, of the nature and implications of the issues being considered, and of the merits of the parties' positions on those issues, from the standpoint of the public interest. Such a group is different from a public employee relations board in that it would not have any formal role in settling the dispute. It would not have to be as legalistic in its procedures, and would be structured to avoid representing only the parties to the negotiations or professional labor mediators or arbitrators. Its constituency is the general public, not the parties to the negotiations.

To act as conduit for information, the committee would need at least the minimal access of the kind provided by the California teacher negotiations legislation, which includes:

1. Disclosure at a public meeting of the governing body by both employer and employee parties of their initial positions (demands).
2. Provisions for public response time and public statements by all interested parties at a subsequent meeting of the body, prior to the commencement of negotiations.
3. A public vote or issuance of an official order (where the executive is bargaining independently of the legislature) by the governing body regarding its initial negotiating position.
4. Disclosure within 24 hours of any new subject of bargaining and publication and distribution through public facilities of that position.

The committee would need the funds to hire its own staff. The Berkeley case study indicates that staff can be as important as access to information. Reliance on the employees of the governing body could be intentionally or unintentionally prejudicial to an independent examination of the issues. The committee and its staff would also need access to all nonconfidential government documents. This would be the same kind of access as would be available to any citizen under freedom of information statutes. In this case, the citizens' committee staff would have both the mandate and the resources to avail itself of its right to such information. Public sector negotiations could be less broadly excluded from open meetings acts, in that their exclusions of "employee application, employment, and retention" do not on their face rule out the myriad public policy considerations that arise in public sector bargaining.

The committee probably would not have mandatory access to the actual negotiating sessions. This would open the whole question of public negotiations. It is an issue that the case studies could not resolve. Therefore, it is inadvisable to prescribe any remedies involving open negotiations without a study of the impact of open, public negotiations on: (1) the negotiations process itself; (2) critical incidents, such as strikes; and (3) the substance of settlements. A citizens' advisory committee might have enough prestige and even political access (in terms of the possible effects on public opinion of its recommendations) that both parties to the negotiations would want to invite it to observe negotiations. The committee members could judge for themselves the utility of such an invitation and would be free to accept or reject it, or to leave the negotiations.

Any disclosure by the committee or its members of what transpired in the negotiations that were observed would have to be negotiated on a tripartite basis among the labor, management, and committee representatives. Labor and management together could set preconditions for observation and reporting. This would force the hammering out of reports that would be less self-serving to either side. This is in contrast to the current practice observed in the case studies, where each side tries to manipulate public opinion through its selective and often one-sided disclosures to the press.

Apart from the need to negotiate disclosure of negotiations as a condition for observing them, the advisory committee would be free to make public statements at any time of its findings of public facts and recommendations. This was the basic strength of the Citizens' Governmental Research Bureau and Public Expenditure Survey of Wisconsin. Failure to get press coverage was a weakness of the Berkeley Citizens' Advisory Committee. This weakness is ironic in light of the local feeling that the press there did a thorough job in covering both phases of the 1975 teacher negotiations.

It should be reiterated that the advisory committee would not legally affect any formal fact finding, mediation, or arbitration as provided by statute or contracts for impasse or dispute resolution. The committee should, however, have access to any and all nonconfidential documents developed by the fact finders, mediators, and arbitrators. Naturally, these parties would have access to materials developed by the citizens' advisory committee. Whether such a committee should be permanent or ad hoc is another consideration. Certain kinds of representation probably could be institutionalized, such as PTA council representation in teacher bargaining situations. A permanent committee would have a chance to build member expertise. This could be particularly important in light of the emphasis on constructing the committee of lay people. On the other hand, the work would be arduous and time consuming.

The committee's "influence," like that of the groups observed in the case studies, would depend on how the parties to the negotiations perceived the committee's ability to constrain them or to exact penalties or provide rewards. Its greatest resource would be its ability to influence public opinion, together with the extent to which public opinion would be perceived by the labor relations decision makers as salient to their own goals. A citizens' advisory committee might stimulate great interest in a labor relations decision at the time of the decision. If the policy makers learned, however, that this public opinion had no perceptable effect at election time, they would be less likely to modify their own decisions according to the desires of the citizens' advisory committee.

While it is called "advisory," the proposed citizens' advisory committee would not necessarily have access to the individual decision makers. The committee's perceived political influence probably would affect its structural access to the decision making process. This raises the consideration that the committee should be able to undertake its own investigations without waiting for any authorization beyond the enabling legislation and the appropriation of funds. In case the legislature should fail to appropriate funds, the members still should have the power to undertake an investigation on their own. This also argues for a semipermanent committee, in that there could be a problem if a governing body failed to appoint the members of the advisory committee. Perhaps the answer could be a committee with overlapping membership, whose members had the power of appointment of part of the membership. In this sense, the committee would be a kind of self-perpetuating public interest group, but one that was publicly funded for the specific purpose of representing the public interest in public sector labor relations.

On balance, formal creation of a citizens' advisory committee on public employee bargaining does interfere with the presumed representation of elected officials. Moreover, it is hard to structure without management domination and affects no special probability of itself being representative of the public. In fact, without resources, it can well become a captive group. Nevertheless, a citizens' advisory group is a politically feasible method of publicizing negotiations and getting information on potentially important governmental policies to the public at large.

OPEN NEGOTIATIONS

So-called open negotiations, tried once in Philadelphia in the midst of the 1972—73 teachers' strike, were not conducive to the settlement. The television coverage apparently hardened public attitudes against both sides. The Milwaukee Council of PTAs tried to get negotiations opened to their own observation in order better to judge the performance of both parties. The president of the board of education was sympathetic to this idea; the teachers' union president was not.

Members of the ministerial alliance were present at some of the negotiations during the 1968 Memphis sanitationmen's strike. Their participation was regarded by both parties and the mediator as detrimental. A key observer was said to have misunderstood the implications of the agreement that was being worked out. He insisted on explicit use of the term "recognition," which was said to have been politically infeasible [2].

The Citizens' Advisory Committee in Berkeley observed both phases of the 1975 teacher negotiations. Contrary to the assumption that they would not be diligent, members covered all the negotiations in shifts, except one night session, to which they were not invited. Their reactions were less in favor of the teachers than of the board of education. During the 1975 strike, when the committee members suggested that teachers be permitted to attend, they were perceived by the teachers' organization leadership as trying to undercut them. It may be concluded from the Berkeley case study that the factor of actually observing negotiations was less important (but probably very influential) than the other information on school finances and politics developed through committee research.

Open negotiations are a form of providing information on bargaining. They are a way to get information on the real issues being negotiated. But they could undermine confidentiality which most professional negotiators believe is essential to an effective negotiating strategy. More persons favored the idea of written or tape recorded transcripts of negotiations to become a part of the public record than favored opening the negotiations to public observers. Such transcripts would not be available until after the agreement had been reached, so they would not reveal negotiations strategies. They would, however, serve as a check on negotiators. Whether such a constraint is good or bad depends upon one's perspective. If both sides knew that there was a possibility of their actions at the bargaining table being judged in public afterwards, they probably would be restrained in what they did or said.

Permitting confidential observers is another possible way to allow citizens to judge negotiations without violating the confidentiality of the proceedings. The parties in Berkeley took this approach when they allowed the members of the Citizens' Advisory Committee to attend but not to comment on the substance of negotiations. The question of who would be allowed to observe the negotiations goes back to the problem of representation.

A common argument against open negotiations is that they inevitably would degenerate into a "circus" or shouting match, without getting down to the serious business of give and take. This argument assumes that each side would attempt to impress its constituents of its steadfastness or militancy. Certainly this is what happened during the negotiations session that was televised in Philadelphia. It is feared that public revelation of bargaining positions will make bargainers inflexible, afraid to take back or offer something once they have taken a public stand. This may be true, but the case studies did not find sufficient examples of open negotiations to permit any such judgment.

Some persons who had observed negotiations thought that as observers they had had just the opposite effect, that their presence had encouraged the elimination of the rhetoric and forced the parties to get down to business. There was no indication from the reports on Berkeley that either side bothered to try to impress the members of the Citizens' Advisory Committee who were attending the negotiations sessions. This might have been due to the fact that all of them were more or less acquainted with one another in the first place.

FURTHER RESEARCH

Two types of basic background research would have facilitated the current study. Both are major, and both lie beyond the scope of the resources for this study. The first is a study of the policies and administrative mechanisms for public employee labor relations decision making (especially negotiations) in use by the jurisdictions which negotiate with their employees. The second is a study of public opinion regarding basic questions pertinent to the representation of the public interest.

Survey of Policies and Administration

In order to study more systematically those phenomena that affect or are hypothesized to affect public employee labor relations practices, more knowledge is needed regarding the universe of these practices. This knowledge can be obtained by a detailed survey of the governments engaged in public employee negotiations. The administration of public employee labor relations in approximately 11,000 government units engaged in either collective bargaining or "meet and confer" is largely uncharted territory. The U.S. Bureau of the Census collects only minimal information on the extent of employee organization, labor relations policies (in terms of collective negotiations or "meet and confer"), work stoppages, and identification of the labor relations officer [3].

In addition, the U.S. Department of Labor compiles largely statewide data on the characteristics of public sector labor relations laws and administrative machinery [4], and on dispute resolution [5]. But no comprehensive data exist on the public employee bargaining administrative process or experience for counties, municipal governments, or school and special districts. State laws tend to provide authorization for the legal framework of bargaining. They do not prescribe the local administrative process for bargaining, nor would they reveal in any detail public interest questions such as the potential for citizen access to the decision making process.

A detailed breakdown of the scope of state enabling legislation and a census of state and local public employee organization membership also was produced by the Advisory Commission on Intergovernmental Relations. But the Commission's report does not describe the local machinery nor discuss the experience under it [6]. A more solid base of information must be developed, if the peculiarities of individual jurisdictions are to be studied further. This is the only way to judge how individual jurisdictions may represent the entire range of possible administrative policies and practices. Identification of critical incidents for the present study had to rely on the literature search and on word of mouth "reputational" knowledge of what particular jurisdictions were thought to be doing. Unfortunately, there is no way to verify whether the network of personal knowledge is comprehensive, without a study of the state of the art. Moreover, it is too difficult for any single researcher to trace the vast web of hearsay and personal knowledge of what particular jurisdictions are doing on given questions relating to the administration of their public employee labor relations program.

A survey of approximately 3,500 of the jurisdictions with the largest number of persons engaged in collective bargaining and/or "meet and confer" negotiations should be done. The object of this survey would be to identify both the range and type of policy procedures used in the conduct of public employee labor relations by the 11,636, states, counties, municipalities, townships, schools and special districts identified by the *1972 Census of Governments* as having procedures to bargain collectively or meet and confer with their employees. The survey would identify the basic charactertistics of administrative machinery and policy, together with selected characteristics of structural and political access found by the present study to be indicative of citizen access and influence on the decision making process for public sector labor relations.

The survey questionnaire to be administered by mail would request such data on the administration of the local labor relations program as follows.

1. Relationship of labor relations office to other officials, such as the executive and legislature, and civil service.
2. Existence of a chief negotiator, extent of dispersed negotiations as among departments.

3. Identification of a policy making body that may set parameters for negotiations, such as negotiations advisory committees, etc.
4. Identification of background and relevant experience of negotiator(s).
5. Extent to which negotiator may exercise independent judgment in negotiations.
6. Extent of direct participation in negotiations by elected officials, consultants, union representatives from out of the jurisdiction, and citizens (defined as persons who are not parties to the bilateral negotiations but who perceive an interest in and attempt to influence the outcome).
7. Scope of bargaining.
8. Mechanisms for developing bargaining positions by management.
9. Mechanisms for developing bargaining positions by labor.
10. Administrative procedures involved in bargaining:
    a. participation by legislative committees
    b. citizen advisory committees
    c. disclosure of positions
    d. public hearings
    e. observation or records of negotiations
    f. ratification procedures
    g. referenda
    h. concurrence or other third party participation in negotiations
    i. relationship of budgetary process to negotiations[a]
11. Negotiations impasse procedures:
    a. identification of third party participation
    b. evaluation of procedures
12. Contract administration procedures.
13. Range of positions or government activities included in bargaining units.
14. Dispute resolution and policy procedures outside the scope of bargaining, such as labor-management committees.

Public Opinion Survey

The case studies suggest that the important issues of the representation of the public interest in public sector labor relations transcend the apparent preoccupation of policy makers with impasses and related critical incidents involving strikes and other illegal work stoppages such as "blue flu." National pollsters have only skimmed the surface of public attitudes toward public sector labor relations questions.

---

[a] Both the existence and evaluations of experience under each above would be determined.

The extent to which the press was perceived in the limited case studies by policy makers, interests, and observers as influential in the governmental labor relations decision making process needs to be verified. It may be that policy priorities are being set in the light of what the press thinks people believe to be critical, namely dramatic incidents. However, there is sufficient evidence in the case studies to indicate that critical incidents aren't as important as the press coverage implies. This evidence suggests that only certain types of work stoppages—those that cause the most direct interruptions of services—are salient. An example of a salient work stoppage would be a teachers' strike. This is not because people are so intimately concerned with what the strike can do to their children's education, as much as the problems associated with having their children remain at home all day, especially for working parents. If this hypothesis is true, then one implication is that emergency day care centers may be the more effective way to handle the problem than trying to end a strike.

Milwaukee's police strike (or "blue flu") in 1971, as well as its city and county public employee strike of 1973, produced hardly a ripple of public concern. Even the press described the public as "apathetic" to these critical incidents. In Memphis, the public showed surprisingly little concern when its garbage accumulated. The eventual success of the sanitationmen's strike depended on an effective economic boycott, not on the interruption of service. Knowledge needs to be developed as to what kinds of critical incidents are perceived as important and why. This would be an empirical study of the public interests in public sector labor relations questions.

The present study was limited to prescribing a definition of the public interest as access to the decision making process. Even as modified to limit it to access to information used in the decision making process, it is still a definition that was imposed. In the absence of public opinion data on the real considerations which may affect public attitudes towards public sector labor relations questions, we had to be satisfied with what was assumed to be the broadest conception of the public interest. This was really a philosophical question, for which real life examples were found in the case studies.

Those studies suggest the need to take a deeper look into public attitudes and opinion on the kinds of questions raised with a limited number of persons who were either decision makers, interest group representatives, or observers. No attempt could be made, with this study's resources, to delve into a broader cross-section of public opinion. Survey research data was available only for Milwaukee and Philadelphia. This was helpful in verifying some of the concepts that emerged from discussions with the persons involved in the situations studied, but none of the surveys had addressed the whole range of considerations affecting the representation of public interest in public sector labor relations.

A systematic effort should be made to inject a set of public sector labor relations questions into the ongoing surveys conducted at the state and local level by public and private scientific polling organizations. Most of these are affiliated with the public opinion institutes or journalism schools of the major universities. These and the other institutions which conduct public policy survey research could be funded to add the appropriate questions to their surveys. Development of questions and interpretation of answers could be done by a coordinating organization, but the actual surveys could be conducted as part of existing survey research efforts.

Appendixes

Appendix A

Model for the Study of Cases of the Representation of the Public Interest in Government Labor Relations

I. **Legal Background**
   A. Type of jurisdiction (municipality or school district)
      1. Labor relations governed by statute
      2. Other basis for authority
         a. Executive order
         b. Common law or de facto practices
   B. Structure of government
      1. Branch(es) of government administering labor relations
         a. Executive and legislative
         b. Executive or legislative
         c. Board or commission
      2. Form of election or appointment
         a. Frequency of election, percent of members elected simultaneously
         b. At large or ward seats
         c. Partisan or nonpartisan elections

II. **Economic Base Data**
   A. Average annual wages (from 1967, if available) of employees involved in critical incident studied
   B. Average annual wages for other employees of same jurisdiction in comparable classes
      1. Organized
      2. Unorganized
   C. Average annual wages for local private sector employees in comparable classes

       1. Organized
       2. Unorganized (where appropriate)
  D. Bureau of Labor Statistics estimates of income levels required for "Lower," "Intermediate," and "Higher" standards of living for jurisdictions being studied
  E. Consumer Price Index (since 1967) for jurisdiction
  F. Sources of funding for labor agreements
       1. Local tax rates (since 1967, if available), property/sales/other
       2. Proportion of local, state, and federal funding of budget

III. Characteristics of Private Sector Labor Force
  A. Percent and types organized
  B. Brief history of organized labor locally
  C. Political activities of local labor movement
       1. Endorse candidates, finance campaigns, work for candidates
       2. Reputation for electing/defeating candidates to offices governing labor relations
         a. Prolabor, antilabor, or neutral
       3. Public sector collective bargaining situations reputedly affecting or being affected by elections
         a. Election campaigns for officials
         b. Referenda on matters affecting labor relations

IV. Labor Relations Background of Jurisdiction
  A. Chronology of public employee relations and development of legal authority
  B. Union ties to government
       1. Independent or "company" union
  C. Organizational structure of bargaining
       1. Coalition bargaining
       2. Independent bargaining

V. Scope of Policy Authority
  A. Nature of labor relations process
       1. Collective bargaining authority, requirements
       2. "Meet and confer," authority, requirements
       3. Other
  B. Scope of negotiations, in policy and practice
       1. Negotiable issues
       2. Management rights
       3. Impact on civil service practices
  C. Antisecrecy/"Sunshine" Law: Effect on negotiations

VI. Structure of Negotiations
    A.   Management
        1. Locii of bargaining authority and administration
            a. Identification of bargaining team
        2. Role of personnel department
            a. Relationship to civil service
        3. Identification of persons who set negotiations parameters
            a. Committee
            b. Other branch of government/other level of government
    B.   Employee organization
        1. Role of international, national, or state organizations
        2. Policy development procedures
        3. Identification of bargaining team

VII. Constraints on Negotiations
    A.   Autonomy of negotiators
    B.   Economic factors
    C.   Role of other branches of government
    D.   Public opinion
    E.   Press
    F.   Other local institutions (e.g., banking community where heavy borrowing is required to fund payrolls either on a short or long term basis)
    G.   Tendency to defer decisions to third parties
        1. Use of arbitrators

VIII. The Public Interest
    A.   Definitions of the public interest
        1. Explicit by participants and observers
        2. Implicit in the situation
    B.   How the parties take account of the public interest in their decisions
    C.   Who represents the public interest
    D.   Feedback from unorganized/organized public(s)
        1. Issues that received feedback
        2. Kind of feedback
            a. Letters
            b. Personal contacts
            c. Public opinion polls
            d. Press
        3. Intensity of feedback
        4. Influence of feedback

IX. **Interests: Identification, Goals, and Methods**
   A. Interest
      1. Individual
      2. Group
         a. Membership
         b. Socioeconomic characteristics
   B. Labor relations policy goals
   C. Audience or target of influence
   D. Methods of direct influence
      1. Lobbying activities
      2. Policy advice
      3. Other
   E. Methods of indirect influence
      1. Campaign activities
      2. Media coverage
      3. Advertisements

X. **Access**
   A. Structural
      1. Management
         a. Formal consultations with negotiators
         b. Appointment to policy committees
         c. Public hearings
            (1) Public can speak at hearings (yes/no)
         d. Observe negotiations
         e. Participate in negotiations
         f. Disclosure requirements:
            (1) Advance negotiations
            (2) During negotiations
            (3) Prior to ratification
            (4) After ratification
            (5) During impasses
         g. Publish contracts
      2. Budgetary process
         a. Coordinate calendar to finalize budget
            (1) Before negotiations
            (2) During negotiations
            (3) After negotiations
         b. Disclosure of labor costs
            (1) Before negotiations
            (2) During negotiations
            (3) After negotiations

3. Public hearings on budget
   a. Public speak at hearings (yes/no)
4. Legislative process
   a. Public hearings
      (1) Before negotiations
      (2) During negotiations
      (3) After negotiations
          (a) Public can speak at hearings
      (4) Publish contracts
      (5) Ratify contracts
5. Referendum
   a. On taxes, contract funding
   b. On contract terms themselves
6. Arbitration-Mediation
   a. Participate in panel selection
   b. Panel membership
   c. Factfinders make recommendations
   d. Hearings by panel in public
7. Judiciary involvement by interests:
   a. Bring suit
   b. Friend of court
B. Political
   1. Officials—consult with "interests"
      a. Chief executive
      b. Chief negotiator
      c. Legislature president
      d. Legislature committee chairman
   2. Electoral process—interests:
      a. Endorse candidates
      b. Finance candidates
      c. Campaign
      d. Run for office
   3. Lobbying—interests:
      a. Contact officials by letter
      b. Contact in person
      c. Volunteer work, services, etc.
   4. Indirect political activities by interests:
      a. Publish position papers
      b. Press coverage
      c. Advertise positions

XI. Influence
    A. Individuals or groups
        1. Own estimates of influence
           a. Issues or goals
           b. Duration of influence
        2. Estimates by others of influence
           a. Issues or goals
           b. Duration of influence

Appendix B

Selected Bibliography

Only those articles and books dealing specifically with the "representation of the public interest in governmental labor relations" are described, together with works referred to in the text.

Arthurs, H.W. *Collective Bargaining by Public Employees in Canada.* Ann Arbor, Mich.: Institute of Labor and Industrial Relations, University of Michigan, Wayne State University, 1971.
The Canadian federal employees' limited right to strike as an example of a "Public Health, Welfare, and Safety" definition of "the public interest."
Barbash, Jack. "Trade Unionism and the General Interest: A Theory of Positive Public Policy Toward Labor." *Wisconsin Law Review* (Winter 1970): 1134–1144, 1970.
Poses a "theory of positive public policy" that transcends the special interests of pressure groups, including labor and management, to account for the social costs of their bargaining results.
Belasco, James A. "Municipal Bargaining and Political Power." *Collective Bargaining and Government: Readings and Cases.* Edited by J. Joseph Loewenberg and Michael H. Moskow. Englewood Cliffs, N.J.: Prentice Hall, 1972, pp. 235–248.
Public employee bargaining is done within the confines of the political system where the mayor dominates city bargaining despite a proliferation of other institutional bargaining arrangements. The "public interest" rests on the discovery of a "mechanism to prevent indiscriminate wage increases to public employees." Budgetary control through the political process, including legislative approval, taxpayer-voter pressures, political competition, and potential interest group activity operates to restrain the upward push on public employee wages in the absence of a private sector market mechanism. The selection suggests wage comparability policies and direct public approval of settlement as additional legal constraint mechanisms.

Bilik, Al. "Toward Public Sector Equality: Extending the Strike Privilege." *Labor Law Journal* 21 (June 1970): 338–356.
An argument against the "sovereignty" doctrine by a union spokesman. Argues that it is in the "public interest" to permit strikes by public employees in order to achieve "equity and the balancing of rights" for public as well as private sector employees.

Burton, John F., Jr. "Local Government Bargaining and Management Structure." *Industrial Relations* 11 (May 1972): 123–139.
Describes the organizational requirements for bargaining policy development and consultations among both executive and legislative branches.

———, and Charles Krider. "The Role and Consequences of Strikes by Public Employees." *Yale Law Journal* 79 (January 1970): 418–440.
Refutes various "public interest" objections to public employee strikes. Upholds political impact of public sector strikes and public employee union activities as legitimate political pressures.

Cassell, Frank H. "Public Hospital Collective Bargaining: A Policy Report to a Board." Unpublished Report, Evanston, Ill.: Northwestern University, 1971.
Advises a hospital management on collective bargaining policy and administrative machinery in terms of the "public interest" in a system which will permit the resolution of as many professional issues as possible away from the bargaining table.

Collins, Thomas W. *An Analysis of the Memphis Garbage Strike of 1968.* Tennessee Institute of Governmental Studies and Research, Public Affairs Forum, Memphis State University, April 1974.
Analyzes local political situation and attitudes towards Memphis sanitationmen from the point of view of the strikers.

Couturier, Jean J. "Chaos or Creativity in Public Labor-Management Relations." *Managing Governments' Labor Relations.* Washington, D.C.: Manpower Press, 1972.
Proposes a permanent board with broad representation of the labor and management parties, legislature, and citizen interest groups to determine when impasse resolution services are necessary, decide the method of impasse resolution, and help choose the impartial body that would resolve the issues.

Craft, James A. "Public Employee Budget Negotiations: Budget Search and Bargaining Behavior." *Public Personnel Review* 31 (October 1970): 244–249.
Describes the patterns of teacher negotiations in California as a process in which either the parties are predominantly interested in finding "misallocations" or "overallocations" in the budget and then mutually reallocate any such funds; or, the parties "negotiate" in the traditional adversary sense of proposals and counterproposals.

Dawson, Paul A. "On Making Public Policy More Public: The Role of Public Interest Groups." Paper presented at the Annual Meeting of the American Political Science Association, New Orleans, Louisiana, September, 4–8, 1973.

Dotson, Arch. "A General View of Public Employment." *Public Administration Review*, 16 (Summer, 1956), 197–211.
Asserts that public employment is a public relationship that must be rationalized in the context of public law. Rationalization is based on the needs and resources

of the two parties—public employee and public employer. The former need their fundamental constitutional rights protected and the latter depend on service delivery by their workers. Their employment relationship embodies the three principles of "democratic effectiveness," "compensatory right," and "equitable advantage."

Flathman, Richard E. *The Public Interest.* New York: John Wiley, 1966.
A discussion of the philosophical concept of the public interest.

Foegen, J.H. "Mediation From Initiation: Hope for Public Labor Relations." *Public Personnel Review* 31 (January 1970): 7–12.
The solution to protecting "the public's interest in the continuous supply of essential services" while retaining for public employees the right to strike is to have a public interest representative at the bargaining table from the beginning of negotiations. Such a party could better mediate any impasse by virtue of intimate familiarity with the negotiations.

——. "Social Responsibility—For Unions Too." *Management of Personnel Quarterly* 8 (Winter 1969): 28–33.
Proposes private–public sector wage comparability as an alternative to public employees' having to strike—and interrupt public services—in order to get fair treatment from their employer.

Gerhart, Paul F. *Political Activity by Public Employee Organizations at the Local Level: Threat or Promise?* Chicago: International Personnel Management Association, Public Employee Relations Library, No. 44, 1974.
An analysis of public employee unions as political special interest groups. Discusses implications of public employee unions as constituencies of the elected officials with whom they bargain. Describes union political tactics and methods of influence.

Horton, Raymond D. *Municipal Labor Relations in New York City: Lessons of the Lindsay-Wagner Years.* New York: Praeger, 1972.
Contrasts the attempt to "depoliticize" governmental labor relations by the Lindsay Administration's delegation of managerial powers to persons not politically accountable, with the Wagner Administration. Criticizes lack of representation of broad public interests in city bargaining due to narrow special interest group access of the unions and the attitude of officials that the interests of "the public" and organized city employees were the same, through the creation of the tripartite Office of Collective Bargaining.

Jones, Ralph T. *Public Sector Labor Relations: An Evaluation of Policy-Related Research.* Belmont, Mass.: Contract Research Corp., 1975.
Summary and evaluation of public sector labor relations *research* studies, not expository writings.

Juris, Hervey A. and Peter Feuille. *Police Unionism.* Lexington, Mass.: D.C. Heath, 1973.
Analyzes the political and economic context of police union power and the political activities of police unions as special interest groups in trying to manipulate the governmental labor relations process to their own advantage.

Kochan, Thomas A. "A Theory of Multilateral Collective Bargaining in City Government." *Industrial and Labor Relations Review* 27 (July 1974): 525–542.
Poses a theory of access to and influence on government labor negotiations by

all other persons who are not direct participants at the bargaining table, ranging from other officials not at the table, such as legislators (who may still impose costs) to citizen interest groups. Describes the range of political relationships involved in governmental labor relations among governmental officials, both appointed and elected, public employee unions, and the general public.

Lippmann, Walter. "The Public Interest." *Essays in the Public Philosophy.* Boston, Mass.: Little, Brown, 1955.

Presents an idealist's view of the public interest as "what men would choose if they saw clearly, thought rationally, acted disinterestedly and benevolently."

Love, Thomas and George T. Sulzner. "Political Implications of Public Employee Bargaining." *Industrial Relations* 11 (November 1972): 18–33.

Collective bargaining analyzed as a political activity in which public officials are held socially responsible by the political process and the laws, rules, and regulations that have been enacted through the political system to govern public sector bargaining. The differences between public and private sector bargaining are the "pressure tactics," including lobbying by labor with the persons with whom they bargain (elected officials). Hypothesizes various degrees of access and influence by public employee unions under various forms of local government. Questions the impact of this political activity on the public interest.

Marshall, F. Ray and Avril Van Adams. "The Memphis Public Employees Strike." *Racial Conflict and Negotiations: Perspectives and Case Studies.* Edited by W. Ellison Chalmers and Gerald W. Cormick. Ann Arbor, Mich.: Institute of Labor and Industrial Relations, University of Michigan, Wayne State University, 1971.

Describes interest groups' goals, methods of access, and influence during the 1968 sanitationmen's strike.

McGrew, Jean B. "Bargaining in Education and the Public Interest." *Journal of Collective Negotiations in the Public Sector* 4 (Fall 1975): 347–357.

Suggests a "negotiations facilitator" who, like Foegen's mediator, would attend negotiations from the onset. After getting the parties to clarify their positions, the facilitator could move beyond the customary mediator's role to that of making recommendations at the request of both parties.

McLennan, Kenneth and Michael H. Moskow. "Multilateral Bargaining in the Public Sector." Edited by Gerald G. Somers. Industrial Relations Research Association. *Proceedings of the Twenty-First Annual Winter Meeting.* Chicago, 1968; Madison, Wis. 1969, pp. 31–40.

Discusses the third party groups which "operate on the fringe of bargaining." Such interest groups have influence on bargaining to the extent that they are able to impose costs upon the parties for their bargaining decisions. Each side attempts to legitimize its own position by getting the support of various segments of the interested community.

———. "Public Education." *Emerging Sectors of Collective Bargaining.* Edited by Seymour Wolfbein. Morristown, N.J.: D.H. Mark, 1970.

Analyzes interest group activity in public education bargaining according to the "multilateral bargaining" model. Describes the behavior and goals of interest groups in Philadelphia teacher bargaining.

Pegnetter, Richard. *Public Employment Bibliography.* Ithica, N.Y.: New York State School of Industrial and Labor Relations, 1971.

Perry, Charles R. *The Labor Relations Climate and Management Rights in Urban School Systems: The Case of Philadelphia.* Philadelphia: University of Pennsylvania Press, 1974.
Identifies basic legal, political, economic, and managerial constraints on Philadelphia teacher bargaining, and analyzes their impact on school policy and service delivery as revealed through the collective bargaining agreement.

Petro, Sylvester. "Sovereignty and Compulsory Public-Sector Bargaining." *Wake Forest Law Review* 10 (March 1974): 25−165.
An absolutist argument against legislation by central governments requiring their subordinate jurisdictions to bargain with public employees as undermining governmental sovereignty. Rejects the private sector analogy in that government's absolute powers of coercion cannot be subject to bargaining with its employees. "Bargaining" by definition implies that the union is sovereign, too. Union sovereignty implies anarchy.

Pezdek, Robert V. *Public Employment Bibliography.* Ithica, N.Y.: New York State School of Industrial and Labor Relations, 1973.

Sarason, Seymour, *et al. The Community at the Bargaining Table.* Boston, Mass.: Institute for Responsive Education, 1975.
Report of field interviews with public education administrators, governing board members, negotiators, mediators, teacher union leaders, legislators, and interest group leaders concerning community interests, representation, and modes of participation in teacher bargaining.

Schubert, Glendon. *The Public Interest.* Glencoe, Ill.: The Free Press, 1960.
A discussion of the philosophical concept of the public interest.

Stanfield, J. Edwin. *In Memphis: Mirror to America?* Special Report. Atlanta, Ga.: Southern Regional Council Inc., April 28, 1968.
A description of events immediately preceding and following the assassination of Dr. Martin Luther King, Jr. during the 1968 Memphis sanitationmen's strike.

───── . *In Memphis: More Than a Garbage Strike.* Special Report. Atlanta, Ga.: Southern Regional Council Inc., March 22, 1968. An analysis of the 1968 Memphis sanitationmen's strike in terms of the role of the civil rights movement.

───── . *In Memphis: Tragedy Unaverted.* Special Report. Atlanta, Ga.: Southern Regional Council Inc., April 3, 1968.
A description of the violence accompanying Dr. King's first march on behalf of the sanitationmen on March 28, 1968. The Report concludes that city officials will resort to police power to overcome strikers.

Stanley, David T. *Managing Government Under Union Pressure.* Washington, D.C.: The Brookings Institution, 1971.
Analyzes the impact of public employee collective bargaining on key functions of local government, especially budgetary decisionmaking.

Summers, Clyde W. "Public Employee Bargaining: A Political Perspective." *Yale Law Journal* 83 (May 1974): 1156−1200.
Questions the direct access of public employee unions as a class of special interest groups to the governmental budgetary process. Lack of access to public

employee bargaining information makes it difficult to hold elected officials accountable for their bargaining decisions. Due to the low profile given to bargaining by both unions and management, the general voting public is not able to identify the linkage between government employee bargaining and budget or service delivery levels.

U.S. Dept. of Commerce, Bureau of the Census. *Labor-Management Relations in State and Local Governments: 1974.* State and Local Governments Special Studies No. 75. Washington, D.C.: USGPO, 1976.

U.S. Civil Service Commission. *Labor-Management Relations in the Public Service.* Washington, D.C.: USGPO, 1972.

U.S. Congress, House, Committee on Education and Labor. *Labor-Management Relations in the Public Sector. Hearings* before Special Sub-Committee on Labor, on H.R. 8677, and H.R. 9730, 93rd Cong., 1st sess., 1974.

U.S. Dept. of Labor. *Current References and Information Services for Policy Decision-Making in State and Local Government Labor Relations: A Bibliography.* Washington, D.C.: USDOL, Labor-Management Services Administration, 1971.

Warner, Kenneth O. and Mary L. Hennessy. *Public Management at the Bargaining Table.* Chicago: Public Personnel Association, 1967.
Questions whether there are procedural checks and balances to protect the public interest in governmental collective bargaining. Concludes that the only way to identify the public interest is through the electoral process. Suggests the creation of a framework that would provide for greater public participation in the public sector bargaining process, largely through access to information regarding bargaining issues and positions.

Wellington, Harry H. and Ralph K. Winter, Jr. *The Unions and the Cities.* Washington, D.C.: The Brookings Institution, 1971.
The political aspects of public employee collective bargaining, together with differences in the market restraints on union power, make the private and public sectors substantially different. Increased public attention to the relationship between public bargaining and taxes and services would constrain union power, but this would require changes in the political process (to increase structural access).

Zeidler, Frank P. "The Public as Third Party." *Labor-Management Relations.* Vol. 1. Englewood Cliffs, N.J.: Public Personnel Association, 1974.
Raises the basic issues of the representation of the public interest in government labor relations.

Appendix C

Public Opinion Poll Data

I. Contents

Public opinion poll data on questions relating to the "Representation of the Public Interest in Public Sector Labor Relations" were available only for the cities of Milwaukee and Philadelphia. These are presented below.

Part 1. The first set of poll data were gathered by the Urban Observatory project of the National League of Cities in Milwaukee in 1970. It was a random cluster sample of 443 households.

Part 2. In December 1974, the Milwaukee Association of Commerce conducted a mail poll of 1,200 randomly selected city residents, of whom 435 responded.

Part 3. The Greater Philadelphia Movement funded Research for Better Schools, Inc., to conduct a probability sample of 1,521 housing units in Philadelphia containing adults over 18. "The sample matched, as closely as possible, the city's population distribution by school district, race, sex, age, education level, income, occupation, and religion." It was conducted in May-July of 1974. There were 691 completed responses.

Part 4. In the spring of 1975, Opinion Research of California conducted personal, in-home interviews with 1,100 persons comprising a representative cross-section of the adult population of the state of California. The study used a modified probability sample, stratified according to geographic areas and population density. It was commissioned by the California Teachers Association.

Part 1. Urban Observatory

Table C.1.a.   Attitudes Towards Public Employee Strikes

Q1.   Some people say that people who provide public services should be able to strike for more pay just like other workers. Others say that city services are too important to let these people strike. Do you think, for example, that teachers or trash collectors should be able to go on strike or not?

No—neither   47%
Yes—both   49%

Q2.   How about policemen and firemen—should they be able to go on strike, or not?

No—neither   62%
Yes—both   37%

Table C.1.b.   Interest in City Politics

Q.   How interested would you say you are in city problems and city politics?

Interest	Percent
Very interested	22
Fairly interested	53
Not too interested	25

Table C.1.c.   Preference for Political Participation

Q.   What do you think is the best way people like you can make themselves heard by the city government? (One to two answers; answers categorized.)

Method	Percent
Contact officials directly	45
Use regular political process	33
Organized group activity—general	11
Organized group activity—peaceful protest	3
Other (does not include violent protest)	4
No way	8
No answer	16

Table C.1.d. Citizen Perceptions of Mayoral Power

Q. Which officials or people do you think really run the local government here in Milwaukee; which people make the most difference in how well the City is run? (One to two answers; answers categorized and mentioned by 6% or more.)

Official	*Percent*
Mayor–Mayor's Office	61
Common Council	41
Police Department	9
No Answer	15

Table C.1.e. Group Membership Distribution of Milwaukee Residents

Type of Group	*Percent of Population with Membership*
General—Civic Affairs	4
General—Education, Youth Service	3
Church-related, Civic Service	2
Neighborhood—Civic Service	1

Table C.1.f. Attitudes Towards Citizen Inputs into School Policy

Q. Do you think that the parents and citizens in this neighborhood have the right amount of say in important decisions about education in the neighborhood schools or not?

Response	*Percent*
Right amount	49
Not right amount	19
No answer	32

Table C.1.g. Attitudes Towards Improvements

Q. What things should be done so they would have more say in the schools? (Question asked of only those who answered "not right amount" to previous question; one to two answers; answers categorized and mentioned by 10% or more.)

Response	*Percent*
Better communication between parents and schools	38
Parents show more interest	23
Neighborhood, community decentralization	12
Stronger PTA's	9
No answer	26

Table C.1.h.   City Employee Pay

Q1.   "Do you think that people who work for the city government usually make *more*, make the *same* or make *less* than they would make if they worked for someone else—say in a business?"

Response	Percent
More	35
Same	34
Less	17
No answer	14

Q2.   "And do you think local government wages and salaries generally should be *higher* than they are now, are they *about right*, or do you think they should be lower?"

Response	Percent
Higher	18
About right	50
Lower	18
No answer	14

Table C.1.i.   Services and Taxes

Q1.   "Considering what people in Milwaukee pay in local taxes, do you think the people generally get their money's worth in services, or not?"

Response	Percent
Yes	35
No	55
No answer	10

Q2.   What is the main reason for this—Why don't people get their money's worth?

Response	Percent
Wrong priorities	26
Inefficient administration	17
Unequal taxes	10
Unequal services	7
No answer	37

Table C.1.j. Services and Taxes

Q1. "As you know, costs keep going up. If a choice has to be made do you think taxes should be raised or services like those on the list should be cut down?"

Response	*Percent*
Taxes raised	32
Services cut	60
No answer	8

Q2. "From what you know, do you think taxes are *too high* here in Milwaukee, *about right*, or are they *too low* to pay for needed services?"

Response	*Percent*
Too high	68
About right	29
Too low	3

Table C.1.k. Employment by City Government

Q1. "Do you or any of your close relatives work for the city government in Milwaukee?"

Response	*Percent*
Yes	18
No	82

Table C.1.l. Education

Q2. "How good would you say is the education children get in the schools in this neighborhood?"

Response	*Percent*
Very good	35
Good enough	31
Not so good	16
Not good at all	4
No answer	14

Part 2.   Milwaukee Association of Commerce

Table C.2.a.   Attitudes Towards Public Employees and Related Matters

Q1.   What pay level do you think government workers *should* receive?

Response	Percent
Less than workers in private employment for equal work	13
The same as workers in private employment for equal work	82
More than workers in private employment for equal work	3
No opinion	2

Q2.   In general, what pay level do you think City and County government employees presently are receiving?

Response	Percent
Less than workers in private employment for equal work	5
About the same as workers in private employment for equal work	21
More than workers in private employment for equal work	61
Don't know	13

Q3.   In general, what is your opinion regarding City and County government employees: a) How difficult are their jobs compared with similar jobs in private employment?

Response	Percent
Much less difficult than in private employment	25
Somewhat less difficult than in private employment	35
Somewhat more difficult than in private employment	9
Much more difficult than in private employment	2
About the same as jobs in private employment	25
No opinion	5

b)   How hardworking are local government employees compared with employees in private employment?

Response	Percent
Much more hardworking than private employees	2
Somewhat more hardworking than private employees	3
About the same as private employees	22
Somewhat less hardworking than private employees	38
Much less hardworking than private employees	32
No opinion	3

Q4. How much of a pay increase (wages plus fringe benefits) do you think City and County employees should get for 1975? (For a one-year increase.)

Response	*Percent*
0–5% increase	46
6–10% increase	27
11–15% increase	7
16–20% increase	5
21–30% increase	1
31–50% increase	1
Over 50% increase	2
No opinion	12
Miscellaneous	1

Q5. How much of a pay increase do you think City and County employees *are demanding* for 1975? (For a one-year increase.)

Response	*Percent*
0–5% increase	2
6–10% increase	6
11–15% increase	12
16–20% increase	18
21–30% increase	11
31–50% increase	6
Over 50% increase	1
Don't know	43

Q6. How would you evaluate City and County tax rates?

Response	*Percent*
Too low	0.2
About right	10
Too high	84
Don't know	6

Q7. If local government is faced with a choice of either raising taxes or cutting services, in general, which would you prefer?

Response	*Percent*
Raise taxes	9
Cut services	73
No opinion	16
Miscellaneous	3

Part 3.   Research for Better Schools, Inc.

Table C.3.a.   Importance of Education to Success

Q1.   How important are schools to one's future success?

Responses	Philadelphia Poll	Gallup, 1973
Extremely important	87%	76%
Fairly important	9	19
Not too important	3	4
No opinion	1	1

Table C.3.b.   Attitudes Towards Small Classes

Q.   In some school districts, the typical class has as many as 35 students; in other districts, only 20. In regard to achievement or progress of students, do you think that small classes make a:

Responses	Philadelphia Poll	Gallup, 1973
Great deal of difference	73%	79%
Moderate difference, or	13	11
Little or no difference	13	6
No opinion	1	4

Table C.3.c.   Money Spent Related to Student Achievement

Q.   In some school districts, about $600 is spent per child per school year; some school districts spend more than $1,200. Do you think this additional expenditure of money makes a great deal of difference in the actual achievement of progress of students—or little difference?

Responses	Philadelphia
Great deal of difference	46%
Moderate difference, or	14
Little or no difference	36
No opinion	4

Table C.3.d. Attitudes Towards Shifting Burden to State

Q.   It has been suggested that State taxes be increased for everyone in order to let the State government pay a greater share of school expenses and to reduce local property taxes. Would you favor an increase in state taxes so that real estate taxes could be lowered on local property in Philadelphia?

Responses	Philadelphia Poll	Gallup 1972
Yes	60%	55%
No	35	34
No opinion	5	11

Table C.3.e. Attitudes Towards Raising Taxes

Q.   Suppose the Philadelphia *public* schools said they needed much more money. As you feel at this time, would you vote to raise taxes for this purpose, or would you vote against raising taxes for this purpose?

Responses	Philadelphia Poll	Gallup 1972	Gallup 1973
For	40%	36%	36%
Against	56	56	56
No opinion	4	8	8

Table C.3.f. School Board Power to Tax

Q.   Raising money for education is presently under the authority of City Council. Do you think that the School Board should be given this authority to raise money for education?

Responses	Philadelphia
Yes	52%
No	42
No opinion	6

Table C.3.g. Attitudes Towards Tenure, Quality Pay, Accountability

Q1. *[Favor teacher Tenure]*	Philadelphia Poll	Gallup 1974	Gallup 1972
Approve	42%	31%	28%
Disapprove	54	56	61
No opinion	4	13	11

Q2.   [Pay teachers on basis of quality, or standard pay scale]

	Philadelphia Poll
Quality of his work	58%
Standard Scale basis	40
No opinion	2

Q3.   Would you favor or oppose a system that would hold teachers and administrators more accountable to the parents for the progress of students?

	Philadelphia Poll
Favor	73%
Oppose	23
No opinion	4

Q4. *[Favor voucher plan]*	Philadelphia Poll	Gallup 1970	Gallup 1971
Yes	76%	43%	38%
No	20	46	44
No opinion	4	11	18

Table C.3.h.   Attitudes Towards Teachers' Voice in Policy

Q.   Should *teachers* have more to say about what goes on within the school in such matters as:

Policy Areas	Yes	No	No Opinion
Curriculum	86%	11%	3%
Administration	80	17	3

Table C.3.i.   Attitudes Towards Parents' Voice in Policy

Q1.   Should the Philadelphia public school *parents* have more to say about what goes on in the school matters of:

Policy	Yes	No	No Opinion
Curriculum	63%	35%	2
Teachers	63	34	3
School rules	60	38	2

Table C.3.j. Attitudes Towards Parents Suing School Board

Q.   Do you think parents should have the right to sue a school district of a student of normal intelligence and without physical disabilities reaches the 6th grade without being able to read?

Responses	Philadelphia Poll	Gallup 1973
Yes	34%	27%
No	63	64
Other	1	—
No opinion	2	9

Part 4.   Opinion Research of California

Table C.4.a.   General Attitudes Towards Right to Collective Bargaining

Q1.   As you probably know, most people in private industry have the right to join unions and to negotiate collective bargaining agreements and contracts with their employers. Generally speaking, do you believe that public employees should or should not have the right of collective bargaining with public agencies?

Response	Percent
Yes, they should	69
No, they should not	26
Don't know	5

Q2.   Whatever your views about collective bargaining for public employees in general may be, do you believe that California's public school teachers should or should not have the right to collective bargaining with their school districts?

Response	Percent
Yes, they should	75
No, they should not	20
Don't know	5

Q3.   Assume that teachers are given the legal right to bargain collectively and to strike under some circumstances. Should this teachers' right to bargain collectively (1) include negotiating educational matters such as class size, educational materials, supplies, discipline, and the physical environment of schools, or (2) should it be limited to negotiating for wages, fringe benefits, and working conditions only?

Response	Percent
Should include educational matters	62
Should be limited to wages, fringe benefits, etc.	32
Don't know	6

Table C.4.b.   Right to Strike

Q1.   Present California law neither permits nor prohibits strikes by public employees. Generally speaking, do you believe that public employees should or should not be permitted to strike?

Response	Percent
Yes, they should	54
No, they should not	42
Don't know	4

Q2.   In your opinion, if every collective bargaining procedure has been tried and exhausted and an absolute stalemate has been reached, do you think that teachers should or should not have the right to strike?

Response	Percent
Yes, they should	59
No, they should not	39
Don't know	2

Q3.   If California law were changed to explicitly permit strikes by public employees, of the following groups which should and which should not be permitted to strike

Group	Should	Should Not	Don't Know
Various, such as state license people, local clerks, stenographers	60	37	3
Public transit workers	55	42	3
College teachers	54	43	3
Refuse collectors	51	47	2
School teachers	50	47	3
All state and local employees	48	47	5
Hospital workers	41	57	2

Group (cont'd)	Should	Should Not	Don't Know
Nurses	37	60	3
Firemen	33	65	2
Policemen	33	65	2
Doctors	32	66	2

Table C.4.c. Strikes Versus Compulsory Arbitration

Q. Do you agree or disagree that if negotiations between public employers and public employees break down, and even after cooling-off periods and other public fact-finding procedures they still cannot agree, then the dispute should be settled by compulsory arbitration with no right to strike?

Response	Percent
Strongly agree	27
Tend to agree	31
Tend to disagree	24
Strongly disagree	10
Don't know	8

Table C.4.d. Public Interest in Teacher Negotiations

Q1. Do you agree or disagree that officials who are elected by the people to establish public policy would be put under unfair pressure by a strike or the threat of a strike which would shut down public services?

Response	Percent
Strongly agree	20
Tend to agree	35
Tend to disagree	25
Strongly disagree	10
Don't know	10

Q2. Do you agree or disagree that if officials such as county supervisors or school board members are elected by the people to establish policy, they would be limited in their ability to really represent the taxpayers if they were pressured by the threat of a strike or by an actual strike which shut down.

Response	Percent
Strongly agree	17
Tend to agree	33
Tend to disagree	26
Strongly disagree	9
Don't know	15

Q3. Do you agree or disagree that if an arbitrator or an elected board of public officials gives a pay raise or otherwise approves an agreement with public workers which results in an increase in the cost of government, such an agreement should not take effect until it has been approved by the voters?

Response	*Percent*
Strongly agree	37
Tend to agree	32
Tend to disagree	17
Strongly disagree	7
Don't know	7

Table C.4.e.   Attitudes Towards Pay Comparability

Q1. Do you agree or disagree that generally speaking, public employees and employees in private industry ought to receive comparable pay for comparable work?

Response	*Percent*
Strongly agree	52
Tend to agree	36
Tend to disagree	5
Strongly disagree	3
Don't know	4

Notes

NOTES TO CHAPTER 1

1. U.S. Department of Commerce, Bureau of the Census, *Labor-Management Relations in State and Local Governments*: *1974* (State and Local Government Special Studies No. 75), Table 1, p. 9.

2. See Clyde W. Summers, "Public Employee Bargaining: A Political Perspective," *Yale Law Journal* 83:1156–1200, 1974.

3. Richard E. Flathman, *The Public Interest* (New York: John Wiley & Sons, 1966), p. 4.

4. Glendon Schubert, *The Public Interest* (Glencoe, Ill.: The Free Press, 1955), p. 199.

5. *Ibid.*

6. *Ibid.*, p. 200.

7. *Ibid.*, p. 201.

8. See Harry Kranz, *The Participatory Bureaucracy* (Lexington, Mass.: D.C. Heath, 1976).

9. U.S. Department of Labor, *Current References and Information Services for Policy Decision-Making in State and Local Government Labor Relations*: *A Bibliography* (Washington, D.C.: U.S. DOL, Labor-Management Services Administration, 1971).

U.S. Civil Service Commission, *Labor-Management Relations in the Public Service* (Washington, D.C.: USGPO, 1972).

Ralph T. Jones, *Public Sector Labor Relations*: *An Evaluation of Policy-Related Research* (Belmont, Mass.: Contract Research Corp., 1975).

Richard Pegnetter, *Public Employment Bibliography* (Ithaca, N.Y.: Cornell University, New York State School of Industrial and Labor Relations, 1971).

Robert V. Pezdek, *Public Employment Bibliography* (Ithaca, N.Y.: Cornell University, New York State School of Industrial and Labor Relations, 1973).

10. See H.W. Arthurs, *Collective Bargaining by Public Employees in Canada* (Ann Arbor: Institute of Labor and Industrial Relations, University of Michigan—Wayne State University, 1971).

NOTES TO CHAPTER 2

1. Milwaukee Urban Observatory, National League of Cities. See Part 1 of Appendix C for selected questions. (Reference to Table C.1.k.

2. Metropolitan Milwaukee Association of Commerce, December 1974. See Part 2 of Appendix C for selected questions.

3. Appendix C, Table C.1.d.

4. Appendix C, Table C.1.c.

5. See Part 2 of Appendix C.

6. See Appendix A for a detailed model.

7. Urban Observatory Poll: 19 to 17 percent.

8. See Appendix C, Table C.1.l.

9. See Appendix C, Table C.1.g.

NOTES TO CHAPTER 3

1. See Pennsylvania Labor Relations Board, *Fact Finding Report and Recommendations*, Case No. PERA F—2472—E (December 18, 1972), p. 2.

2. See Appendix C, Part 3 for relevant public opinion poll data.

3. See Philadelphia *Evening Bulletin*, December 16, 1973.

4. Seymour Sarason, *et al.*, *The Community at the Bargaining Table* (Boston: Institute for Responsive Education, 1975).

5. *Philadelphia Inquirer*, March 23, 1973.

NOTES TO CHAPTER 4

1. Lucy R. Mason, *To Win These Rights: A Personal Story of the CIO in the South* (New York: Harper, 1952), p. 105.

2. *Memphis Press-Scimitar*, January 2, 1940.

3. Benjamin Aaron, "Labor Relations Law," Lloyd Ulman, ed., *Challenges to Collective Bargaining* (Englewood Cliffs, N.J.: Prentice-Hall, 1967), pp. 113—114.

4. For a detailed discussion of third party interest activities during the 1968 strike, see: F. Ray Marshall and Avril Van Adams, "The Memphis Public Employees Strike," in: W. Ellison Chalmers and Gerald W. Cormick, eds., *Racial Conflict and Negotiations: Perspectives and Case Studies* (Ann Arbor: Institute of Labor and Industrial Relations, University of Michigan—Wayne State University, 1971).

5. House Bill No. 916, 4—3—75, Sec. 9(c) (9) (G).

6. See Bibliography, Appendix B.

7. Marshall and Van Adams, *op. cit.*, p. 95.

8. *Ibid.*, p. 105.

NOTES TO CHAPTER 5

1. Letter of January 29, 1975, Vasconsellos to D. Todd.
2. *Ibid.*, and Letter of April 17, 1975, Vasconsellos to C. Walker.
3. League of Women Voters of California, *Education Kit*, January 1975.
4. California School Boards Association, "Guidelines for Implementing the New Meet and Confer Legislation," *Newsgram*, December 16, 1974.
5. California Teachers Association, *Negotiations*, "Position of the CTA Negotiations Department Regarding Implementation of the Public Notice Provisions of the Winton Act," undated memorandum.
6. *Newsgram, op. cit.*
7. *Education Kit, op. cit.*
8. Undated memorandum: J. Vasconsellos to J. Brooks (CSBA).
9. *Negotiations, op. cit.*
10. *Newsgram, op. cit.*
11. *Negotiations, op. cit.*
12. *California Teachers Association* vs. *San Francisco Unified School District*, Petition for Writ of Mandate, No. 687–622, March 19, 1975, Exhibit F.
13. *Education Kit, op. cit.*
14. Letter of February 5, 1975 to J. Vasconsellos.
15. Letter of February 5, 1975, Joseph M. Brooks (CSBA) to J. Vasconsellos.
16. *Negotiations, op. cit.*
17. *Ibid.*
18. See Appendix C, Tables C.4.a., C.4.b., C.4.c., C.4.d.
19. California Teachers Association, *Action*, March 14, 1975, p. 6.

NOTES TO CONCLUSIONS

1. See Appendix C, Table C.3.e.
2. See also F. Ray Marshall and Arvil Van Adams, "The Memphis Public Employees Strike," in W. Ellison Chalmers and Gerald W. Cormick, eds., *Racial Conflict and Negotiations: Perspectives and Case Studies* (Ann Arbor: Institute of Labor and Industrial Relations, 1971), p. 91.
3. U.S. Bureau of the Census, *1972 Census of Governments*, USGPO, 1972, Vol. 3, No. 3.
4. U.S. Department of Labor, Labor-Management Services Administration, Division of Public Employee Labor Relations, *Summary of State Policy Regulations for Public Sector Labor Relations* (Washington, D.C.: USGPO, 1973). *Scope of Bargaining in the Public Sector* (Washington, D.C.: USGPO, 1972). *Collective Bargaining in Public Employment and the Merit System* (Washington, D.C.: USGPO, 1972).
5. *Dispute Settlement in the Public Sector: The State of the Art* (Washington, D.C.: USGPO, 1972). Also see Jean J. Couturier, "Chaos or Creativity in Public Labor-Management Relations," in Chester Newland, ed., *Managing, Governments' Labor Relations* (Washington, D.C.: Manpower Press, 1972).
6. Advisory Commission on Intergovernmental Relations, *Labor Management Policies for State and Local Government* (A Commission Report) (Washington, D.C.: USGPO, 1969).

Index

Access, see also: individual interest groups by name; Access mechanisms
defined, 2, 4-7
discussed, 173-87
influence, relationship of access to, 7, 8, 156, 194-98, 203
information, access to, 150, 199-203
  Berkeley, 130-34
  Memphis, 98
  Milwaukee, 41
public interest, see: Public interest, definitions, access to information
political
  defined, 6, 10, 149
  discussed, 150, 156, 173, 177, (table) 176, 185-87, 202, 203
    Memphis, 95-100
    Milwaukee, 33, 43
    Philadelphia, (table) 54-55, 60, 62
  influence of, 195, 196-98, 202
structural
  defined, 6, 9, 10, 20, 149
  discussed, 150, 173-74, (table) 174-75, 176-85, 203
  citizens excluded, 165-66
  Berkeley, 105-09, 125-28, 131-35, 14-45, 156, 177, 196, 201-02

  Memphis, 95, 195, 196
  opposition by black community, 177, 178, 185
  Milwaukee, 27-28, 29, 33, 38, 40-41, 43, 177, 185, 195, 196, 201-02
  Philadelphia, 60, 62, 185, 195, 196, 201-02
influence of, 196, 203
political access, compared with, 2, 6, 20, 149, 150, 155, 173, 178, 185, 200, 210
and elected officials, 185-86
and union political power, 185-86
influence, 194-98
  Milwaukee, 33, 202
  Philadelphia, 202
press coverage, 199, 200
study proposal, 213-15
unions, access through, 28, 33, 34-37, 43, 86, 100, 170-71, 178, 204-05
Access mechanisms, see also: Access, political, structural; Appendix A; individual interest groups by name
advisory committees (citizen), 107, 109, 125-28, 135, 137, 141-42, 145, (table) 174-75, 177, 178, 183, 205-11
arbitration, see: third parties, citizens as, below

caucuses, citizen access to, 109, 110,
    111, 132, 145, 202
"Community at the Bargaining
    Table," see: tripartite nego-
    tiations, below
consultations
  with citizens, (table) 174, 178–
    179
  with officials, (table) 176, 186
contracts
  publication, 34, (table) 174, 179–
    80
  ratification, (table) 175, 182
  referendum, 98–99, 134, 201
court action, see: litigation by citi-
    zens, below
disclosure of negotiating positions,
    12, (table) 174, 179, 203–06,
    see also: information access,
    below
  Berkeley
    California law, 9, 105–09, 119,
      127, 129–30, 136, 145, 169
      (table) 174, 179, 195, 196,
      199, 202, 206, 209, see also:
      Rodda Act; Vasconsellos
      Amendment
    League of Women Voters of
      Berkeley, 126, 202
    League of Women Voters of
      California, 136, 169, 177, 178,
      191, 195, 202
  Memphis, 96, 98, 204
  Milwaukee, 33–34, 43, 204–05
    Citizens' Governmental Re-
      search Bureau, 27
  Philadelphia, 60, 61, 204
electoral activities, (table) 176, 186
factfinding, see: third parties,
    citizens as, below
hearings, public, 9, 12, (table) 175,
    179, 181–82, see also: Budget
    process
  Berkeley, 110, 125–27, (table)
    174, 179, 182, 191
  Memphis, 96–97, 179
  Milwaukee City, 34, 43
  Milwaukee schools, 40–41, 179
  Philadelphia, 60, (table) 174,
    179, 182
information, access to, 150, 155,
    199–203, 205
  Berkeley, 120, 130–34, 146
  Memphis, 98
  Milwaukee, 41
litigation by citizens, (table) 175,
    182

Milwaukee city, 32
Milwaukee schools, 41, 200
Philadelphia, (table) 243
  enjoin PFT, 45–46, 47–48, 49,
    50, 58, 60, 62, 63–64
  Parents' Union suit, 48, (table)
    55, 56–57, 182
  Welfare Rights Organization suit,
    57
lobby, (table) 158, (table) 176, 186,
    195
open meetings laws, see: "Sun-
    shine" laws, below
open negotiations/public observers,
    12, 183, (table) 184, 209–10,
    211–13
  Berkeley, 131–34, 140–41, 144,
    145, 166, 177, 179, 183,
    (table) 184, 202, 212, 213
  Memphis, 96, 98, 179, 211–12
  Milwaukee, 30, 33, 38–39, (note)
    39, 177, 211
  Philadelphia, 57, 62–63, 177, 211
referenda, 9, (table) 175, 182–83
  Berkeley school tax, 134, (note)
    134, 145, 182–83, (table)
    246
  contracts, 98–99, 134, 201
  Memphis city taxes, 98–99, 134,
    182–83
  Milwaukee city, 34
  Milwaukee schools, 41
  Philadelphia, 63
"Sunshine" laws, 5, 183, 185, 201,
    209
  Berkeley, 183, 184
  vs. executive sessions, 127–28,
    129, 141, 185
  California (Brown Act), 106,
    127–28, 183
  League of Women Voters of
    California, 127, (note) 127
  Pennsylvania, 183
  Tennessee, 97, 183
  Wisconsin, 31, 33, 41, 183
third parties, citizens as, (table)
    175, 183
  Berkeley, 109, 141–42, 183
  Milwaukee, 27, 34, 178, 183
  Philadelphia, 60
tripartite negotiations, 18, (table)
    174, 179, 195, 200, 201, 203
  "Community at the Bargaining
    Table," 53, 60
  Berkeley
    minority demands, 126, 131,
      135, 136, 171, 191

support, 135
    union opposition, 135
  Milwaukee, 43
  Philadelphia, 62
Accountability, see: Representation
American Federation of Labor (AFL),
    early days in Memphis, 70
American Federation of Labor-Council
    of Industrial Organizations, see
    AFL-CIO
AFL-CIO Labor Councils
  Berkeley, 114 (note) 114, 172
    influence, 138, 146
  Memphis, 75, 79–81, 84–85, 171–
    72
    as an interest group, 85, 88
    on public employee pensions, 93
    support tax referendum, 99
  Milwaukee, 22, 23, 172
    influence, 197
  Philadelphia, 50, 51, 171–72
    general strike threat ("Day of Con-
      science"), 49, 58, 163, 167,
      189, 196, 197, 198, 202
    as an interest groups, 53
    access, (table) 55
    goals, (table) 54, 58
    methods, (table) 55, 58
    influence, (table) 55, 63–64,
      66, 167, 189, 196, 197, 202
American Federation of State, County,
    and Municipal Employees
    (AFSCME)
  Memphis, Local 1733
  Memphis, Local 1733
    access through AFSCME to
      negotiations, 86, 170–71,
      178, 198
    black community attitudes to-
      wards, 78, 80–83, 86, 88, 91,
      95, 98, 99–100, 104
    hospital workers, see: Memphis
      hospital workers
    influence, 100, 102, 198
    interest group relations, 81, 86–87
    attitude towards mayor, 73
    national AFSCME relationship,
      79–80, 85
    oppose open negotiations, 98
    political influence, 78–79, 80,
      81–83, 87, 100
    public attitudes towards, 76
    public interest
      AFSCME leader's definition,
        92
      AFSCME represents, 91
    right to strike, 99

sanitationmen, see: Sanitation-
    men, negotiations; Sanitation-
    men's strike tactics, 78, 80,
    87, 94–95, 102
  tax referendum support, 99
  Milwaukee, 24
  1973 city-county work stoppage,
    32, 157, 167, 200, 216
  opposition to open negotiations,
    (note) 39
  press coverage of wage data, 35–36
American Federation of Teachers, 52
Americans for Democratic Action
    (Philadelphia)
  access, (table) 55
  goals, 53, (table) 54, 56, 62
  influence, (table) 55, 64
  methods, (table) 55, 56
Asian Alliance/Task Force (Berkeley)
  access issue, 126
  representation, 117, 121, 122, 127

Banks (Philadelphia)
  influence, 65
  role, 46–47
Berkeley Federation of Teachers
  election activity, 114
  influence of Citizens' Advisory
    Committee, 136
  membership, 116
  representation on Citizens' Fiscal
    Review Committee, 131
  strike vote, 110–111
Berkeley Pupil Personnel Association,
    116, 131
Berkeley Teachers Association
  budget information, 128
  data use complaint, 139
  election activity, 114
  influence of Citizens' Advisory
    Committee, 136
  membership, 116
  no layoffs position, 124
  representation on Citizens' Fiscal
    Review Committee, 131
Berkeley teachers' strike (1975), 9,
    109, 111–12, 118, 119, 134,
    140–45, 157
Berkeley Unified School District
  Board of Education, see:
    School board
Blacks, see: Minority interests
Board of education, see: School
    board
Boycott, see: Minority issues, Mem-
    phis, economic boycott

Milwaukee
city, 24–25
schools, 38
Philadelphia, 52
Collins, Thomas W. (note) 69, 101
Committee on the Move for Equality
(Memphis), 85
Common council, see: City council
Concerned Black Parents (Berkeley),
see also: NAACP
access demands, 126, 135, 136, 171
representation, 110, 117, 122, 127
Concerned Women of East Memphis
and Shelby County
access, 94, 102
goals, 85, 87, 102
methods, 102–03
influence, 94, 102–03
press, 94, 103, 192, 194
public interest groups, 169
Congress of Industrial Organizations
(CIO), early days in Memphis,
70, 71
Critical incidents
defined, 8–9, 12, 20
discussed, 167, 192–93, 200, 201,
203, 214, 215
Berkeley, 109, 112
Memphis, 157, 192
Milwaukee, 21
Philadelphia, 45, 157, 192
press attention to, 192, 199, 216
Crump, E.H., 70–71, (notes) 70–71,
81, 102

Dawson, Paul A., 26, 29, 192
Democrats, 23, 25, 51
Disclosure, see: Access mechanisms;
Collective bargaining, legisla-
tion, California disclosure law

Electrical Workers, International
Brotherhood of, 96

Federal Mediation and Conciliation
Service, 85, 98
Firefighters
Memphis, 70, 71, 72, 89, 99
Flathman, Richard E., 2

Governmental structure
Berkeley, 112, 146
Memphis, 72, (note) 72, 73, 75
Milwaukee
city, 22
schools, 37
Philadelphia, 50

Home and School Council (Philadelphia), see: Parent-Teachers
Association
Hortonville, Wisconsin, 1974 teachers'
strike, (note) 45

Influence
of access types, structural compared
with political, 194–98
of citizens' advisory committees
(conceptual), 210–11
defined, 7–8, 70, 149, 187–94
discussed, 187–98, see also individual
interest groups
Berkeley, 135–39, 187, (table)
187, (table) 188, 189, 196
AFL-CIO, 138
Asian-black communities,
135–37, 191
of budget crisis, 138
California Teachers Association,
salary data, 139, school board
election, 113
Chamber of Commerce, 138, 146
city council, 138
Citizens' Advisory Committee,
114–15, 135–38, 142, 143–46
163, 196, 206, 207, 212
of disclosure law, 196, 202
election of school board, 114,
138
on factfinding panel, 144–45
League of Women Voters of
Berkeley, 136, 137, 191, 196
League of Women Voters of
California, 136, 195
press, 139, 143–44, 206
students, 136
Memphis, 100–03, 187, (table)
187, (table) 188, 189, 196
AFSCME, 100, 198
boycott, 80, 89–90, 101, 102,
104, 189, 196, 216
business community, 100–01,
103
city council, 100–01
Concerned Women of East Memphis and Shelby County, 94,
102–03
mayor, 100–02
Martin Luther King, Jr.,
assassination, 89–90, 92, 101–
02, 191, 198
Memphis Gas Light & Water
settlement, 96–97
Ministerial Alliance, 100–01,
104, 198, 211–12

President of the United States,
101-02
press, 101-02, 103-04
strike threats and fear of
violence, 95, 103, 191
Milwaukee city, 34-37, (table)
187, (table) 188, 189, 196
Association of Commerce, 30,
196-97
common council
employee vote, 24
labor, 23, 197
Citizens' Governmental Research
Bureau, 34-35, 42, 196
labor, 23, 35, 159, 163, 197
mayor, 25, (table) 235
Milwaukee County Property
Owners' Association, 36
press, 33, 34, 35-57, 192, 193,
204-05
Public Expenditure Survey, 35-36,
196, 207
Milwaukee schools, 41-42
Citizens' Governmental
Research Bureau, 42
Citizen Recall, 42, 44
PTA Council, 41-42
Philadelphia, 52, (table) 55, 63-
65, 187, (table) 187, (table)
188, 189, 196
Americans for Democratic
Action, (table) 55, 64
AFL-CIO Labor Council, (table)
55, 63-64, 66, 167, 189, 196,
197, 202
banks, 65
Citizens' Committee on Public
Education, (table) 55, 61-63
city council, 62
Home & School Council, (table) 55
labor vote, 50-51
League of Women Voters of
Philadelphia, (table) 55, 64
mayor, 61-62, 192-93, 197,
204
Parents' Union, (table) 55,
61-62, 63-64
President of the United States,
58
Urban Coalition, (table) 55, 63,
196
Urban League, (table) 55
U.S. Assistant Secretary of
Labor, 63-66
Welfare Rights Organization,
(table) 55, 64
press, (table) 55, 65

press as a special type of influence,
189, (table) 190, 191-94
measures, 10, 149, 187, (table) 187,
(table) 188
Interest groups, see also individual
groups by name
defined, 3, 4, 12, 15, 19, 20, 150,
167, 169, 203
identified
Berkeley, 117-23, 167
Memphis, 85-88
Milwaukee city, 25-31, 167
Milwaukee schools, 38-40
Philadelphia, 48, 52-58, 167
public interest groups
defined, 26-28, 39, 52, 53, 167,
169, 192, 199, 203
identified
Berkeley, 118, 121, 133-34,
145, 167, 169
Memphis, 83, 92, 104, 169
Milwaukee, 26, 28, 39, 167, 169
Philadelphia, 53
special interest groups,
defined, see: public interest groups
identified, 169-73
business, 170, 172, see also:
Business community
civil rights, 170-71, see also:
Minority interests
educational activists, 170
labor, 163, (table) 164
Memphis, AFL-CIO, 85, 88
Philadelphia, AFL-CIO, 53,
171-72
parents, 170
press, 30, 53
taxpayers, 169, 170, 172-73,
see also: Taxpayers' interests
Interest motivation, see also: Access,
political
causes, 156-59
as constraint on decision makers,
163, 189, 210-11
Memphis, 100-01, 104
Milwaukee, 32, 37-38, 44
Philadelphia, 65
Interests, see: Interest groups;
Minority interests; Taxpayers'
interests
International Ladies Garment Workers'
Union, 49, 61

Jewish Community Relations Council
(Philadelphia), 64

King, Rev. Martin Luther, Jr.

Budget process
  access, (tables) 174-75, 179, 180
  Berkeley
    access, 128-29, 146-47
    Citizens' Advisory Committee,
      130, 133, 135, 138
    crisis, 110, 111, 124, 128-29, 145,
      147
    influence, 138
    strike, 140
  Memphis, 96-97, 100, 179, 180
  Milwaukee
    access, 34
    Citizens' Governmental Research
      Bureau, 27-28
    Public Expenditure Survey of
      Wisconsin, 28-29
    school budget, 40-41, 179
  New York City's fiscal plight, 1, 166
  Philadelphia, 46, 50, 60, 147, 179,
    180
Business community, see also:
      Chamber of Commerce; indi-
      vidual interest groups; Tax-
      payers' interests
  Future Memphis, 85, 88
  influence, 100-01
  interests, 85, 87, 89-91, 94, 172
  strike threats, 95, 103, 202

California Legislative Counsel, 107
California School Boards Association,
    107-09, 120-21
California School Employees Associa-
    tion, Local 1
  membership, (note) 116-17
  observer status, 132, 166
  strike, 110-11, 116
California Teachers Association
  AFL-CIO attitude on strike (note)
    114
  budget information, 128
  disclosure implementation position,
    108-09
  salary data source, 139
Canadian Public Service Staff Rela-
    tions Act, 16
Catholics parochial schools interest,
    53
Certificated Employees Council
    (Berkeley)
  Citizens' Advisory Committee
    observer status, 131-32
    representation on, 137
  composition, 106, 116
  disclosure requirements, 127, 129
  interests, 137

  negotiations, 109-12, 116-17
  no layoffs position, 123
  open negotiations, 132
  press, 139, 204
  strike, 112, 140-44
Chamber of Commerce
  Berkeley, 118, 138, 146
  Memphis, 85, 87-88, 100, see also:
    Business community
  Milwaukee, 26
    goals, 30
    influence, 30, 196-97
    poll data, 13, 30, (Tables) 238-38
  Philadelphia, 53
    goals, 57, 62
    methods, 57
Chief negotiator
  Berkeley, 115, 128, 130, 132, 141,
    163
  Memphis, 72, 84, 95-96, 163
  Milwaukee
    city, 24-25, 43, 163
    schools, 38
  Philadelphia, 52, 59, 60, 63, 163
Citizens' Committee on Public Edu-
    cation in Philadelphia, 53
  access, (table) 55
  goals, 53, (table) 54, 56, 60-61,
    177, 178
  influence, (table) 55, 61-63
  methods, (table) 55, 56
City Club (Milwaukee), 26
City Council
  election influences
    Milwaukee, 23, 24, 25, 33, 37,
      197
    Philadelphia, 50-51
  influence on negotiations
    Memphis, 100-01
    Philadelphia, 197
  negotiations role
    general, (table) 175, 180-81
    Memphis, 83-84, 95-98, 166,
      180-81, 182, 195
    Milwaukee, 22, 24-25, 37, 43,
      166, 180-81, 182, 195
    Philadelphia, 46, 47-48, 50, 52,
      61-62, 66, 180-81, 182, 195
Citizen Recall (Milwaukee)
  access, 32
  goals, 39, 172
  influence, 42, 44
  methods, 39
Citizens' Advisory Committee
    (concept), 107, 138, 206-11
Citizens' Advisory Committee on
    Negotiations (Berkeley)

access, 109, 126, 127, 129, 131–32,
　134, 136, 137, 141–42, 145,
　177, 178, 183, 202, 205, 212
　observe negotiations, 132, 140–41,
　　144, 145, 166, 179, 202
　open negotiations, 131–32, 134,
　　177, 212, 213
budget crisis, 128–29, 130, 131, 133,
　140, 146
creation, 109–10, 117, 122, 126–27,
　178, 183
disclosure, 129–30, 205–06
goals, 118, 122, 123, 124, 132, 137–
　38, 142–43
influence, 114–15, 135–38, 142,
　143–46, 163, 196, 206, 207
press, 133, 141, 193, 205
public interest group, 169
representation
　of Certificated Employees Council,
　　137
　on Citizens' Fiscal Review Com-
　　mittee, 131
　on factfinding panel, 142, 144–45,
　　183
　of management, 122, 135, 140–41,
　　142, 143, 145–46, 169, 207
　of minority interests, 123, 126,
　　135, 136, 137, 171, 191
　of interest groups, 117–18, 122,
　　127, 133–34, 136, 206
　strike, 140, 142–43
staff, 128–29, 133, 146, 205, 207
strike role, 112, 119, 140–45
taxpayers' interest, 172
Citizens' Budget and Finance Com-
　mittee (Berkeley)
　budget crisis, 128
　creation, 126, 178
　disclosure, 131
　goals, 118, 121–22, 124, 137
　representation
　　of, 117–18, 121, 131
　　on Citizens' Advisory Committee,
　　　122, 127, 137
　　on factfinding panel, 142
　　on Citizens' Fiscal Review Com-
　　　mittee, 131
　tripartite negotiations, 135
Citizens' Fiscal Review Committee
　(Berkeley), 131
Citizens' Governmental Research
　Bureau (Milwaukee), 25
　access, 28, 33–34, 39, 43, 177, 178,
　　183, 201, 205
　goals, 27–28, 29, 34, 39, 43, 172
　influence, 34–35, 42, 196

methods, 28, 33, 35, 196, 207
press, 35, 36, 191, 193, 207
public interest group, 26, 27, 28, 43,
　167, 169, 172
Civil service, see also: Personnel
　director
　negotiations role, 22, 27, 84
Closed shop in public employment,
　(note) 19
Collective bargaining
　California, compared with "meet
　　and confer," (note) 105, 106,
　　111, 112, 116
　closed negotiations, 2, 5, 201
　confidentiality, 202–03, 212
　issues, see also: individual interest
　　group goals; Minority interests;
　　Public interest, definitions
　Berkeley
　　negotiations, 110–11, 121–24,
　　　132, 138, 145
　　strike, 112, 118–19, 134, 140–
　Memphis
　　dues check-off, 74, 90–91, 92
　　grievances, 93
　　"meet and confer," 83–84, 104
　　promotional policies, 93
　　recognition, 72, 90–91, 92
　　self respect, 90
　　wages, 74–76, (table) 77, 87,
　　　(note) 92, 92–93, 95
　Philadelphia
　　strike, 46–50, (note) 59
　legislation, see also "Sunshine" laws
　California
　　disclosure law, 9, 105–09, 119,
　　　129–30, 136, 145, 169, 177,
　　　179, 188, 195, 196, 199, 202,
　　　205, 206, 209
　　Rodda Act, 106, (note) 112,
　　　119, 182
　　Vasconsellos Amendment, 105,
　　　106–09, 117, 119
　　Winton Act, (note) 105, 106, 107,
　　　112, 116, 145, 182
　Landrum-Griffin Act, 81
　Memphis, 81, 83–84, 89, 92, 97,
　　104
　Milwaukee, 21, 38
　Pennsylvania law, 45–46, 63, 64,
　　66
　Tennessee House bill, 99
"professionalism," 163, 166, 183,
　185, 201, 205
structure
　Berkeley, 106, 115–17
　Memphis, 83–85

influence of assassination, 89–90,
92, 101–02, 191, 198
strike role, 69, 74–75, 76, 80, 89–90,
91

Labor, organized, see also: individual
organizations by name
access through, 28, 33, 34–37, 43,
86, 100, 170–71, 178, 204–05
political power of, general, 156,
159–63, (table) 161, (table)
162, 185–86
Berkeley, 113–15, 138, 146, 159,
172
Memphis, 69, 70–71, 75–76, 79–
83, 93–94, 99, 100, 102, 178,
198
AFSCME, 78–83, 100
Milwaukee, 22–25, 44, 159. 163.
197
Philadelphia, 45, 50–51, 61, 189,
see also: AFL-CIO Labor
Council, general strike threat
private sector unions' attitudes towards public employees,
general, (table) 164, 185
Berkeley, 114, (note) 114, 171–72
Memphis, 80–81, 85, 88, 93–94,
99, 101, 171–72
Milwaukee, 23, 171–72
Philadelphia, 51, 171–72, see also:
AFL-CIO Labor Council,
general strike threat
public attitudes towards, general,
3, 5, 18, 19, 151, (table) 160
Berkeley, 112–13, 119, (tables)
243–45
Memphis, 70–76, (table) 77–78,
81
Milwaukee, 22–23, 37–38, 202,
(table) 234
Philadelphia, 50–51, 60, 67, 159
Landrum-Griffin Act, 81
League of Women Voters
Berkeley, 117, 119–20
access, 126, 202
disclosure, 126
goals, 118–21, 124, 126, 137, 196
influence, 136, 137, 191, 196
press, 144
public interest group, 133–34, 145
representation on citizens' committees, 121, 122, 127, 134,
137, 145
strike, 119
taxpayers' interest, 135
tripartite bargaining, 135

California
access, 136, 169, 177, 178, 191,
195, 202
disclosure
lobby, 105, 120
implementation, 107–09, 119
goals, 119–20
influence, 136, 195
methods, 120
pay study, 111
public interest group, 121, 167,
169
press, 139
"Sunshine" law, 127, (note) 127
Philadelphia
access, (table) 55
goals, (table) 54, 58, 60
influence, (table) 55, 64
methods, (table) 55, 58

Marshall, F. Ray, 101–02
Mayor
election influences
Memphis
1971, 82, 92, 159, 192–93,
197–98
1975, 81–82, 100, 104, 197,
198
Milwaukee, 24
Philadelphia, 172
influence in negotiations
Memphis, 100–01
Milwaukee, 25, 37, 43, (table) 235
Philadelphia, 52, 60–61, 65–67,
192–93, 195, 196, 197, 200,
204
negotiations role
general, 146–47, 166
Memphis
1968, 73–74, 79, 83, 88–89, 90,
91–92, 94, 101–02, 103
1975, 84, 95–98, 104, 166,
195, 198
Milwaukee, 22, 24–25
Philadelphia, 47–52, 60, 172–73
Meany, George, 58
"Meet and confer," see: Collective
bargaining, California, Memphis
Memphis Commercial Appeal, 103
Memphis Gas, Light, and Water Board,
96–97
Memphis hospital workers
FMCS, 85, 98
press, 78, 94, 95, 103
recognition, 71, 72, 76, 78, 85, 87,
89, 90, 94, 98, 102–03

Memphis sanitationmen's strike
(1968), 69, 71, 72-75, 78, 79,
81, 94, 101-04, 157, 159, 170,
172, 191, 192, 193, 198, 202,
204
Merit system, see: Civil service
Metropolitan Milwaukee Association
of Commerce, see: Chamber
of Commerce
Milwaukee Board of School Directors,
see: School board
Milwaukee city-county employees'
strike (1973), 32, 157, 167,
200, 216
Milwaukee Council of PTAs, see:
Parent Teachers Association
Milwaukee County Property Owners'
Association, 26
access, 29-30
goals, 29-30, 172
influence, 36
methods, 36
Milwaukee police "blue flu" (1971),
200, 216
Milwaukee Teachers Education Association, 38, 39, 40
Milwaukee teachers' strike (1975),
32, 41-42, 118, 157, 200
Ministerial Alliance (Memphis)
access, 98, 179, 211-12
goals, 86-87, 99-100, 104
influence, 100-01, 104, 198, 211-
12
methods, 86-87
Minority interests
Berkeley
access as a racial issue, 126,
129-30, 135, 136, 138, 145,
146
Citizens' Advisory Committee,
122, 137, 140
educational enrichment, 111, 118-
19, 123-25, 138, 142, 171
influence of blacks and Asians,
135-37, 191
PTA, 121
Memphis
AFSCME
civil rights v. special interests,
78, 79-83, 86, 88, 90-91, 95,
98, 99-100, 104, 198
tactics, 78, 90
black taxpayers, 79, 88, 91, 99, 104
economic boycott, 74, 78, 85, 86,
90, 93, 94, 198
influence, 80, 89-90, 101, 102,
104, 189, 196, 216

issues, 72, 73, 157, 170-71, 202
political access v. structural, of
minority community, 177-78,
185, 195, 202
school population, (note) 99
school tax, 99
strike fears, 95, 100, 191
Milwaukee Urban League, 171
Philadelphia
issues, 48, 51, 53, 56, 171
public interest definition, 58
school population, 56, (note) 56
teachers, 64

National Association for the Ad-
vancement of Colored People
Berkeley, 117, see also: Concerned
Black Parents
disclosure, 126, 127, 130
goals, 124, 126
representation, 122, 127
Memphis, 85, 86, 99
National Education Association, 38
National Labor Relations Act, 16
New York City, fiscal plight, 1, 166
New York State School of Industrial
and Labor Relations, Library,
13
Newark, New Jersey, 1971 teachers'
strike, (note) 45
Newspapers, see: press

Organized labor, see: Labor, organized;
individual organizations by
name

Parent Teachers Association
Berkeley, 117
disclosure, 126, 127
goals, 110, 118-19, 121
representation
on citizens' committees, 121,
122, 127
of minority interests, 118-19
Milwaukee
access, 41, 177, 178, 211
goals, 38-39, 40, 170
influence, 41-42
methods, 39
press, 191
representation, 38
Philadelphia
access, (table) 55
goals, (table) 54, 57, 63
influence, (table) 55
methods, (table) 55, 57
representation, 53

Parents' Union (Philadelphia)
  access, (table) 55
  goals, (table) 54, 56
  influence, (table) 55, 61–62, 63–64
  methods, 48, 53, (table) 55, 56–57,
    182
Pennsylvania Public Employee Rela-
    tions Act, 45–46, 63, 66
Pennsylvania State Education Asso-
    ciation, 49
People United to Save Humanity
    (Memphis), 85, 86
Personnel director, see also: Civil
    service
  Memphis, 84, 95–96
  Milwaukee, 24, 35
Philadelphia Board of Education, see:
    School board
Philadelphia Federation of Teachers,
    46–52, 56, 58, 59, 63, 64–65
Philadelphia teachers' strike (1972–
    73), 45–67, 118
  chronology, 46–50
  civil rights, 171, 172, 179, 192
  hearings, 182
  influence of, 156, 166, 167, 189
  open negotiations, 179, 211
  press coverage, 191, 196, 197, 200,
    202
  saliency, 157
  TV coverage, 211, 212
Police
  Memphis, 70, 71, 72, 89, 99
  Milwaukee "blue flu," 32, 200, 216
Press, see also: Public opinion
  coverage in general, 192, 199, 200,
    204, 210, 216
  Berkeley
    coverage of negotiations, 111,
      139, 192, 193, 203, 205, 210
    affirmative action policy, 139
    Berkeley Gazette, 139, 143,
      144, 192, 199, 203
    board of education, 139
    Citizens' Advisory Committee,
      133, 141, 193, 205, 207
    League of Women Voters of
      California, 139
    League of Women Voters of
      Berkeley, 139
    influence, 139, 143–44, 206,
      207
  Memphis
    coverage of 1968–69 and 1975,
      191–92
    access to information through,
      96

editorial positions, 78, 91, 193
    Memphis Commercial Appeal,
      103
    strike threats, 78, 94–95, 103,
      192, 194
    influence, 103–04
  Milwaukee
    coverage in general, 31–32, 36–
      37, 191, 192, 193, 205
    anti-secrecy act, 31, 33
    as an "interest," 25, 30–31
    interest group coverage, 34, 36,
      193
    Milwaukee Journal, 30–31, 32,
      33
    Milwaukee Sentinel, 30, 35, 39
    open negotiations, 33, 39
    right to strike, 30
    unorganized public, 33
    influence, 33, 34–37, 191, 204–
      05
  Philadelphia
    as an "interest," 53, (table) 54–
      55
    influenced, 65, 191, 192, 193
    strike coverage, 60, 61, 64, 65,
      191
    on public interest, 67
    influence, 149, 189, (table) 190,
      191–94, 199, 200, 204, 205–
      06, 210, 216
"Professionalism" in bargaining, see:
    Collective bargaining, "pro-
    fessionalism"
Public Expenditure Survey of Wiscon-
    sin, 26
  access, 35, 202–02
  goals, 28–29, 172
  influence, 35–36, 196, 207
  methods, 29, 35–36, 196
  press, 35, 36, 191, 193
  public interest group, 28–29, 172
Public, see: Interest groups
Public interest
  concepts, 1–8, 10, 13, 14, 18, 19,
    151, 150–55, 167, 199–203
  definitions
    ability to pay, see: taxpayers
    access, structural, 216
    affirmative action, 110, 111, 121,
      122, 123–24, 138, 139, 142,
      145
    balance of power, see: union-
      management
    civil peace
      Memphis, 69, 78, 87, 88–89, 90,
        92, 157

Philadelphia, 59
press, 95
comparability of wages, see: parity
continuity of services, 14–15, 150,
(table) 152–53
constitutional rights of employees,
14, 18–19
constraints on employers and employees, 14, 18, 150
costs-benefits/services tradeoff,
59, 151, (table) 152–53, 169,
170, 201
due process, 151, (table) 152–53,
155
Berkeley, 124
Milwaukee, 28, 38, 43
employee equity, 151–52, (table)
152–53, 170
equitable settlements, 14, 18, 36,
150, 151, (table) 152–53
efficiency of government, 14, 17–
18, 150, (table) 152–53
Milwaukee, 31
essential services, 14, 15
Milwaukee, 31, 44, 150
harmonious public employee relations, 69, 82, 88–89
labor peace, 59, 72
inconvenience, avoiding, 14, 15,
150
justice, economic and social
Memphis, 86, 88, 100, 150, 151
management rights, 151, (table)
152–53, 155
Berkeley, 122, 124
Milwaukee, 31
Philadelphia, 182
merit system, 14, 19–20, 150
parity (private and public workers'
pay), 151, (table) 152–53,
155, 170, (tables) 238, (table)
246
Berkeley, (note) 123, (table)
246
Milwaukee, 28–29, 30, 31, 40,
(table) 238
Memphis, 88, 92
pluralism, 6–7, 163, 173
productivity, 27, 29
public health, safety, welfare, 14,
16–17, 150
Memphis, 95
Philadelphia, 45, 47, 48, 58
quality of education
Berkeley, 124
Milwaukee, 40
Philadelphia, 58

quality of services, service delivery,
151, (table) 152–53, 155
Milwaukee, 31
salary increase, no
Berkeley, 119, 132, 138, 142
school funding, increase
Berkeley, opposition, 118
Milwaukee, 40
Philadelphia, 59, 66
self-respect of workers
Memphis, 90–91
sovereignty of government, 14, 17
Berkeley, 124, 134
Memphis, 88–89, 91
stable collective bargaining, 14,
19, 150
taxpayers, ability to pay, 151,
(table) 152–53, 155
Berkeley, 123–24
Memphis, 88, 91, 104
Milwaukee, 31
teacher accountability
Berkeley, 121, 122
Milwaukee, 40
Philadelphia, 58
union-management balance of
power
Memphis, 92
Milwaukee, 31
Public interest groups, see: Interest
groups
Public opinion, see also: Press
apathy, 12, (table) 154, 156–57,
186, see also: Interest motiva-
tion
Berkeley, 157
Memphis, 76, 93, 157, 216
Milwaukee, 32, 36, 157, 200, 216
Philadelphia, 47
feedback, 12, 44, 157, (table) 158,
159, 186
Berkeley, 110, 123
Memphis, 93–94, 98, 100
Milwaukee, 32, 36, 41, 44
polls
California Teachers Association
(Opinion Research of Califor-
nia), 13, 113, 123, (note) 134,
233, (tables) 243–46
Greater Philadelphia Movement
(Research for Better Schools,
Inc.), 13, 50, 200, 223, (tables)
240–43
Harris (Louis) Poll, 159, 194,
(table) 194
Metropolitan Milwaukee Associa-
tion of Commerce, 13, 23, 30,

31, 233, (tables) 238-39
Urban Observatory, 12-13, 22,
    23, 25, 31, 37, 233, (tables)
    234-37
research proposal, 215-17
unorganized public
    defined, 11, 12
    discussed, (table) 176, 186-87
        Berkeley, 110, 111, 123, 134,
            136, 144, 203-04
            press influence turnout, 139,
            204
        Memphis, see also: Minority
            interests
            no polls, 76
            press focus public attention,
            103
            referendum, 99
            support for mayor in 1968, 73,
            94
        Milwaukee, 31, 32, 33
            press focus public attention,
            37
            elected officials' impressions,
            44
        Philadelphia, 50, 59-60, 67
            reactions during strike, 47-48,
            49, 50
            news reports of attitudes, 60,
            67
            reactions to televised negotia-
            tions, 65
    influences on
        citizens' advisory committee role
            role, 203-04, 208-09, 210-11
        press, see also: Press, influence,
            200-01, 204, 205-06, 210

Railway Labor Act, 16
Race, see: Minority interests
Recognition
    Berkeley, (note) 112, 116
    Memphis
        hospital workers, 71, 72, 76, 78,
            85, 87, 90, 94, 98, 102-03
        sanitationmen, 72, 90-91, 92
    Milwaukee, 24, 38
    Philadelphia, 64
Representation
    accountability of decision makers,
        18, 150, 151, 155, 156,
        163-67, 199, 200-03, 208
    concept, 3, 8, 149
    elected officials, 3, 31-32, 59,
        92, 163, (table) 165, 166-67,
        (table) 168, 173, 177, 201,
        202

of interests, 10, see also: individual
    groups by name
Berkeley
    board of education, 125-28,
        135, 146
    Certificated Employees Council,
        106, 116, 137
    Citizens' Advisory Committee,
        117-18, 121-22, 123, 126,
        127, 133-34, 135-37, 140,
        141, 142-43, 171, 191, 206,
        207
        as concept, 138, 206-11
        on Citizens' Fiscal Review
            Committee, 131-32
        on factfinding panel, 142,
            144-45
        of management, 122, 135-36,
            140-41, 142, 143, 145-46,
            169, 207
        of minority interests, 135, 136,
            137, 171, 191
    Citizens' Budget and Finance
        Committee, 118, 121, 122,
        127, 131, 137, 142
    League of Women Voters of
        Berkeley, 121, 122, 127, 134,
        135, 137, 145
    League of Women Voters of
        California, 169
    minority interests, 110, 117,
        121-23, 127, 135, 136
    PTA, 118-19, 121, 122, 127, 131
    students, 136, 144
    taxpayers, 113, 135, (table) 245
    tripartite negotiations, 131, 135,
        136
Memphis, see also: AFSCME as a
    civil rights group; Minority
    interests
    AFSCME, 79, 91, 95, 104
        on AFL-CIO Council, 84
    city officials, 91-92
    Concerned Women of East Mem-
        phis, 102
    mayor, 73, 92
Milwaukee
    Citizens' Governmental Re-
        search Bureau, 26, 169
    city officials, 30-31, 43-44
    common council in negotiations,
        24, 181, 195
    PTA, 38
    Property Owners', 29
    Public Expenditure Survey, 28
    Wisconsin Employment Rela-
        tions Commission, 34, 183

Philadelphia
  city council in negotiations, 62
  Citizens' Committee view, 61–
    62, 62–63
  school board nominating panel,
    50, 60–61
Republicans, 51, 113
Rodda Act (California), 106, (note)
  112, 119, 182

San Francisco, 1975 mayoral election, 1
Sanitationmen (Memphis), negotia-
    tions
  1968, 69, 71, 72–75, 78, 79, 81,
    94, 101–04, 157, 159, 170,
    172, 191, 192, 193, 198, 202,
    204
  1969, 87, 94, 101–04
  1975, 9, 69, 86–87, 92, 104
School board
  Berkeley
    Citizens' Advisory Committee
      influence, 137–38, 142,
      144–45
    disclosure policies, 109–110,
      125–28, 129–30, 182, 191
    election influences, 111, 113–15,
      146
    executive session, 127–28, 129,
      141, 143, 185
    negotiations
      chronology, 109–12
      open, 131–34, 144
      positions, 115–16, 125–28
      press, 139
      strike, 140–45
      superintendant, 115–16, 125
  Memphis, 87
  Milwaukee
    election influences, 37–38, 39
    negotiations role, 37, 38, 182
  Philadelphia
    appointment, 50
    financial role, 46, 50, 66
    negotiations role, 50, 52, 61, 141,
      182
Schubert, Glendon, 3
Southern Tenant Farmers Union, 70
Special interest groups, see: Interest
  groups
Stanfield, J. Edwin, 101
Strike ban
  as a definition of the public interest,
    14–15, 16–17
Strike, right to in public employment
  California, public attitudes towards,
    113, (tables) 244–45

Harris Poll, 159, (table) 194
Memphis
  black community attitude, 99
  Chamber of Commerce and inevi-
    tability, 100
  mayor's attitude on illegality, 73,
    89, 91–92, 104
Milwaukee, 21
  PTA, 38–39
  editorial positions, 32
  Pennsylvania law, 45–46, 63, 66
  press coverage, 193–94
  Tennessee law, 83, 89
Strike threats, 157, 167
Memphis
  black community, 79, 90, 104
  business community, 87, 89–90,
    172, 189
  city council, 101
  hospital workers, 1969, 71, 76,
    78, 87, 94, 95, 102, 103
  press reaction, 78, 94–95, 103,
    192, 194
  sanitationmen, 1963–68, 71
  white community, 89–90, 93,
    94, 103
Philadelphia, 163, 167
  AFL-CIO Labor Council, general
    strike ("Day of Conscience"),
    49, 58, 163, 167, 189, 196,
    197, 198, 202
  influence, (table) 55, 63–64, 66,
    167, 189, 196, 197, 202
Strikes, see: Berkeley teachers' strike
  (1975), Memphis sanitation-
  men's strike (1968), Milwaukee
  city-county employees' strike
  (1973), Milwaukee police
  "blue flu" (1971), Milwaukee
  teachers' strike (1975), Philadelphia teachers' strike (1972–
  73)
"Sunshine" laws, general, 5, 183, 185,
  201, 209
  California Open Meetings (Brown)
    Act, 106, (note) 127, 127–28
  Memphis city council circumven-
    tion, 97
  Milwaukee *Journal* and, 31, 33
  Milwaukee schools, 41
  Wisconsin Employment Relations
    Commission ruling, 33

Taxes, see also: Taxpayers' interests
  Berkeley, 134, 138, 145, 183
  California, 111
  Memphis, 75, 76, 99, 104

Philadelphia, 46–50, 204
referenda, 182–83
Taxpayers' interests
  ability to pay, 1, 2, 17, 31, 88, 91,
      104, 123–24, 151, (tables)
      152–53, 155
  Berkeley, 118, 121, 135, 172
  California poll data, (table) 245
  fringe benefits, 35
  Memphis
    access to city council, 96
    blacks, 79, 88, 91, 99, 100, 104
    business community, 87–88, 91
    unions, 80, 93–94, 165
  Milwaukee
    city, 167
    interest groups, 26, 27, 28–30, 39,
        172
    poll data, (tables) 236–37,
        (table) 239
    schools, 37–38
  pension costs, 2, 27, 93
  Philadelphia
    influence, 64, 66
    mayor, 59, 60, 67, 172–73
    poll data, (tables) 241
    press, 192, see also: Influence, press
  as a special interest group, 169,
      170, 172
  union members, 80, 93–94, 163,
      (table) 164
Teamsters, International Brotherhood
    of, 49, 114
Tennessee House bill, 99
Timberlane, N.H., 1973 teachers'
    strike, (note) 45
Truman, Harry S., 5

U.S. Assistant Secretary of Labor
  influence, 63–66
  role Philadelphia teachers' strike,
      49–50, 58, 61
U.S. Congress, 5
U.S., Under Secretary of Labor, 85, 90
U.S., President
  Memphis sanitationmen's strike
    influence, 101–02
  role, 74, 85, 90, 91, 98, 198
  Philadelphia teachers' strike role, 58

U.S. Secretary of Health, Education,
    and Welfare, 47
Union of State Governments
    (Pennsylvania), 48
Unions, see: Labor, organized; indi-
    vidual organizations by name
Urban Coalition (Philadelphia)
  access, (table) 55, 179
  goals, 48, 53, (table) 54, 56
  influence, (table) 55, 63, 196
  methods, (table) 55, 56, 171, 198
Urban League
  Memphis, 85, 86
  Milwaukee, 171
  Philadelphia, 53
    access, (table) 55
    goals, (table) 54, 57, 60
    influence, (table) 55
    methods, (table) 55, 56, 57

Van Adams, Avril, 101–02
Variables, dependent and independent
  defined, 7–8, 149
Vasconsellos Amendment (California),
    105, 106–09, 117, 119
Vasconsellos, John (California
    Assemblyman)
  amendment author, 105
  interpretation, 107–08

Welfare Rights Organization
    (Philadelphia)
  access, (table) 55
  goals, 48, 53, (table) 54, 57
  influence, (table) 55, 64
  methods, (table) 55, 57, 60
Winton Act (California State Educa-
    tion Code), (note) 105, 106,
    107, 112, 116, 145, 182
Wisconsin Citizens for Legal Reform,
    see: Citizen Recall
Wisconsin Employment Relations
    Commission
  Anti-Secrecy Act ruling, 33
  citizen access, 34, 183
Wisconsin Municipal Employment
    Relations Act, 21, 38

✳

About the Authors

Richard P. Schick was the project director and principal researcher for the National Civil Service League's contract with the U.S. Department of Labor, Labor-Management Services Administration, Office of Policy Development for whom this study was conducted. He was also a Senior Program Analyst for the U.S. Congress, Commission on the Organization of the Government of the District of Columbia. Prior to joining the League, Dr. Schick taught political science. His doctoral dissertation was on *National Emergency Strike Legislation: Proposals Since the Taft-Hartley Act.*

Jean J. Couturier is a Professor of Public Management and Director of Northwestern University's Graduate Public Management Programs. He was formerly the Executive Director of the National Civil Service League. Earlier, Mr. Couturier was for seven years an AFL—CIO union representative of public employees. He organized New York City's public hospital, professional, and clerical employees and became director of 56 New York State government employee locals with responsibility for administration, staff, negotiations, lobbying, research, and training. Mr. Couturier is a founder of the American Consortium for International Public Administration and of the Academy for Code Administration. He has published over 40 articles and edited several books on government employment and employee relations.

In their work with the National Civil Service League, a public interest group, Msrs. Schick and Couturier have advised governmental agencies at the federal, state, and local levels, as well as public administration societies and citizens' groups, on public employment and related policy issues.

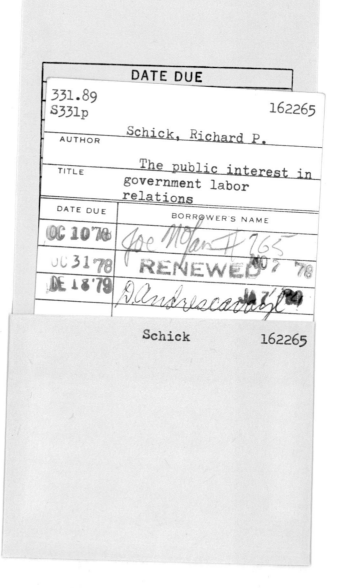